Visual Arts
Units for All Levels

Mark Gura

International Society for Technology in Education
EUGENE, OREGON • WASHINGTON, DC

National Educational Technology Standards for Students Curriculum Series

Visual Arts Units for All Levels

Mark Gura

Publications Director: *Courtney Burkholder*
Acquisitions Editor: *Jeff V. Bolkan*
Production Editor: *Lynda Gansel*
Production Coordinator: *Maddelyn High*
Graphic Designer: *Signe Landin*
Book Sales and Marketing Manager: *Max Keele*
Copy Editor: *Kathy Clayton*
Indexer: *Seth Maislin, Potomac Indexing*
Book/Cover Design and Production: *Kim McGovern*

Library of Congress Cataloging-in-Publication Data

Gura, Mark.
   Visual arts units for all levels / Mark Gura. — 1st ed.
      p. cm. — (National educational technology standards for students curriculum series)
   Includes index.
   ISBN 978-1-56484-242-8 (pbk.)
   1. Art—Study and teaching. 2. Art and technology. 3. Educational technology.   I. International Society for Technology in Education. II. Title.
   N85.G87 2008
   707.1—dc22

                                                                                    2008015425

First Edition
ISBN: 978-1-56484-242-8

Printed in the United States of America

International Society for Technology in Education (ISTE)
Washington, DC, Office:
      1710 Rhode Island Ave. NW, Suite 900, Washington, DC 20036-3132
Eugene, Oregon, Office:
      175 West Broadway, Suite 300, Eugene, OR 97401-3003
Order Desk: 1.800.336.5191
Order Fax: 1.541.302.3778
Customer Service: orders@iste.org
Book Publishing: books@iste.org
Rights and Permissions: permissions@iste.org
Web: www.iste.org

About ISTE

The International Society for Technology in Education (ISTE) is the trusted source for professional development, knowledge generation, advocacy, and leadership for innovation. A nonprofit membership association, ISTE provides leadership and service to improve teaching, learning, and school leadership by advancing the effective use of technology in PK–12 and teacher education.

Home of the National Educational Technology Standards (NETS), the Center for Applied Research in Educational Technology (CARET), and the National Educational Computing Conference (NECC), ISTE represents more than 85,000 professionals worldwide. We support our members with information, networking opportunities, and guidance as they face the challenge of transforming education. To find out more about these and other ISTE initiatives, visit our Web site at **www.iste.org**.

As part of our mission, ISTE Book Publishing works with experienced educators to develop and produce practical resources for classroom teachers, teacher educators, and technology leaders. Every manuscript we select for publication is carefully peer-reviewed and professionally edited. We look for content that emphasizes the effective use of technology where it can make a difference—increasing the productivity of teachers and administrators; helping students with unique learning styles, abilities, or backgrounds; collecting and using data for decision making at the school and district levels; and creating dynamic, project-based learning environments that engage 21st-century learners. We value your feedback on this book and other ISTE products. E-mail us at **books@iste.org**.

About the Author

MARK GURA has been an educator for more than three decades. The former Director of Instructional Technology for the NYC public school system, Gura is a thought leader in this emerging field. He draws on his extensive background as a literacy, science, and arts teacher in promoting the creative use of technology to provide highly motivating, relevant activities for students. He has done extensive work in preparing teachers to be effective instructors in the digital age, designing and implementing professional development for thousands of teachers. Gura writes regularly for *Converge Magazine* and numerous other publications, and consults on matters of education and instructional technology throughout the New York City area. He co-hosts The Teachers Podcast (www.teacherspodcast.org) and invites readers to investigate technology and visual art teaching further at his blog Visual Art and Technology (http://visualartunits.blogspot.com). He lives with his wife Maria in Teaneck, New Jersey.

Contents

Appendixes

SECTION **1**

Incorporating Technology
in the Visual Arts Classroom

CHAPTER 1

Using This Book

THIS BOOK IS FOR ALL MEMBERS of learning communities who want greater insight into the potential that visual art holds as a vital dimension of 21st-century learning. While rooted in the most basic and ancient of human needs and behaviors, art is as relevant today in the Information Age as it was in the print and pre-print eras, perhaps even more so.

Many members of school communities will have their intellectual lives enriched by the materials and ideas in this book. Art and technology teachers may instinctively understand that integrating both art and technology into classroom activities will enrich them greatly, but all teachers will find value in this integration. This book provides the approaches and projects that will enable them to do what may have previously seemed beyond their reach.

Likewise, art teachers who are interested in bringing technology into a teaching practice that is centered on traditional approaches and materials will find here what they need to bring their classroom fully into the digital age.

Technology teachers interested in grounding their classroom activities in highly motivating and relevant subject-based curriculum will find new sets of practices here as well—ones that reinforce and extend their current curriculum.

Technology staff developers, coaches, and specialists will find the connections needed to support the teachers they work with. The approaches and activities here will help them better integrate technology into classrooms through the implementation and creation of technology-supported art activities that are tied to general curriculum in a great many ways.

Above all, educational generalists of every stripe will find many interesting paths to travel as they weave their current courses of study into rich, multi-textured tapestries following two dynamic threads of human thought: creativity and communication.

As will quickly become apparent, the activities in this book are not aimed simply at enriching traditional teaching and learning but have the potential to impact whole student communities profoundly. By tapping the power of technology and art, student exhibits, performances, and publications are made not just doable but, after a simple learning curve, easy and natural to implement. Such activities, performances, and products are the glue that can hold together a community of learners and focus and fuel it to go further and faster in its explorations.

Getting Started

As will be seen throughout this book, basic school technology items are all that's required: relatively up-to-date computers, a few printers, inexpensive digital cameras, LCD projectors, scanners, Internet access, and some common software. Most schools have much of this on hand already, and doing the activities in this book need not require much investment of scarce funds. A great effort has been made in presenting the projects to show how low- or no-cost Web-based resources can be used. Many of the logistics of actual classroom implementation are open ended and left up to the teacher, ensuring that no specific ratio of devices is necessitated. Devices may be shared according to specific classroom conditions.

Teachers who work on visual art projects with their students understand that sharing materials (paints, crayons, scissors, glue, etc.) among students, as well as grouping students for the sharing of resources and responsibilities, comes with the territory. But this doesn't represent a significant consideration in making activities work. In fact, in view of our new understanding about the social, collaborative, and interpersonal skills that make up an important segment of 21st-century learning, this added dimension can be a great plus.

Outcomes

By participating in the projects included in this book, students will benefit from and satisfy national, state, and local standards established for both visual art and technology.

Learning About Technology

The table below describes how the National Educational Technology Standards for Students (NETS•S) are connected to the instructional units and how technology impacts how we think, learn, and communicate.

TABLE 1. How the NETS•S connect to the units

NETS•S	Connections to the units
1. Creativity and Innovation Students demonstrate creative thinking, construct knowledge, and develop innovative products and processes using technology. Students: a. apply existing knowledge to generate new ideas, products, or processes b. create original works as a means of personal or group expression c. use models and simulations to explore complex systems and issues d. identify trends and forecast possibilities	Using computers and other digital devices, software, and online resources, students acquire and analyze information and graphic materials to solve problems and satisfy design requirements involved in making original works of art. Students: a. research and interpret findings, framing their own works of art (products) within the context of the history of art, using this knowledge as a point of departure for their own ideas and approaches b. employ digital tools and resources to create original art individually and/or collaboratively c. make use of the unique ways that technology aids the artist in visualizing, processing, and presenting works of art d. understand the underlying purpose and logic of works of art, extrapolating beyond art they've studied directly, creating original approaches and works of their own
2. Communication and Collaboration Students use digital media and environments to communicate and work collaboratively, including at a distance, to support individual learning and contribute to the learning of others. Students: a. interact, collaborate, and publish with peers, experts, or others employing a variety of media and formats b. communicate information and ideas effectively to multiple audiences using a variety of media and formats c. develop cultural understanding and global awareness by engaging with learners of other cultures d. contribute to project teams to produce original works or solve problems	Using a variety of digital graphic processing and authoring tools, students create works to communicate ideas, feelings, and sensibilities as well as employ a variety of traditional and interactive Web resources to facilitate their sharing. Students: a. collaborate with peers and others in the creation and "publishing" of their work by a variety of means: digitally assisted traditional "hard copy," portable digital media, and Web-based format b. share works of art in progress and related information concerning their creation with collaborating peers and mentors; share completed works with a variety of audiences, as well as information documenting their evolution, evaluation, and criticism c. research art works addressing global cultural themes and present them via interactive Web resources, inviting and responding to feedback from worldwide audiences d. produce works of art collaboratively, employing digital resources as well as sharing materials, tools, resources, and ideas and expertise in their production

(Continued)

Learning About Art

The table below describes how the National Standards for Arts Education (NSAE; Visual Arts) are expressed in the context of instructional units that highlight the application of technology to the study, creation, and sharing of art. For the sake of clarity and simplicity, only the Content Standard portion of the NSAE is shown. See appendix B for the full version of the standards, which includes the Achievement Standard portion as well.

TABLE 2. How the National Standards for Arts Education (Visual Arts) connect to the units

NSAE (Visual Arts)	Connections to the units
Content Standard 1 Understanding and applying media, techniques, and processes	Students use digital graphics and authoring tools in a variety of ways to create original works of art and methods to share them, as well as extend the use of traditional art materials, techniques, and processes. Students demonstrate the above by analyzing art-making challenges and selecting effective approaches, methods, tools, and resources (digital and traditional) with which to address them. This use reflects authentic understanding of how personal ideas and experiences can be expressed with the use of technology tools and resources.
Content Standard 2 Using knowledge of structures and functions	Students demonstrate an understanding of how effective images and three-dimensional works express underlying organizational principles. Graphics and communication technologies are among the approaches and resources used to accomplish this. Furthermore, students are familiar with and sufficiently competent to employ these principles in the creation of their own works of art, using technology and traditional tools and resources to produce effective works based on them. These principles include items such as proportion, line quality and variety, contrast of value (lightness and darkness), and the relationships of color combinations. Students create art works that address these specifically, selecting digital tools designed to aid in working with them. Students use digital tools to manipulate structures and functions in organizing visual statements (e.g., drawing figures by ordering and joining basic shapes)—effectively arranging constituent elements of a whole work by adjusting and balancing the size and placement of shapes in proportion to one another; calculating the temporal design aspects of sculpture in the round; and utilizing the affective triggers produced by color combinations. Furthermore, students take advantage of technology's ability to easily produce multiple versions by creating alternative and contrasting versions of art works.
Content Standard 3 Choosing and evaluating a range of subject matter, symbols, and ideas	Students use communications, search, and other technology functions to research and select a variety of images (realistic and nonobjective), including abstract shapes and symbols, as well as conceptual contexts in which to place and employ them in making works of art. These are presented to viewers in real-world two-dimensional/pictorial, three-dimensional/sculptural, and virtual environments using traditional approaches to establishing space, as well as new digital approaches and combinations of the two. These include the use of technology to create linear presentations (e.g., animation) and nontemporal presentations (e.g., through hyperlinked media authoring tools).

(Continued)

TABLE 2. *(Continued)*

NSAE (Visual Arts)	Connections to the units
Content Standard 4 Understanding the visual arts in relation to history and cultures	Students approach art-making challenges within the context of the history of making art, as well as in relation to the societies and cultures that developed and practice them. Students use technology tools and resources to research and understand the history of art and its many developments, genres, movements, and artist exponents. Similarly, they understand the culture and society that developed specific art types, techniques, and approaches. This understanding extends to the physical, political, economic, and other factors that establish the background against which art may be fully understood as a human endeavor. Students extrapolate from such research and activities, developing a vocabulary of skills and understanding on which they may draw from when making original works using technology-based and traditional tools and resources.
Content Standard 5 Reflecting upon and assessing the characteristics and merits of their work and the work of others	Students understand how to analyze art works for intention and purpose, connection to context, and for success in implementation. They use communications and other technologies to locate appropriate source material, explanations, and commentary, and to communicate their own reflections on art movements and works. Students are effective at describing and analyzing art works and articulating their assessment and suggestions orally, graphically, and in writing, and they select the most effective and appropriate tools (including digital) in order to do so. In demonstrating competencies in analysis of art, students include historical and cultural references, as well as insights into methodologies and techniques used in their creation. They adapt art-making tools and approaches to use in illustrating and explaining their reflections and assessments, and they employ appropriate digital tools to communicate and to give and receive feedback.
Content Standard 6 Making connections between visual arts and other disciplines	Students use digital communications resources to facilitate their research and analysis of art works for underlying themes and to enable them to make clear connections to works done in other art forms such as literature, dance, drama, and music. Students use their skills in other disciplines and technology use related to them to extend the scope and value of their visual art works.

Connecting the NETS•S to the NSAE (Visual Arts)

The NETS•S and the National Standards for Arts Education (NSAE) are organized around differing formats; consequently, they do not align easily, as each has its own set of overarching goals and concerns, and these are expressed from different perspectives. Still, a side-by-side comparison is useful for the readers of this book and all those who would wisely use technology to support teaching and learning involving visual art. The table below is organized with the NETS•S as the initial focus to which the NSAE are applied. In some of the items below an NSAE standard may be directly related to more than one NETS•S standard; therefore the lettered performance indicators of some NETS•S are re-ordered to better align visually with the corresponding NSAE items.

TABLE 3. How the NETS•S and NSAE (Visual Arts) relate in the units

NETS•S (Technology)	NSAE (Visual Arts)	How the NETS•S and NSAE relate in the units
1. Creativity and Innovation Students demonstrate creative thinking, construct knowledge, and develop innovative products and processes using technology. Students: **a.** apply existing knowledge to generate new ideas, products, or processes **b.** create original works as a means of personal or group expression **c.** use models and simulations to explore complex systems and issues **d.** identify trends and forecast possibilities	**CS-1 Understanding and applying media, techniques, and processes** **a.** Students select media, techniques, and processes; analyze what makes them effective or not effective in communicating ideas; and reflect upon the effectiveness of their choices **CS-2 Using knowledge of structures and functions** **a.** Students generalize about the effects of visual structures and functions and reflect upon these effects in their own work **b.** Students employ organizational structures and analyze what makes them effective or not effective in the communication of ideas	Visual art is inherently involved with creation of works of art (products) and innovation in the use and adaptation of processes to support it. An essential component of art instruction involves learning the means of making images: media, techniques, and processes. In creating these and in organizing them into finished, expressive, original works, students learn about and employ visual structures and functions. Technology can make handling these challenging activities something all students and teachers can achieve. By producing art works in multiple versions and providing ways to pre-visualize their further development, experimentation is encouraged and supported.

(Continued)

TABLE 3. *(Continued)*

NETS•S (Technology)	NSAE (Visual Arts)	How the NETS•S and NSAE relate in the units
2. Communication and Collaboration Students use digital media and environments to communicate and work collaboratively, including at a distance, to support individual learning and contribute to the learning of others. Students: b. communicate information and ideas effectively to multiple audiences using a variety of media and formats c. develop cultural understanding and global awareness by engaging with learners of other cultures a. interact, collaborate, and publish with peers, experts or others, employing a variety of media and formats d. contribute to project teams to produce original works or solve problems	**CS-1 Understanding and applying media, techniques, and processes** b. Students intentionally take advantage of the qualities and characteristics of art media, techniques, and processes to enhance communication of their experiences and ideas **CS-4 Understanding the visual arts in relation to history and cultures** a. Students know and compare the characteristics of artworks in various eras and cultures b. Students describe and place a variety of art objects in historical and cultural contexts **CS-5 Reflecting upon and assessing the characteristics and merits of their work and the work of others** a. Students compare multiple purposes for creating works of art b. Students analyze contemporary and historic meanings in specific artworks through cultural and aesthetic inquiry c. Students describe and compare a variety of individual responses to their own artworks and to artworks from various eras and cultures	Making art is an activity directed at communication. As digital works can be saved and shared via portable media and the Internet, technology facilitates collaboration in this process, while eliminating the limits of location and distance. By applying technology-based graphic media and the techniques by which they are used, student communication is made easier and more effective, with far greater opportunities to share, exhibit, publish, and reach authentic audiences. Audiences, in turn, are empowered to interact with student artists, give feedback, and share their own artistic efforts. Art represents both a common platform for the content of exchanges, and a universal language to express it. A major component of art as a content area is its appreciation, critical analysis, and written and oral description to support these. This dimension represents a rich body of opportunities to facilitate communication between students.
3. Research and Information Fluency Students apply digital tools to gather, evaluate, and use information. Students: a. plan strategies to guide inquiry c. evaluate and select information sources and digital tools based on the appropriateness to specific tasks b. locate, organize, analyze, evaluate, synthesize, and ethically use information from a variety of sources and media d. process data and report results	**CS-3 Choosing and evaluating a range of subject matter, symbols, and ideas** a. Students integrate visual, spatial, and temporal concepts with content to communicate intended meaning in their artworks b. Students use subjects, themes, and symbols that demonstrate knowledge of contexts, values, and aesthetics that communicate intended meaning in artworks **CS-6 Making connections between visual arts and other disciplines** a. Students compare the characteristics of works in two or more art forms that share similar subject matter, historical periods, or cultural context	For much art making, artists must collect raw visual material that they will approximate, refine, adapt, and organize as they work toward a finished piece. Technology-based resources such as Internet-based collections of images and search engines, greatly facilitate finding "source" material and simultaneously support the observation of intellectual property rights rules. Such resources furthermore support student efforts to investigate how artists have traditionally handled design challenges similar to the ones they are themselves addressing. Investigating common threads in works, genres, and movements is a highly valuable dimension of studying art that informs and enriches the production of original work. Using technology-based resources facilitates this immensely.

(Continued)

TABLE 3. *(Continued)*

NETS•S (Technology)	NSAE (Visual Arts)	How the NETS•S and NSAE relate in the units
4. Critical Thinking, Problem Solving, and Decision Making Students use critical thinking skills to plan and conduct research, manage projects, solve problems, and make informed decisions using appropriate digital tools and resources. Students: a. identify and define authentic problems and significant questions for investigation b. plan and manage activities to develop a solution or complete a project c. collect and analyze data to identify solutions and/or make informed decisions d. use multiple processes and diverse perspectives to explore alternative solutions	**CS-1 Understanding and applying media, techniques, and processes** a. Students select media, techniques, and processes; analyze what makes them effective or not effective in communicating ideas; and reflect upon the effectiveness of their choices b. Students intentionally take advantage of the qualities and characteristics of art media, techniques, and processes to enhance communication of their experiences and ideas **CS-3 Choosing and evaluating a range of subject matter, symbols, and ideas** b. Students use subjects, themes, and symbols that demonstrate knowledge of contexts, values, and aesthetics that communicate intended meaning in artworks **CS-4 Understanding the visual arts in relation to history and cultures** c. Students analyze, describe, and demonstrate how factors of time and place (such as climate, resources, ideas, and technology) influence visual characteristics that give meaning and value to a work of art	Conceiving and executing art projects embodies all the planning, researching, and critical analysis of stages of progress that other types of projects do. Through the use of technology functions (such as file-version management), pre-visualization applications (such as storyboards and graphic organizers), and e-publishing template menus, students are supported in making informed and effective decisions in creating works of art. Progress analysis involves reflection on aspects of success and failure, identifying problems in implementation and pursuing solutions and selecting appropriate options as they emerge. This involves investigating and evaluating media and tools and the practices by which they are best employed. While professional artists have traditionally provided themselves with an expanded body of process on which to draw by using exploratory devices (such as preliminary sketches, color studies, and thumbnail compositions), as well as tools (such as the camera obscura, pantograph, and light box); the cost, time, and space investment, as well as requisite skills needed for these resources have precluded students' use. Technology now puts a wide range of similar resources within the grasp of the average student.

(Continued)

TABLE 3. *(Continued)*

NETS•S (Technology)	NSAE (Visual Arts)	How the NETS•S and NSAE relate in the units
5. Digital Citizenship Students understand human, cultural, and societal issues related to technology and practice legal and ethical behavior. Students: a. advocate and practice safe, legal, and responsible use of information and technology b. exhibit a positive attitude toward using technology that supports collaboration, learning, and productivity c. demonstrate personal responsibility for lifelong learning d. exhibit leadership for digital citizenship	**CS-1 Understanding and applying media, techniques, and processes** a. Students select media, techniques, and processes; analyze what makes them effective or not effective in communicating ideas; and reflect upon the effectiveness of their choices b. Students intentionally take advantage of the qualities and characteristics of art media, techniques, and processes to enhance communication of their experiences and ideas **CS-5 Reflecting upon and assessing the characteristics and merits of their work and the work of others** a. Students compare multiple purposes for creating works of art b. Students analyze contemporary and historic meanings in specific artworks through cultural and aesthetic inquiry c. Students describe and compare a variety of individual responses to their own artworks and to artworks from various eras and cultures	Art is a particularly rich body of content through which cultures, societies, and their values and issues may be studied. Technology facilitates and enriches studying, understanding, and reports on what's learned. Art is also a perfect lens through which intellectual property and copyright issues may be understood, especially so in view of the ways that digital technologies have profoundly impacted this area. The capacity to create effective art works and share them globally is greatly enhanced and extended through technology: art provides the structure and rationale for content and technology, the tools with which to produce it as well as the media by which it may be mass exhibited and published. Making art is a means of understanding one's world and expressing reflections, feelings, and opinions about it, and provides a purpose for and means by which individuals may embrace lifelong learning. Furthermore, positively and respectfully reviewing the work of others, as well as giving and accepting feedback are indispensable facets of study in this area.

(Continued)

TABLE 3. *(Continued)*

NETS•S (Technology)	NSAE (Visual Arts)	How the NETS•S and NSAE relate in the units
6. Technology Operations and Concepts Students demonstrate a sound understanding of technology concepts, systems, and operations. Students: **a.** understand and use technology systems **b.** select and use applications effectively and productively **c.** troubleshoot systems and applications **d.** transfer current knowledge to learning of new technologies	**CS-1 Understanding and applying media, techniques, and processes** **a.** Students select media, techniques, and processes; analyze what makes them effective or not effective in communicating ideas; and reflect upon the effectiveness of their choices **b.** Students intentionally take advantage of the qualities and characteristics of art media, techniques, and processes to enhance communication of their experiences and ideas **CS-2 Using knowledge of structures and functions** **a.** Students generalize about the effects of visual structures and functions and reflect upon these effects in their own work **b.** Students employ organizational structures and analyze what makes them effective or not effective in the communication of ideas **c.** Students select and use the qualities of structures and functions of art to improve communication of their ideas **CS-6 Making connections between visual arts and other disciplines** **a.** Students compare the characteristics of works in two or more art forms that share similar subject matter, historical periods, or cultural context **b.** Students describe ways in which the principles and subject matter of other disciplines taught in the school are interrelated with the visual arts	Digital tools and resources employed in the study, creation, and sharing of works of art are applications that fully embrace and express the underlying principles, systems, and operations of important technologies. Using these applications to support art activities provides a highly meaningful and focused opportunity for students to understand technology systems and to explore and discover their potential as productivity tools. Artists universally analyze their tools—exploring, probing, and pushing their capabilities and limits, as well as modifying and repairing them when necessary. In analyzing art challenges through their structures, functions, and organizational principles, students are afforded a vocabulary through which they may understand the potential and workings of technology tools that are designed specifically for or adapted to the needs of art. Technology-based research resources facilitate the study of connections found within art genres and movements, art-making cultures and societies, and functions and products of art and other disciplines.

About the Model Established

This book, and the projects it presents, is intended as a model for the use of school technology to enable the inclusion of visual art in the curriculum. It also provides a model for rich, subject-driven, and appropriate technology integration across the curriculum.

The projects are intended as real and important curriculum for a broad spectrum of students. However, it is not expected that they will be implemented exactly as presented. A visual art project is a unit of study that is flexible and can be modified and tailored in many ways to fit grade and learning level, to meet the specific needs of a class, and to take advantage of available resources. In truth, a visual art project is best implemented when a teacher embraces it and adds a degree of her own (and her students') personality, background, interests, and creativity; making it something that is truly their own.

Prerequisite Skill Set

To participate in these projects it would be useful for teachers and students to know some basic technology skills such as using an operating system; Web navigation and searching; file management; and the operations and functions of word processing—save, save as, cut, copy, paste, insert, import, adjust size or color, style, and print. Knowledge of the basics of peripheral devices such as LCD projectors, digital cameras, and scanners will be helpful, too.

What You Will Learn or Need to Learn

Through involvement with this book and its projects, a variety of highly useful technology skills will be addressed. The projects may be seen as an opportunity to learn (or better learn) these skills and to do so in the ideal context of the skills being embedded in the work. Skills are learned or reinforced in a "just-in-time" manner to just the right depth of understanding.

Some of the skills covered will be: working with graphics files (selecting, saving as, converting, importing, etc.), creating slide shows, hyperlinking multimedia, digital animation, virtual reality, and others.

How You Can Acquire the Skills You Need

A good number of the skills mentioned above would not be ordinarily acquired unless one were involved in the type of project covered in these pages. Generally, they are not difficult to learn. The context in which they are used offers learners insights that help in their learning, as well.

Furthermore, the information that accompanies these resources, as well as the information provided by their "help" functions, along with an extensive body of tutorials and resources found on the Web, make learning these skills relatively easy.

Today's learners are active learners who have come to understand that getting the information they need no longer exclusively involves being told or shown person-to-person. Technology items (the type of nonspecialist, consumer-oriented items referenced in this book) are manufactured with ease of use in mind and with self-directed learning information on demand, as well. Experimentation, trial and error, and self-directed research for the information (when it is wanted) are all dimensions of the new understanding about learning that will make acquiring the technology skills needed here relatively easy.

Also, simply asking knowledgeable peers and colleagues, directly and informally, is a simple but highly useful approach toward learning, as is making comparisons and connections to previously learned software and technology skills and knowledge. In a sense, it's perfect—the projects here serve as models for informal learning of the skills needed to do them; a very 21st-century educational reality. By embracing this and including it in the class discussions around these projects, we can enrich them and make them even more relevant.

Models for Collaboration

The projects here serve as foci for collaborations that might not often take place in schools otherwise. Some questions may arise: Will the school's current technology resources suffice for a selected project? If acquiring new resources is being considered to do these projects, are they the best ones for the job? How does one operate the hardware, software, or other resources needed? Are the files, software, and devices compatible? These questions might represent difficult obstacles for teachers working in isolation. However, working on these projects is the perfect rationale for quick or extended collaborative work between professionals—subject area teachers and technology teachers or specialists—as well as between school-based specialists and district-level technology coordinators, and so forth. Parents and community-based organizations also may be approached for an assist with the enrichment of the school's network and relationships in general.

About the Projects

The projects are structured activities that involve classic visual arts content and concerns. Each of them involves one or more important facets of digital technology use. The projects cover the gamut of art-making approaches, including drawing, painting, design, drafting, and printmaking, as well as sculpture and three-dimensional design. Similarly, as has always been the case in well-constructed art activities implemented by traditional means, these projects are contextualized within general and art-specific historical and cultural studies, and they involve ancillary research. Furthermore, the projects call for reflection, analysis and criticism, and the language and communicative means to accomplish these endeavors.

There are several important differences, however, about how these technology-supported projects unfold as students work on them. In many cases, the difficulties of hand-eye coordination and facility with fine motor skills involved in the art and craft of drawing and painting are skirted. Those students who have a natural bent for them will not be discouraged or forced to abandon these interests. However, the extreme impediments these requisite skills and abilities often present to student artists will likely rarely make their presence known in these projects. This issue models developments in the real world, too. The computer's ability to "make easy" the drawing of straight lines, compound curves, and other difficult-to-accomplish chores has freed the average person (and now the average student) to explore his or her taste, sensibilities, and creativity. It is important for students to know this and to experience this liberation, as technology now empowers them to be artists in whatever way most successfully makes student art projects valuable to them.

Similarly, printmaking, publishing of art-laden books, and the creation of slide shows, animations, fine art photographs, and virtual reality pieces (which until recently were the province of a few with access to limitless funds, resources, and highly skilled technicians) are now possible for all through the presence of digital technology.

Additionally, research, an essential element in many dimensions of studying and making art, was once an undertaking that involved the expenditure of great amounts of time, specialized skills, and access to a well-provisioned library; however, good research is now within the grasp of all who have access to the Web.

Above all, what has been avoided in this book is the glorification of superficial visual effects and the unsophisticated favoring of these effects over time-proven aesthetic values. This work does not promote the taking of shortcuts that would effectively bypass the interwoven disciplines that make up the field of visual art and threaten to render its study meaningless. In short, these projects preserve what is good in classic visual art activites. They will also expand and enrich the opportunities available to the average student.

These projects are presented as a spectrum that may be done in its entirety or sampled by implementing just one or two. They do not necessarily build on one another to create a sequential course of study. Rather, taken as a whole, they give a view of the many varieties of approach to making art that may be valuably undertaken by students while presenting a broad spectrum of technology skills. Furthermore, they illustrate how the two are inextricably intertwined and related. Above all, they show an approach that teachers can profitably replicate or tailor in order to produce similar projects on their own.

Each project illustrates and models how an important background context for its implementation can be established through independent (or group) student research and/or focused classroom discussion. And, of course, each project offers an activity directed toward the production of original work by the students, which thereby embeds and demonstrates specific, standards-aligned learning.

All of the projects culminate with a sharing activity, whether it be an exhibit, publication of the work, or some combination of the two. Interdisciplinary connections are embedded in or suggested for a great many of the projects presented.

Also, an approach to assessing student products and performance is included in the book, as well as notes and tools that address specific facets or dimensions of the assessment.

Finally, numerous Web resources are suggested for each project, which will give teachers and students a starting point in finding important background material, as well as links to resources and how-to explanations that are sure to impact the implementation of each project.

CHAPTER **2**

Technology and School Art Programs

ALTHOUGH NOT OFTEN SPOKEN OF formally, technology-using teachers have long understood the natural and powerful connection between visual art projects and technology use in the classroom. There are important reasons why this is so and understanding them will make the implementation of art projects and technology practices easier and more effective.

Technology Can Transform Art

Technology can impact just about every facet of making and understanding art. It can provide artists with a rich source of reference material. It allows them access to a virtual canvas where they can both recreate old techniques and discover new artistic possibilities. Once the art is created, technology makes it much easier to use, share, and store the artwork and its related materials.

Visual Reference Materials for Artists

Artists have always drawn from observation, either from real-life models or from graphic representations used as reference. Before mass produced images were available, obtaining reference information involved making drawings or prints of models in generic poses or doing studies of the works of famous artists of previous eras.

When photography was developed, artists naturally took advantage of this quick way of capturing valuable visual reference material. Early photography, however, was an art in its own right, with a difficult skill set to learn. Artists increasingly took advantage of it as it became easier, less expensive, and more portable.

With the development of commercial printing, mass-produced images were used by artists for reference information and inspiration. For example, the impressionists were highly influenced by inexpensive reproductions of Japanese wood block prints and post-impressionists such as Gauguin were known to save photos clipped from magazines from which subjects and graphic ideas were borrowed.

As the era of commercial illustration came into its own, it became common practice for professional illustrators to maintain vast personal libraries of "scrap": commercially produced and mass-distributed images from which poses, faces, gestures, and other essential information could be retrieved quickly and reliably.

Nowadays, the Web and various browsers have made this aspect of art easier than ever before. Search engines can ferret out much of what is needed by artists quickly and efficiently. Furthermore, once mined, these images can be processed digitally in a wide variety of ways that can actually begin the process of making original art directly from the reference materials.

Making Images

Through a variety of digital technology applications, a great many of the classic image-making techniques that artists have employed through history can now be done virtually, including: drawing, painting, drafting, and photography. Some of these effects are startling. Some drawing and painting tablets, for instance, can produce subtle effects, such as wet into wet watercolor, that are hard to distinguish from traditional versions.

Furthermore, as well as replicating traditional methods, technology has introduced new dimensions to art making. Image processing is a good example. With this widely used technique, images already created, whether by digital photography (generated through a paint program) or simply via scanned files of traditionally produced images, can be manipulated and transformed to bring out unseen or un-thought-of qualities and possibilities.

The ability of technology to copy at will allows endless experimentation on images, while the original is preserved and available to be reverted back to, if and when that option makes most sense to the artist. This has particular meaning for students and their teachers.

Storing and Archiving Images

Artists tend to accumulate finished works, studies, and reference material. Keeping all of this data safe and organized so that it can be located when needed can be a daunting task. Student artists have special needs in this regard, as well.

Professionals have come to accept digital copies of their original works done in traditional materials as their final copy. For schools this approach holds particular promise. Limited physical space is available to schools to store student art work for long periods of time. By creating digital versions, hard copy originals can be sent home after a designated time. The digitals can then serve as a record of the work completed for purposes of grading or portfolio development and as a reference for future work. Additionally, digital video, animation, and virtual reality make new types of sharing and archiving of work possible.

Applying Images

Technology has evolved into a series of methods and processes by which imagery can be inserted into a variety of important communication items such as books and printed material, Web sites, digital videos, and PowerPoint slide presentations. Also, through the use of digital transfer media, imagery can now be applied to a greater variety of physical objects than previously possible. As a result, new art forms, particularly three-dimensional ones, are possible.

Sharing Art Work

Ultimately, artists want their work to be seen. Although much of it is personal and is produced in order to satisfy personal needs, the process of presenting one's work to an audience lends a purpose and focus to every aspect of its production that cannot be achieved though other means. Technology can facilitate this important dimension and lend important new approaches and capabilities to it.

Technology Helps Extend What Art Programs Can Do

A visual arts program is something that schools nearly always would like to offer as part of their overall instructional program. The reality, however, is that it is often a difficult goal to achieve. In addition to providing space, time, and materials, finding a qualified visual arts instructor can be difficult, too. Furthermore, a visual arts curriculum that is relevant, compelling, and aligns well to the rest of the school's instructional offerings is often either hard to find or unavailable altogether.

Many schools that do have art programs would like to find ways to freshen them up, make them more relevant, or reinvent them wholesale in order to bring this part of the curriculum, one that really ought to bring sparkle and distinction to a school, in line with other aspects of 21st-century education.

On both scores, this book offers many insights and approaches to make these goals achievable. Technology has changed almost all of the work of the intellect in our world and its potential to impact the visual arts equally so. In fact, in many ways beyond the world of school, the arts have been vastly transformed by the emergence and application of digital technologies. And although these changes may not have found their way into our schools yet, the sooner we make this happen, the sooner our young people will benefit. They are growing increasingly impatient with the pre-technology era form of education offered them currently, visual arts included.

Bring Visual Art Instructional Programs into the Digital Age

As discussed previously, many new possibilities in visual art have been brought into being by the emergence and application of technology. It is to the credit of artists and art professionals that while new tools are embraced wholeheartedly, core values of craft, technique, and message continue to be adhered to in this age of digital technologies.

It is important to bear in mind, as technology-supported visual arts programs are conceived for schools, that technology should be approached as an enabler—something that can make what's been done successfully over the years better, more effective, and more relevant. Technology should not be used to supplant the best of what's been achieved in visual arts education but to enhance it and make it more accessible. Above all, it is not a way to make instant art or to do instant visual art projects that require little of students. It is not a vehicle to involve students in superficial, effects-oriented activities that do not provide challenge, opportunity for reflection, and discipline. Making visual art is a serious undertaking that involves insight and discipline and the enhancements of technology should not make this any less so.

Teach Students about Technology as They Learn Art and Other Content Impacted by Art

The lessons and activities in this book will offer schools wonderful advantages in preparing students to become global citizens of the 21st-century. Not only will they get a fine grounding in the conceptual basis of art and the techniques through which it is created, but they will be given a unique window through which they can perceive the workings of digital technologies, their applications, and how they affect human creativity and communication.

Visual art projects establish a context in which students learn about art. With the addition of technology, they learn about vital new tools and resources that are now used ubiquitously in the world beyond school. Furthermore, the study of art involves the study of a great many things across the various disciplines that comprise human knowledge. Art is vital to publishing and literature, and there are many opportunities through visual art projects, particularly technology-supported ones, to learn and apply literacy skills. The same is true in the areas of the various hard and soft sciences.

Technology Makes Art Projects More Accessible and Practical

Through the use of technology, art can become part of the general instructional program without the difficulties of acquiring the resources required by traditional studio art courses. Computer-based art can be created without the dedication of additional space, without mess, and in many cases without the acquisition of expensive materials. Furthermore, it can be applied in ways that unify the school community by breathing life and inspiration into school-wide projects.

Technology Can Help All Teachers Use Art to Teach

Most important of all, the techniques and approaches shared in this book will make it far easier for all educators to make visual art an integral part of the learning experience across the curriculum. These activities make use of technology in a way that eliminates the need for talent in any aspect of the creation of art. The focus is on understanding, the exercise of taste and creativity, and reflective and analytical thought processes.

Furthermore, the activities are conceived to provide not only great insight into the meaning and function of art in society and human life but to dovetail with the study of language and humanities and their roles in the various disciplines across the curriculum.

Well, What About Talent?

All art students and teachers face the issue of talent at some point. It is interesting to note that many individuals identified as talented artists themselves often express doubt that talent truly exists or that it can be defined in any meaningful way. This book has been written from the position that talent is not a necessary element of learning and understanding art or even of making wonderful art. Consequently the activities presented here do not require any previous training or special ability, particularly in the area of technique.

Rather, the explorations outlined involve the making of informed decisions, the exercise of taste and sensibility, and the joys of focused invention. Design standards, parameters, and guidelines are emphasized so that meaning is maintained. The amount of "anything goes" rope afforded student artists is kept to a meaningful limit so that the aspect of "too much" that often comes with enthusiastic but inexperienced students' art making will not be enough to hang themselves with.

Technology is so powerful and so capable of creating startling visual effects on its own that the unguided can easily be dazzled by the light emanating from the monitor without wondering "why"? In the face of all the bells and whistles, and tricks that computers can make images sit up and do, this book steers a course deep beneath the surface, presenting classic issues, concerns, and themes in the production of visual art. The effects presented are clearly tied to exploring the crux of making art better and enhancing the expression of time-less themes that do well from their new technology.

Covered techniques include drawing, painting, sculpture, and three-dimensional art, as well as art that has stemmed from the emergence of new media such as digital video, digital animation, and hyperlinked multimedia. Presented are not only the "how to's" but also the "what to's" and "why to's." Classic themes such as landscape, portrait, still life, and figure study are presented. Established methods and approaches like collage, multiples, and works in series are relied upon to provide structure to a field of study so vast that loosing one's way can almost be expected save for the presence of well-drawn maps. The projects are rooted in the history of art, as well as in the surveying of and reflecting on the art produced by many differing cultures at particular time periods.

Ubiquity

This book is directed primarily at the use of common, ubiquitous office-type technology; a resource set of technologies that are relatively easy to learn and use. Furthermore, what's useful to teachers is technology applications that are affordable and within reach of school budgets, and these are the highlighted resources in this text.

Technology is the ultimate enabler. It has democratized the media, enabling photographers, videographers, print and online publishers, recording artists, and anyone who wishes to assume these roles to provide media inexpensively and at will. Technology can make accomplished visual artists of all students and teachers, as well. This book is directed to making that happen in a meaningful way.

CHAPTER 3

Visual Art Projects and Project-Based Learning

THE TEACHING OF VISUAL ART and the inclusion of visual art in the teaching of core subjects are areas in which the implementation of project based learning is a comfortable and easy match.

Making art and doing projects go hand-in-hand, or perhaps they are really two sides of the same coin. The making of any work of art is a project and conforms to the classic format of having a preparation phase; a beginning, middle, and conclusion; and then a continuing series of reflection and sharing activities. This process, and its work and learning flow, are at the very essence of projects. And of course, a product is created, too, another defining aspect of learning projects and one that students relate to in particular.

Unlike visual art, however, other subject areas often are difficult contexts in which to integrate traditional curriculum and project-based learning. Importantly, more than just content, visual art represents an instructional medium by which this integration can be accomplished. In the study of language arts, science, mathematics, social studies, and other areas, approaching learning and teaching by completing a visual art project is a way to introduce valuable content as a learning project.

Although project-based learning may seem like a new approach to teachers of core subjects, this is not the case for art teachers or teachers who incorporate art as part of their curricular repertoire. Often, though, they understand it by virtue of instinct and self-directed exploration. They may not be aware that what they've been doing has a conceptual name and conforms to a philosophical goal of pedagogy.

Conversely, teachers who have yet to make project-based learning part of the instructional program and who may be struggling with the challenge of conceiving how to bring it into their classrooms, will find that including art projects is a perfect way to do so. Art projects serve as a convenient model for those attempting to understand or visualize how projects can drive and structure learning experiences. A visit to the Web sites of many professional organizations associated with teaching various subject disciplines will reveal an acknowledgement of the value of integrating art into teaching, along with suggested links and entry points. Visual art projects can make the implementation of these ideas practical and effective.

In a sense, the projects of great artists include more than just their works and masterpieces. The development of their styles and techniques can also be seen as projects. Furthermore, projects easily and effectively form a context by which other aspects of the discipline of art (i.e., art history, design theory, appreciation, criticism, and connoisseurship) combine to make a meaningful whole.

The logical "ends" of art projects are products. Whether these are traditional products, such as drawings and paintings, or nontraditional products, such as Web pages, the point of an art project is the creation of an end product. Consequently, the integration of art into traditional, non-art-involved student products, like reports, can add numerous, wonderful dimensions to such standard classroom fare.

Recognizing the production of student art products as project-based learning, however, offers much more than simply ascribing a pedagogical concept to activities that have long been undervalued in the hierarchy of education values. Visual art projects involve many dimensions of learning and can involve students doing independent research, engaging in focused group discussions, explaining their thinking through accountable talk, comparing and contrasting great ideas seen in the masterworks of important historical figures, and more.

Many dimensions of project-based learning across the curriculum are facilitated through the implementation of visual art projects and may include the following:

- Addressing multiple intelligences and differentiated learning styles

- Providing opportunities for students to apply basic skills and background knowledge they've learned in a variety of subject areas

- Providing extended learning experiences

- Effectively engaging and motivating students, particularly at-risk or hard to reach students

- Providing opportunities for collaborative learning

- Moving instruction from teacher-centered to student-centered

- Fostering higher-order thinking skills and problem-solving skills

- Incorporating interdisciplinary learning

- Providing learning experiences that are authentic, relevant, and connected to real-world activities that take place outside the classroom

- Fostering meaningful mentor–mentee relationships between students and teachers

- Providing a context in which teachers collaborate and engage in peer planning and coaching

- Providing a meaningful context for product (portfolio) and performance assessment

Most important, today's digital technologies can make all aspects of visual art projects more accessible and doable. Teachers and students who would be challenged to make project-based learning part of the learning experience through traditional means will find great support through the focused use of technology.

CHAPTER **4**

Getting Tooled Up

WHAT WILL YOU NEED to complete the projects listed in this book?

Computers and Connections

At the most basic level, the class will need some computers in order to implement these units. For the most part, any functioning, more or less latter-day computer will enable much of what's described here. Although obviously advantageous, a one-to-one student to computer ratio is not a necessity. Much of what's suggested can be accomplished with a dozen or so computers for a class, or a three- or four-to-one ratio of students to computers.

An Internet connection will make for a much richer experience. School computer labs, often with carrel-like work areas that offer little table space and an isolating experience for students, are less than ideal for visual art projects, which require more of a classroom-like setting. If this traditional lab setting is all that's available in a school, a good compromise would be to teach the class partially in a traditional classroom with desks that can be grouped for collaborative projects and plenty of room to lay out materials and works in progress (as well as to store work), and part of the time in the lab for the intensive computer-using portions of the units. If laptops are used, much of this problem can be avoided. However, a word of advice—unlike the manipulation of information tools, it is difficult to manipulate image-making software with the trackball or membrane mouse substitute built into laptops. At a nominal cost, a class set of mice can be added, making the laptop a far more effective tool set.

Peripherals

In addition to computers, the following peripheral devices will greatly extend the capability of the art program.

Mouse for laptops. Using a mouse is recommended because of the difficulty in manipulating image-making software with the trackball or membrane mouse substitute built in to laptops.

LCD Projector. An important aspect of art projects involves whole group discussions in which images and other resources are shared. An LCD projector is an invaluable teaching tool in sharing images, videos, animations, and Web sites among an entire class. An interactive white board can make the projector even more functional.

Digital Camera (and Digital Video Camera). Beyond the simple photographing of student art work for archiving purposes, a digital camera is essential for creating visual reference material and for generating the images necessary for virtual reality and animation projects.

Flatbed Scanner. Transforming images created in traditional materials into digital files is an essential capability for manipulating images digitally and archiving projects and importing them into presentation applications.

Drawing Tablet and Stylus. Drawing can be a highly challenging skill set, even when done with the most sensitive of materials. A mouse can be clunky and difficult to maneuver and control for drawing. The stylus gives much better sensitivity and control while the drawing tablet interface can provide a startling spectrum of effects.

Consumables

The following items are as critical as computers and peripheral devices.

Portable Storage. These are perfect for storing, back-up, and quick and easy transferring of student work from one computer to another. Floppies, flash drives, CDs, and DVDs are indispensable. They can also be viewed as a publishing medium with which student work can be duplicated and distributed.

Paper. Although all printers use paper, the quality and weight of the paper is rarely considered. Beyond the standard 20 lb. white paper, the teacher who wishes to effectively guide student artists through projects that involve hard copy printing should understand that the type of paper used will impact a project and often greatly enhance the final results obtained. A paper's finish will greatly influence the appearance of the ink or toner. Reflective, polished, matte, textured, and toned papers should be considered for many of the projects. Heavy stock, too, can add a great deal to a product. Check the printer's specs to see the types of papers that the manufacture recommends using.

Ink and Toner. In addition to giving vibrant and accurate colors and rich blacks, toners and inks have other properties that must be considered. Of particular interest is water fastness and the way the ink will mix with traditional art materials in projects that call for such mixed media.

Transfer Media. Some projects call for special transfer media. One common type is heat transfer paper, often used to produce T-shirts. This is a simple material to use. An image is printed in the usual way but onto a special paper. When subjected to the heat of a handheld iron, the printed design is transferred to a cloth that it has been placed against it. A similar material, although not requiring heat, can produce decals that can be applied to almost any surface. Art supply stores, craft stores, hobby shops, and the Internet are good sources for information about and purchases of these materials.

Software

Rather than present a vast list of specific software, it is far more practical to describe these applications in terms of their functions. Although the number of different titles is extensive and growing all the time, the *types* or *categories* of software make up a much smaller group. Needless to say, there is an overlap—some applications may be hybrids of two or more types. By understanding what various programs accomplish and the approaches they take to do so, student and teacher artists develop an instinctual, as well as a reflective, understanding of how to make happen the visual effects they need for their work. With a little experience it becomes clear that there are often several ways to accomplish a given task or effect, and this understanding is helpful in determining the most practical and effective path to take.

Here is a partial list of software functions commonly used in making technology-supported visual art projects:

- Draw (line, auto shapes, erase, etc.)
- Paint (brush, air brush, fill, etc.)
- Adjust highlights, shadows, contrast, etc.
- Cut
- Paste
- Copy
- Crop
- Grab
- Save and Save as
- Move/Nudge
- Adjust size
- Insert/Import image

Some of these are functions that are also used in software not directly associated with making art. And, of course, much of the software used isn't really specifically created as an art material at all, but rather is appropriated for that use. Programs such as Microsoft Word and PowerPoint are useful for art projects, as are graphically oriented Web authoring pieces such as Dreamweaver or WebBlender. In fact, many types of software offer potentially important applications for visual art.

TABLE 4. Software types and titles used in the projects and samples

Project	Software or other Technology Application	Use
Unit 1 Still life	Drawing (in Word) Picasa Photo Sharing Web Gallery	Draw with AutoShapes
Unit 2 Geometric abstraction	Drawing (in Word)	Draw with Line and AutoShapes functions
Unit 3 Ukiyo-e	Picasa photo-editing software	Increase contrast and eliminate gray tones
	Painting software	Strengthen black outline and erase middle tones Paste images into the picture
Unit 4 Holiday surprise calendar	Drawing software	Draw basic images
	Scanner	Scan drawing completed with conventional materials
	Web/Multimedia authoring tool	Create links between the various screens developed for the project
Unit 5 Time warp photos	Photo-editing software	Crop, make sepia, and add special effects to digital photos
	Painting software	Add faux aging details to photos
Unit 6 "Devolving" drawings—animal series	Image processing software	Increase contrast
	Painting software	Transform photo to contour drawing
	Drawing software with AutoShapes function (Word)	Assign and cover with a basic shape each structural component of the figure Transform the drawing to an abstract design Combine all separate images into a single combined work
Unit 7 Surrealist collage	Photo-editing software	Crop and adjust contrast of raw images
	Painting software	Alter images, eliminate portions, add details, strengthen lines, paste processed images into final piece, etc.
Unit 8 Hard-edge design	Drawing software with AutoShapes function (Word)	Fill a line grid with shapes and colors/tones
Unit 9 Enviroscapes (drafting)	Drawing (or other drawing enabled) software with AutoShapes and Line drawing functions (PowerPoint)	Draft a precise floor plan drawing
	Thumbnail Gallery software (JAlbum)	Present all works in coordinated fashion for sharing

(Continued)

TABLE 4. *(Continued)*

Project	Software or other Technology Application	Use
Unit 10 Box sculpture	Photo-editing software	Crop, adjust contrast, etc. of reference images
	Word processing (or other) software that facilitates the easy insertion and adjustment for size of images	Print out multiple copies in varied sizes
	Digital video-editing software	Create a "video" file composed of numerous still digital photos taken of the sculpture
	YouTube (or other) online video sharing resource	Share work
Unit 11 Mask making	Drawing software with AutoShapes capability (Word)	Plot a large oval to mark the size and shape of a human face
	Photo-editing software	"Process" a variety of found graphics for inclusion as design elements in the project
	Word processing software	Adjust size and print multiple hard copies of images
	Scanner	Digitize hard copy work
	Painting software	"Finish" various aspects of the final image
Unit 12 Origami	Photo-editing software	Crop, adjust contrast, etc.
	Painting software	Eliminate unwanted material, isolate image to remain
	Word processing software with drawing functions (Word)	Adjust size and orientation of images, copy and paste in quantity to create pattern
	Digital photos and PDF files	Create e-Book to share work
Unit 13 Graphic mobiles	Photo-editing software	Crop, isolate segments of reference graphics, adjust contrast, and apply effects
	Word processing software with drawing functions (Word)	Use AutoShapes to create a linear frame for the images, adjust size, and print multiple copies of images
	GIF Animator software	Create a shareable 2 D "showcase" piece to announce and share 3-D work
Unit 14 Cutout sculptures	Photo-editing processing software	Adjust contrast of raw graphics
	Painting software	Transform photographic material to contour drawing
	Word processing software	Adjust size and print out graphics
	Virtual reality software	Archive and share finished work
Unit 15 Stained glass sculpture	Drawing software with AutoShapes and Line tool functions (Word)	Draw basic graphics
	Word processing (or other) application that facilitates easy insertion of images and adjustment of their size, copy and paste, etc.	Adjust size of graphics and produce multiple copies

(Continued)

TABLE 4. *(Continued)*

Project	Software or other Technology Application	Use
Unit 16 Digital zoetrope	Painting software	Draw series of images
	Presentation software (PowerPoint)	Create series of slides from images then present and share them
Unit 17 Clay animation	Digital Photography	Capture various stages of clay model as separate 2-D images
	Animation software "Frames"	Present images rapidly in sequence to create the illusion of animated movement
Unit 19 Digital storybook	Scanner	Digitize hard copy art
	Painting software	Sharpen lines in scanned drawings
	Word processing function	Create frame in which to place drawing and generate text for captions
	Presentation software (PowerPoint)	Create a digital image with embedded hyperlinks
Unit 20 Virtual sculpture	Digital photography	Create basic images that capture various views of the 3-D work in 2-D
	Simply VR	Incorporate separate photos into a cohesive virtual reality piece

Photo-editing/Image Processing Software

The Web abounds with free or low-cost, downloadable photo-editing software. A simple Web search will turn up many possibilities. Popular online photo sharing resources such as Picasa, Flickr, and Kodak Easy Share Gallery permit photo editing online, as well as storing and sharing of edited photos.

Picasa offers both online editing and software that can be downloaded to a computer, where it can be used independently. Consequently, it is a useful resource—one that was used to produce numerous samples given in this book. It is a handy item to reach for when a quick but effective "crop" of an image needs to be performed. Other software titles of note are GIMP (free) and Pixel. Both are offered in compatible Windows and MAC versions as well as for other operating systems. Although these software titles were developed for use by the multitude of amateur photographers out there, they permit the artist to import any image saved in a standard digital file format. Once imported it can be adjusted or transformed with a broad set of effects and functions.

Adobe's Photoshop Elements is available at a moderate price (or for a free 30-day trial download). It is commonly provided with school computers. Elements has typical photo-editing functions, however, it is more robust while remaining highly accessible for students. It also offers many features that go beyond the basic free photo-editing tools, including animation and flipbooks, slide shows that allow for the inclusion of sound, a GIF animator, and advanced organizing and sorting. It is a worthwhile next-level-up application.

Drawing/Painting

What's the difference between painting and drawing applications? For the sake of this book, I feel this issue should be understood in the same sense that one would wonder about the difference between drawing and painting as art-making techniques. Drawing is essentially associated with line, or by extension, shapes that are defined by line. Painting is associated with shapes defined as masses, and with fields of color or tone. Still, there are numerous areas of overlap where a definitive judgment about whether a work of art is a drawing or a painting isn't always clear. Van Gogh is known as a painter, yet his technique can often be seen as drawing with paint. Similarly, Seurat, also known as a painter, did many of his famous preparatory drawings by using charcoal to cover his paper with masses—in other words, drawings without lines. Or are they really paintings created with a drawing material?

In order to free readers to concentrate on making art, I've avoided burdening them with any more technical details than are absolutely necessary. However, in an effort to offer a complete understanding, from the technical standpoint, painting programs are often considered those that create bitmap images, also known as raster graphics, which are composed of little bits of tone. Drawing programs are those that produce vector graphics, or pictures created by plotting continuous lines. However, to confuse matters, it is not uncommon for graphics programs to have a foot in both worlds.

On a more practical level for school-based artists, forgetting about the technical designation of a program is liberating. I recommend concentrating on the feature sets, the art effects that can be rendered with the program. Common drawing functions used are lines, shapes, and borders. Common painting functions are brushes (airbrush or spray), and graduated tones. Still, it is common for a program labeled as either type to have both sets of functions, which is why I lump them together.

A great many drawing tasks can easily be accomplished in WordPerfect, Microsoft Word, and PowerPoint (which offers word processing as part of its function set) programs. Word is of particular value, not only because it is provided with so many school computers but also because it offers so many drawing functions. Many of these functions, however, are not well known or easy to locate the first time the program is used. A good many free tutorials on the Web list the various drawing functions of Word, where to find them, and how to use them (see particularly Florida Gulf Coast University www.fgcu.edu/support/office2000/word/graphics.html). A young artist could produce an impressive body of work using nothing but Word. It is a gem of a program for artists and well worth the effort to explore.

Presentation/Slide Show Software

Most school computers come with either PowerPoint or Keynote (Macintosh). However those who find themselves without a slide show application can choose from many low-cost varieties on the Web. Many of these programs offer a free trial period of 30 to 60 days. Digital Photo Slide Show 2003.1, which can be downloaded from the CNET Download site at www.download.com/3000-2193-10062346.html, is one worthwhile example.

Animation

Although PowerPoint and other presentation software can be adapted for the purpose of student animation, FRAMES (Tech4Learning) is a low-cost software made specifically for this purpose. A 30-day free trial is available on the Web (registration required). Other downloadable options (free or low-cost) are listed on About.com at http://animation.about.com/od/referencematerials/a/freesoftware.htm.

GIF Animators

These programs are widely available on the Web at very modest prices, and a few free versions can be found, as well. However, many of the programs for sale also offer a free trial period—enough access to complete a project or two, and definitely helpful in experimenting with and deciding whether this type of software is a resource you want to use on a regular basis. A worthwhile example is called Easy GIF Animator.

Thumbnail Gallery

There are many galleries available through quick downloads, many of which are free, offer free trial versions, or are low-cost shareware. A particularly easy-to-use and functional example is JAlbum (http://jalbum.net), which is free and available for Windows, Mac, and other platforms.

Web/Multimedia Authoring Tool (WebBlender)

Beyond static drawn and painted images, artists now make pieces that incorporate sound, video, a variety of animation types, and hyperlinks to other content or to specified foci for the viewers attention within a piece off art. Some software can be adapted for this purpose; PowerPoint, in fact, can do all of the above, and Word can do some of it. However, there are wonderful, fun to use, kid-friendly programs available that aren't prohibitively costly. A highly worthwhile one is WebBlender.

Virtual Reality Software

Specialized software is available to "stitch together" digital still photos to create a virtual reality piece of either the "spin" variety or the panorama variety. A low-cost title called Simply VR is available, which is quite easy to use and gives professional results.

Screen Capture Pieces

A useful technique is to capture a piece of artwork exactly as it is displayed on the computer's monitor. Macintosh computers come with this feature built in, while in Windows the procedure is to use the "Print Screen" key and then "paste" the capture into Paint, where it can be saved and manipulated. Beyond these basics, a great many low-cost items available on the Web offer many more features and options. One good choice is SnagIt.

Mixing Software Types

As a little experience is gained in drawing and painting, becoming comfortable with beginning a piece in one type of software, importing it into another, and then perhaps finishing it in a third (or back in the first one) will pay terrific dividends. Many of the samples shown in this book were completed by an artist working in and toggling back and forth between Word, Paint (or another painting program), Picasa (or another photo-editing/image processing program), and a scanner. Of course some projects involve other software types listed in this unit, as well. The wonderful thing about this approach is that what develops is not a memorized list of what can or should be done with any given software program but rather a set of instincts about which software can be used to accomplish a project.

For Windows users, a good place to begin is with Paint, which is included as an accessory with the Windows operating system. However, experimentation with a variety of simple programs is a prescription for insight-fueled success. Simply trying and playing with a variety of software is a good way to learn.

Two free downloadable drawing/painting software titles available for all common operating systems (Windows, MAC, and others) are Tux and ArtRage. Tux is intended for early-through upper-elementary levels. Its attractive, easy-to-use interface allows students to perform a great many art tasks. ArtRage is a more sophisticated, highly functional program that accomplishes fine art-making operations.

Online Digital Resources

Online digital resources are particularly useful for sharing art work.

Blogging Resources

Remarkably easy to set up and use, blogs are a highly useful instructional resource with applications across the curriculum. For art projects, they provide a vital way to share links to online work as well as student writing about art projects, which makes them the key to many curricular connections between art and other subject areas.

Because some educators may have security concerns with any online resource, I recommend they consult their school or district's Internet Appropriate Usage Policy before undertaking a project with a Web presence. Most policies simply clarify the set of issues that comes with Web use, rather than prohibiting it. In general, though, I recommend registering with a large company that exerts control over the use of its resource, or one that is closely associated with the needs of teachers. A great many teachers use blogs without experiencing any problems. A few blog resources used by teachers include:

- Blogger: www.blogger.com
- WordPress: http://wordpress.com
- TeachAde: www.teachade.com

Online Photo Sharing

Picasa, Flickr, Kodak Easy Share Gallery, Photobucket, and many others offer an easy and elegant way to upload digital photos of student art, as well as any images of student art that have been saved in standard graphics file formats, to a customized virtual gallery. Not only are these a wonderful way to store and display student art, but simply e-mailing or otherwise distributing the link to the appropriate page makes sharing the work easy and effective.

Online Video Sharing

Similar to the photo-sharing sites, free, easy-to-use online sharing resources for digital videos are abundant. A few often used by educators are:

- AOL Video: http://video.aol.com
- Ourmedia: http://ourmedia.org
- YouTube: www.youtube.com
- TeacherTube: www.teachertube.com

Search Engines

Because much of making art with technology involves using the Web to perform the traditional function of finding reference images, search engines that were created for research are essential. Google Images is a good standby to turn to. Others that ferret out images well are Live Search and Picsearch.

Software Friends

Here are a few titles that will prove exceptionally useful, easy to use, practical, and cost effective: Word, PowerPoint, Paint, Picasa, Simply VR, ImageBlender, WebBlender, and Photoshop Elements

Tech to Go

There is an abundance of free or low-cost resources available that can be used by teachers in engaging students in worthwhile art activities. This book attempts to provide activities that reflect an understanding that tooling up to do technology-supported art need not require much expenditure, providing of course that the teacher is willing to do some research, inquiry, and preparatory experimentation. Whenever possible, relatively ubiquitous software (e.g., Word, PowerPoint, and Paint) are used as examples in order to demonstrate that projects can be completed without the acquisition of an entirely new set of resources. In New York City, the annual Tech to Go conference features such resources and many thousands of teachers have become adept technology users and integrators by following this approach.

However, it will become clear that the Tech to Go resources all represent a perfect place from which to begin, and once teachers and students are familiar with making art with technology, their instincts will eventually lead them to the desire for more sophisticated and specialized resources.

Other Useful Resources

Below is a list of items that bear investigation for anyone interested in beginning or deepening an involvement with teaching art through the use of technology.

Software Tutorials

Although formal professional development is made available from time to time, much can be learned from basic online tutorials. Bear in mind that the instructional integration aspect of using the software has largely already been covered in this book. So what's left to master is the technical side of the software. But fear not—the vast majority of the programs covered in this book are by nature simple to use. Essentially, using them involves reading directions and a little experimentation. The online tutorials will shed a great deal of light.

General Tutorial Sources

About.com: http://about.com

ExpertVillage: www.expertvillage.com

Specific Tutorials

Graphics (Florida Gulf Coast University):
www.fgcu.edu/support/office2000/word/graphics.html

Improving Your Digital Pictures with Picasa:
http://www.informit.com/articles/article.aspx?p=418012

Of Particular Value

ArtsEdge (Kennedy Center/Marco Polo): http://artsedge.kennedy-center.org

Art Education Associations (Princeton Online):
www.princetonol.com/groups/iad/aeai/aeai.html

Incredible @rt Department: www.princetonol.com/groups/iad/

Internet School Library Media Center: http://falcon.jmu.edu/~ramseyil/arteducation.htm

Electronic Media and Online Arts Resource Center: www.cedarnet.org/emig/nj.html

Federal Resources for Educational Excellence:
http://wdcrobcolp01.ed.gov/CFAPPS/FREE/displaysubject.cfm?sid=1&subid=22

ArtsEdge Standards: http://artsedge.kennedy-center.org/teach/standards.cfm

Kathy Schrock's Guide for Educators:
http://school.discovery.com/schrockguide/arts/artarch.html

National Art Education Association: www.naea-reston.org

Free Software Downloads

Free Downloads Center: www.freedownloadscenter.com/Search/drawing_W1.html

Tux Paint (free download drawing program): www.newbreedsoftware.com/tuxpaint/

All Graphic Design (many free trials of graphic software): www.allgraphicdesign.com/imagedrawing.html

Freebyte's Guide to Free Graphics Software: www.freebyte.com/graphicprograms/

Online Art Museum Directories

Index of Art Museums Worldwide: www.zdom.com/art/kaloustguedel/worldartmuseums.htm

Mother of all Art and Art History Links Page—Museums (site sponsored by the School of Art & Design at the University of Michigan) www.art-design.umich.edu/mother/museums.html

Museum Network: www.museumnetwork.com

Virtual Library museums pages: http://icom.museum/vlmp/

Public Domain Image Collections and Resource Sites

Eduscapes—Teacher Tap: http://eduscapes.com/tap/topic98.htm

Princeton Online Incredible @rt Department: www.princetonol.com/groups/iad/links/clip art.html

Springfield Township High School Virtual Library: http://mciunix.mciu.k12.pa.us/~spjvWeb/cfimages.html

U.S. Fish and Wildlife Service Digital Library System: http://images.fws.gov

Wikipedia—Public domain image resources: http://en.wikipedia.org/wiki/Public_domain_image_resources

General Art Tutorials

• Art Kids Rule: http://accessarts.org/ArtKids/Tutorials/Drawing/

• Knowledge Hound: www.knowledgehound.com/topics/art.htm

• TutorialMan: www.tutorialman.com/digital_art/page1/

CHAPTER **5**

Working with Graphics Files

A GOOD DEAL OF THE USE of technology to support learning in the area of visual art involves saving and using graphics as digital files. Creating original images in drawing and painting programs, scanning images, taking digital photos, making use of images found on the Web, and other techniques that are part and parcel of the process of making technology-supported art all involve saving work in one file format or another. These files may be imported into an application and resaved in the same format (or in a different one altogether), in order to further the work and to accommodate the requirements of presenting, publishing, or disseminating it.

To produce technology-supported student art projects it will be necessary to have a basic understanding of graphic file formats. This is a broad, complicated, engrossing, and potentially confusing area. Therefore, it is important to keep some perspective when approaching this subject in order to avoid getting too deeply involved in the technical aspects of digital graphics. Investing too much time, effort, and attention can be distracting from the core work at hand— the creation of works of art.

What really matters with graphics files is simply that they must be used and that some of them will permit the artist to realize his or her vision and others may not. Some formats are compatible with the programs in which you want to do your work and others are not. Some files allow for the capture of images that are clear and well defined; others are not so well defined. Some formats save as large files, an aspect that can slow down or prevent them from being imported into other applications, making them difficult to store, or difficult to transfer online.

As with all art resources, the awareness of the artist and his attitude toward their use will govern much of his success or failure in the use of the digital files. Knowing the format a piece of art is in at any given part of the process is important, as is knowing which "save as" format options will be available to choose from when he reaches the end of the process stage he is working on. In a sense, most of it boils down to *size, resolution*, and *compatibility*.

Above all, an experimental attitude is beneficial. Trial and error with file formats will lead to discoveries and understandings. Comparing notes with others doing similar work and encountering the same issues is also a fruitful approach.

Some file formats are specialized or related to a particular software type, program, or device. However there are some common ones that student artists will find necessary and unavoidable.

During the course of a year or semester a class may find use for many different formats, but for the sake of classroom management it may be wise to specify certain formats for specific tasks within the projects. Allowing students freedom of expression is important, but supporting them by setting parameters that reflect a vetting of what will work and what may be problematic is important as well. As with all other aspects of the projects modeled in this book, teachers are encouraged to try all the technical aspects of the production of a work of art on their own before assigning it to students. Additionally, questions about file formats should be directed to the school or district technology coordinator who may be able to clarify format issues easily.

Formats

The following are several simple guidelines to begin an understanding of graphics file formats. File formats are identified by the three- or four-letter extension at the end of the file name. Students and teachers preparing technology-supported visual projects will definitely use common formats that include GIF, JPEG, TIFF, and PDF.

Images intended to be viewed on a screen, particularly those used in Web sites, should be in JPEG, GIF, or PNG format.

Student work meant to be printed may produce best results if saved as a TIFF. TIFF is a versatile format and is useful when scanning images and should be explored for its possibilities.

> **Note.** There are two basic types of graphics file formats: bitmap and vector. Vector files save images by breaking them into simple shapes and then reconstructing them when the file is opened. These types of files are not a good choice for the Web. The other type is a bitmap image, which interprets an image as series of very small squares. Consequently, increasing the size of a bitmap image will reduce resolution because the squares from which it is composed are forced to increase in size proportionately as well. Vector images don't have this drawback.

Another common format encountered in student art projects is PDF. Most closely associated with Adobe's Acrobat software, PDF files represent a way to save work in a highly stable and largely unchangeable format that is relatively small in size and uploadable for sharing via Web sites. PDFs can be used to produce and share e-books and have many uses for student projects.

Many other formats exist. Some of these are proprietary or associated by name with specific software or digital devices. In these cases though, they are usually compatible with one of the basic types described above, and they behave much the same as the generic format does. A little Web research will quickly clear up these relationships.

See the Web resources listed at the end of this section for content that goes into deeper explanation of file formats and working with them.

Converting Files. Essentially, converting an image from one format to another involves opening it in one application in a given format and then saving it as another file format. Of course, not every application accepts all formats or gives the ability to save in all formats. Some image processing software in common use by schools, such as Photoshop Elements, offer a wide variety of options. However, a simple Web search using the key words "file converter" or "free file converter" will turn up numerous low-cost or no-cost programs created especially to aid in the conversion of files. Contacting the software publisher about recommended ways to convert the file options put out by that software, may prove to be helpful. Alternately, the Web abounds with discussion forums of application users and graphics enthusiasts. Posting a question in a forum or blog will likely elicit the help and advice desired.

File Size. You can determine the size of a file by selecting the file's "properties" function.

A Little Further

As you gain experience, embracing a few refinements of understanding will serve your class projects well. The following are a few tips that go a little further.

Converting by "Save As" or "Export"

Many software programs will allow file conversion by using the "save as" function and then simply selecting the type of file format desired, but others may require the file to be saved first and then "exported" as a different format. If the file format desired is not available as a save or export option in the program being used, you may want to simply open it in another program simply for the sake of using that program's file format options. If no program is available to do this, try searching the Web for one of the many free or low-cost file converters.

It is important to make certain that files are saved in their original format, as well as the converted format, in case the conversion is unsatisfactory and the original is needed again.

JPEG versus GIF

Generally it is best to save photos as JPEG and to save line art as GIF. Similarly, black-and-white images often works best in GIF, and images that require a range of grays work best as JPEG.

Compression of JPEG files

Many software programs allow artists to choose a compression setting in which to save JPEG files. High compression will produce a small file. However, the lower the compression the clearer the image quality.

Changing the Dimensions of a Graphic

Much of the difficulty and disappointment in using graphics files is experienced when images are "sized." Bitmap images lose quality when their size is changed, but vector graphics don't offer as much of a problem in this regard. If the image loss in bitmap is unacceptable (for most uses a small degree of loss is OK), a better result may be achieved by backtracking and saving the file after selecting a size close to the one needed in the final product or version.

Web Resources with Information about Graphics Files

All Graphic Design: www.allgraphicdesign.com/graphics/graphicsclip artanimations/ clipartgraphics/fileformats/bitmaprasterimages/graphicsfileformats.html

Scan Tips: www.scantips.com/basics09.html

Timothy Arends—Your Guide to Graphic File Formats: http://members.aol.com/arendsart/pages/infopgs/filetype.html

Prepressure: www.prepressure.com/library/file-formats

Graphics File Formats: A Quick Reference: www.Webopedia.com/quick_ref/graphics_formats.asp

Printernational: www.printernational.org/graphic-file-formats.php

How to Create PDF Files: www.techlearning.com/db_area/archives/TL/2003/05/inservice.php

CHAPTER **6**

Sharing
Student Art Work

PRODUCING ART WORKS is but one part of the full spectrum of learning experiences related to art. Reviewing, evaluating, and analyzing art, as well as engaging in productive, enlightening conversations about it, represent another leg of the journey, and sharing the work through exhibitions, publishing, or other approaches completes it.

Sharing art work is especially important because much of art is inherently oriented toward producing something for an audience. Not only does sharing the work give a sense of completion—by providing a culminating event—it focuses the work from the very beginning, giving it a perspective, a filter through which its purpose and efficacy can be measured.

Finally, as with all communicative products received by audiences, published or exhibited work invites feedback. This feedback is invaluable in helping the student artists understand the effectiveness of the selected theme and their approach to it. It also authentically creates the sense of a continuous process in which work and the feedback it receives are folded into further attempts and the processes by which they are best tackled.

Two chapters of this book are devoted to the intricacies of how to share student art work through a variety of exhibition and publishing approaches, one is devoted to two-dimensional work and the other to a variety of three-dimensional projects. These are presented as projects, not art-producing projects but art-exhibiting and publishing projects. Both of these include individual, small group, and whole class aspects.

The table below lists the many approaches to sharing student art that are presented as parts of the instructional units in the book. Many of these projects have applications other than those specifically cited within the units, so readers are encouraged to look for applications that can be transferred from one project to another.

TABLE 5. Approaches to sharing student art

Unit / Project	Sharing Approach	Comment
Unit 1 **Still life**	Picasa Web Album—used as student-annotated online thumbnail gallery. Student explanations can be inserted as captions.	
Unit 2 **Geometric abstraction**	Student works joined together as modules to form a large group work. A digital version of this can be imported into slide show software such as PowerPoint in order to project a wall-sized version of the work.	
Unit 3 **Ukiyo-e**	Distributed as hard copy multiples, traditional exhibition on walls, public slide show, or online gallery.	
Unit 4 **Holiday surprise calendar**	Run on a public access kiosk; uploaded to class Web site.	
Unit 5 **Time warp photos**	A traditional exhibition of hard copy printouts of the student photos; a kiosk-based digital exhibition using photo-gallery software; a PowerPoint slide show of the class's body of work on this project; a Web site carrying a photo-gallery version of the work.	
Unit 6 **"Devolving" drawings—animal series**	Exhibition on the wall; copy works to CDs and distribute or attach as file to e-mail.	
Unit 7 **Surrealist landscape**	Exhibition on wall enhanced with slide show of details of hard copy work. Slide show e-mailed as invitation.	
Unit 8 **Hard-edge color study**	Thumbnail gallery using Flickr Web album.	
Unit 9 **Enviroscapes (drafting)**	Exhibition on wall or a virtual exhibit via a thumbnail gallery.	
Unit 10 **Box sculpture**	Online video made from stills.	
Unit 11 **Mask making**	Exhibit on the wall (flat version, three-dimensional version, both together); exhibition of photos of masks in progress.	
Unit 12 **Origami**	eBooks; exhibition of diptyches on wall; virtual reality exhibit.	

(Continued)

TABLE 5. *(Continued)*

Unit / Project	Sharing Approach	Comment
Unit 13 **Graphic mobiles**	Digital photos and captions explaining process (or video); GIF Animation distributed by e-mail or on disk.	
Unit 14 **Drawn sculptures**	Table-top exhibit; virtual reality exhibit	
Unit 15 **Stained glass sculpture**	Virtual reality presented through LCD projector in public space	
Unit 16 **Digital zoetrope**	Computer lab or kiosks	
Unit 17 **Clay animation**	Theater-style animation festival using LCD projector in public space	
Unit 18 **Sharing student art**	Graphics, invitation, poster, etc.	
Unit 19 **Digital Storybook**	Distribute hard copies of finished books; project digital version (interactive white board) in public setting or run on computer kiosks; upload finished books to photo sharing album resource on Web	
Unit 20 **Virtual Sculptures**	Kiosk exhibits of virtual sculpture pieces	

CHAPTER **7**

Assessing Digital Art Projects

LIKE PRACTITIONERS OF OTHER SUBJECTS, visual art educators have developed sets of standards to serve as frameworks for planning and assessing programs, activities, and student performance. Many sets of standards have been developed, but generally the professionals who have worked on them have come to similar conclusions about the dimensions of teaching, learning, and assessing in this area, and consequently they are often quite similar.

A comparison of visual arts standards (although they may be organized differently) will reveal that they generally cover student learning about the materials, techniques, processes, and approaches; as well as the functions and structures involved in creating art. Standards contextualize visual art learning through history and cross-cultural connections; and the address the intellectual structures involved in analyzing, comparing, criticizing, and communicating about art.

Additionally, attention is paid to learning about the strong and important connections visual art has with the study and understanding of other disciplines.

It is not enough for a standards document to simply list all the topics involved in establishing the content of visual art. If it is to assist in assessment, the document must offer support in determining how much has been learned and how well. Therefore, a useful framework will include both "content" standards and "performance" or "achievement" standards.

These standards documents typically "spiral," which is to say that the same standards are applied to students across grade- and age-levels, but they offer a different amount of detail at each level. The specifics of the content and the nature and depth of the performance or achievement increase as the student progresses through his or her career. This approach is effective because it enables the students, over time, to sustain familiarity with the broad spectrum of ideas and skills involved, giving them the opportunity to focus deeper as they return to them at a later date. This is also important for bodies of lessons like those in this book, as all of the projects presented are relevant and worthwhile across the grade levels, although it is for the teacher to present them in ways appropriate for the level at which students are functioning.

The standards used in this book are the National Standards for Arts Education (Visual Arts). The complete standards can be found in appendix B and on The Kennedy Center ArtsEdge (Thinkfinity–MarcoPolo) Web site at: http://artsedge.kennedy-center.org/. The Web site states: "The standards outline what every K–12 student should know and be able to do in the arts." The standards were developed by the Consortium of National Arts Education Associations through a grant administered by the National Association for Music Education.

Note: The standards documents referred to in this section make specific references to what are considered new resources such as: "computer graphics, media technology, digital works, software, and electronic media." While it is encouraging that the use of technology is recognized and acknowledged by these documents as being legitimate and worthwhile, it is presented as a separate category, apart from more traditional art-making processes like painting, drawing, printmaking, sculpture, and so on.

However, technology has blended with traditional approaches in ways that will never be reversed. Technology is no longer separate from the traditional techniques but has become part and parcel of those approaches to making art. Furthermore, technology has changed the study and creation of art, as well as the horizon of possibilities of every dimension of the world of art in ways that far outstrip those anticipated by the student achievement found currently. These new dimensions of the use of technology in the creation of art are reflected fully in the art projects described in this book.

Above all, the use of technology in these pages illustrates not how technology can be added on to existing art projects and the processes they employ, but how it is inseparable and achieves something truly new in its approach to making art, while maintaining timeless qualities in the art produced.

Using Rubrics for Visual Art Projects

The visual art project is a type of student work that requires an assessment approach different from the written tests that have traditionally been the standard for core academic subjects. Furthermore, many accomplished art teachers would assert that, if done properly, a model visual art project will engage, inspire, and enlighten students in ways that truly are their own reward. In such a situation, grades become a far lesser goal. However, grading is an established institution and the grading of art projects must usually be included as part of school culture.

More than simply an ethical and effective method for assessment, the use of rubrics can add much to the learning experience. A great many rubrics, including those for visual art, have been created, and a little research will turn up many examples. Appropriate rubrics can be used as is or can serve as models for instruments created specifically for the project at hand.

In essence, rubrics are simple. On one hand the criteria or aspects of the student work on which the grade is to be formed are listed. On the other is a scale of the degree of quality to which the student has addressed and realized those facets of the project. Usually both dimensions of scoring are annotated and defined so as to aid the scorer in assuring that all project facets are scored and that the decision as to the level of performance for each is an informed one. The following section provides a useful, if very general, example.

Going Further...

The New York City Department of Education's "Blueprint for Teaching and Learning in the Arts—Grades K–12" is a particularly interesting start. This document embraces the ideas detailed previously, but it adds additional dimensions that may prove highly valuable in planning the breadth of visual arts projects as well as in assessing student performance. It is available as a PDF document at http://schools.nyc.gov/projectarts/Media/Blueprint/Blueprint intro for art.pdf

This document picks up the thread of the concept of interdisciplinary connections and goes into particular depth about the connection to learning in the area of literacy. The document's overview section states: "Each of the arts has its own vocabulary and literacy, as well as its own set of skills that support learning across the curriculum. For example, although musical notation is a language all its own, a student who develops skills in reading musical notation is at the same time developing skills useful to learning reading. Similarly, the careful observation of a work of art resembles the close reading of a text—one that includes making observations and drawing inferences. Generally, the arts provide students with inexhaustible subjects about which they may read and write, as well as engage in accountable talk.

The full section gives a framework that maps out specific areas in the instructional program where these ideas can be effectively placed, as well as describing the types of activities that may be used to bring them to life. The activities fall into the areas of looking at and discussing art; developing visual arts vocabulary; reading and writing about art; and problem solving, interpreting, and analyzing art.

As will be seen in the accountable talk section, these approaches not only effectively extend and enrich visual art projects, but they lay the groundwork for assessment that is based on the extended process of working and learning, as opposed to simply evaluating the outcome of a single project expressed as a work of art.

The NYC document explores two other areas of particular interest. One is the community and cultural resources strand, in which an important dimension of learning relates to understanding, accessing, and using resources such as museums. Although this was originally intended for New York City students who have a vast number of museums, studios, and community-based organizations nearby, the Web presence of the vast majority of such institutions makes this approach applicable and doable for students in any location with Internet access. Although many teachers and students would gravitate toward these resources instinctually, formally making this aspect of visual art learning one of the criteria for doing and assessing a project lends an important dimension to the experience. One aspect that will be helpful is the student Web site review form. This form structures and guides the experience, as well as provides an easy basis for assessment.

The second area of interest is the strand on careers and life-long learning, which includes "career-building skills learned in arts activities and required in all other fields of endeavor: goals setting, planning, and working independently and in teams." Many of the projects introduced in this book include such skills, and it may prove highly valuable to formalize this aspect by including a criteria in the assessment rubric to account for them. The use of technology, which is often accompanied by projects planned around the way that individuals share resources, establishes a clear, real-world rationale for focusing on these skills.

And Further...

Learning about visual art involves such (visual arts) standards as "recognizing the societal, cultural, and historical significance of the arts," "connecting art to other disciplines," and "understanding the visual arts in relation to history and cultures."

Consequently, visual art projects may be seen as providing important vehicles for learning important aspects of other subject areas. It may prove valuable, therefore, to align visual art projects with the standards of language arts, social studies, and perhaps other areas. A survey of popular standards documents in those areas, furthermore, will reveal references to visual art and technology.

The following table demonstrates how a rubric may be used to assess student art work. Similarly, its specific application and use have been illustrated in most of the book's chapters.

TABLE 6. Suggested rubric for student visual arts projects

Grading Criteria	Excellent	Proficient	Partially Proficient	Incomplete
Completion of the Project	All portions of the project are completed successfully at a high level.	Most portions of the project are completed successfully at a high or satisfactory level.	Some important (and other) portions of the project are completed successfully at a satisfactory level.	Few of the project portions are completed successfully at a satisfactory level.
Research and Preparation	Conducted the needed research/preparation in a way that allows for a full level of participation in the project.	Conducted the needed research/preparation in a way that allows for a high level of participation in the project.	Conducted the needed research/preparation in a way that allows for a satisfactory level of participation in the project.	Conducted the needed research/preparation in a way that allows for a minimal level of participation in the project.
Theme and Concept	Fully understood the concepts and goals of the project. Understood the contextual background content. Understood how to apply the above in the creation of an original work.	Understood a good deal of the concepts and goals of the project. Understood the contextual background content to a high degree. Understood how to apply the above in the creation of an original work to a high degree.	Understood some of the concepts and goals of the project. Understood the contextual background content to a degree. Understood how to apply the above in the creation of an original work to a degree.	Did not adequately understand the concepts and goals of the project. Did not adequately understand the contextual background content. Did not adequately understand how to apply the above in the creation of an original work.
Technical Proficiency	Demonstrated a very high degree of understanding and mastery of the concepts and skills involved in the techniques required of the project.	Demonstrated a good degree of understanding and mastery of the concepts and skills involved in the techniques required of the project.	Demonstrated a satisfactory degree of understanding and mastery of the concepts and skills involved in the techniques required of the project.	Did not demonstrate an adequate degree of understanding and mastery of the concepts and skills involved in the techniques required of the project.
Technology Use	Demonstrated a very high degree of understanding of the technology concepts and skills involved in the techniques required of the project.	Demonstrated a good degree of understanding of the technology concepts and skills involved in the techniques required of the project.	Demonstrated a satisfactory degree of understanding of the technology concepts and skills involved in the techniques required of the project.	Did not demonstrate an adequate degree of understanding of the technology concepts and skills involved in the techniques required of the project.
Creativity-Expression	Conceived, developed, and executed a work of art that is highly original and that takes full advantage of the medium's possibilities.	To a good degree, conceived, developed, and executed a work of art that is original and that takes full advantage of the medium's possibilities.	To a satisfactory degree, conceived, developed, and executed a work of art that is somewhat original and that takes advantage of some of the medium's possibilities.	Did not conceive and execute a work that is original or takes good advantage of the medium's possibilities.

The projects in this book are special visual art projects because technology plays a major role. This difference is easily accommodated in their assessment by including technology-use criteria as well as the more traditional art criteria listed in Table 6.

Using the rubric to calculate a grade is a relatively simple matter:

1. Assign a point value to each criteria in the left-hand column of the rubric. If there are 5 criteria, then each may be given a value of 20 points maximum. However, the teacher (or class) may decide to weight the value of criteria differently.

2. Once the maximum value of each criteria is established, then the rating within that criteria will receive anywhere from 100% to 0% of that criteria's portion of the overall grade, depending on the rating given when moving from left to right across the rubric.

Several chapters offer additional assessment items that go in different directions, or deeper. These suggestions are included below for convenience, as they may be applied or adapted to a variety of projects, in addition to the chapter in which they are found.

From Unit 1: Table Top Still Lifes

Project Components	Excellent	Proficient	Partially Proficient	Not Sufficiently Proficient or Incomplete
Artistic Growth The student has used this activity as an opportunity to expand his/her understanding of art and how it is made. The variety and level of the work shows increased mastery of techniques and the ability to plan art works.				

From Unit 3: New Images from the Floating World

Project Components	Excellent	Proficient	Partially Proficient	Not Sufficiently Proficient or Incomplete
Graphic Relevance All graphic elements are easy to read; the purpose behind their inclusion is clear; they add to the visual impact and help tell the story of the piece.				

From Unit 5: Time Warp Photo Portraits

Requiring the student to explain the process followed and the decisions made will greatly enrich the assessment dimension of the project. The following chart will facilitate the assessment.

Explains the Art Work Produced through Participation in the Project

Prompt	RATING OF EXPLANATION		
	Exemplary	Satisfactory	Unclear
How does the way you posed the photograph cue the viewer to the time and place you would like him or her to perceive in the photo?			
What objects, backgrounds, or other information-giving elements did you include in your photo to place it within an historical context?			
What photographic qualities did you give the photo to date it?			
What elements did you add to the photograph as a physical object to make it appear authentic to the time and place you selected?			
Give examples of authentic photos on which you modeled yours.			

From Unit 7: Surrealist Landscape in Mixed Media

Art as Report

Because one of the purposes of this project is to communicate what's been learned about a subject to an audience, treating it as a visual report can enrich its assessment. Accordingly, the following criteria might be applied to this project.

- Quality of information: Are sufficient details given? Are they accurate?
- Is the information presented in a way that effectively communicates the content?
- Is the theme presented in a way that will effectively interest the viewer?

From Unit 16: Digital Zoetrope: Animated Drawings

The point of a collaborative project is, at least in part, for students to learn about collaboration itself. How well do the students handle themselves in the working team situation, and how well do they contribute to the group's efforts? The following rubric (or one that is similar) will help focus assessment of these dimensions.

Aspects of Collaboration	Excellent	Proficient	Partially Proficient	Not Sufficiently Proficient
Contribution to the group effort Expends effort; applies personal talents and abilities toward completion of the project.				
Assumes responsibility or leadership Helps the team direct its efforts; takes initiative to complete the project.				
Works effectively with others Listens to teammates and values their opinions; cooperates and shares in the work; is willing to compromise in order to complete the project.				

From Unit 20: A Virtual Sculpture Exhibit

In addition to learning related to the *creation* of works of art, sharing art through exhibitions or other methods represents a body of knowledge and understanding that must also be learned. Items to include in a checklist or rubric to help assess the exhibition of works might include:

- Was an appropriate piece of sculpture chosen from the student's overall body of work as the representative piece for the exhibit?

- Was the piece presented effectively in the photo shoot (i.e., was an effective and appropriate base and backdrop created)?

- Were the photos taken effectively (properly illuminated, and focused with appropriate distance of piece from camera, appropriate and effective increments of rotation, etc.)?

- Were the photos effectively incorporated into the VR experience of the sculpture?

Accountable Talk

The Institute for Learning (at the University of Pittsburgh) defines accountable talk with the following statement: "Talking with others about ideas and work is fundamental to learning. But not all talk sustains learning. For classroom talk to promote learning it must be accountable—to the learning community, to accurate and appropriate knowledge, and to rigorous thinking. Accountable talk seriously responds to and further develops what others in the group have said. It puts forth and demands knowledge that is accurate and relevant to the issue under discussion. Accountable talk uses evidence appropriate to the discipline (e.g., proofs in mathematics, data from investigations in science, textual details in literature, documentary sources in history) and follows established norms of good reasoning. Teachers should intentionally create the norms and skills of accountable talk in their classrooms."

In reviewing and rating a student's work, the practice of accountable talk can be an important companion to performance assessments facilitated by the use of rubrics. Having the student explain the decisions made and the results achieved in the production of a work can give great insight into the quality of the performance. By directing a series of standard questions to all members of the class, whose responses will be reviewed in light of the same rubric, the answers take on the dimension of being accountable to the community of learners. An oral discussion grade may be given on its own or may be inserted into the rubric as a section.

It should be noted that accountable talk is but one of nine Principles of Learning in the Institute for Learning's material, and this component may be best understood as part of an interdependent continuum of principles: 1) Organizing for Effort, 2) Clear Expectations, 3) Fair and Credible Evaluations, 4) Recognition of Accomplishment, 5) Academic Rigor in a Thinking Curriculum, 6) Accountable Talk, 7) Socializing Intelligence, 8) Self-management of Learning, and 9) Learning as Apprentice.

The form on the following page was developed to aid in the recording, analysis, and assessment of accountable talk and may prove useful as a model upon which teachers can base similar instruments to aid in their support of learning through visual art projects.

Some other considerations to take into account:

- Include the students in the process of creating rubrics. Brainstorming is a good approach to their creation. The students will have a far greater stake in the project and see more validity in their grades if they play a role in creating the grading guide.

- Generally speaking, rubrics function as instruments to facilitate summative assessment. They can, however, be used to give students feedback about their progress in partially completed projects, assuming a formative function as they cue young artists to mid-course corrections in their work.

Figure 1.
Principles of learning
observation sheet—
Accountable Talk

Features and indicators of accountable talk	Evidence of teatures or indicators	Notes
Accountable to Learning Community Participants: • are engaged in talk • are listening to one another • elaborate and build upon ideas and each other's contributions • ask each other questions aimed at clarifying or expanding a proposition		
Accountable to Knowledge Participants: • make use of specific and accurate knowledge • provide evidence for claims and arguments • recognize the kind of knowledge or framework required to address a topic		
Accountable to Rigorous Thinking Participants: • use rational strategies to present arguments and draw conclusions • construct explanations and test understanding of concepts • challenge the quality of each other's reasoning.		

© 2004 University of Pittsburgh

Special Dimensions to Grading Visual Art Projects

Art projects, particularly technology-supported ones, are somewhat unique student learning products. Because many of them involve saving work as digital files, copied and saved easily, it is possible to retain a record of the various stages of the art work it goes through in its development. This technique offers the great advantage of getting snapshots of the student artist's work process and decisions.

Web Resources

Chicago Public Schools, Instructional Intranet: Tips for choosing rubrics: http://intranet.cps.k12.il.us/Assessments/Ideas_and_Rubrics/Rubric_Bank/Choosing_Rubrics/choosing_rubrics.html

CHAPTER 8

Copyright and Intellectual Property Rights

MANY PROJECTS IN THIS BOOK involve students searching for and using reference images as part of the process of producing their own original work. By doing so they join a vast and historic body of artists who have made the reference to and/or the appropriation of images produced by others an aspect of their own work process.

Famous artists, from Marcel Duchamp to Andy Warhol, have appropriated images virtually unchanged, presenting them or incorporating them into their own work. This is an accepted dimension of making art, and a survey of museum collections will produce many examples. Although this is legitimate from the artistic point of view, this practice that has the potential to produce copyright problems.

Wholesale appropriation of images, however, is not an approach taken in any of the projects described in this book. The practice of using reference images—images on which new ones may be based or which provide information for an artist to use in creating original works—is taken in a few of the projects in this text. Using reference material is not copying or reproducing anything; it is simply mining graphic information to use in the production of an original work. This approach has been used by artists for a long time and was a part of the creation of a broad range of well-known works that range from famous impressionist paintings to popular illustrations for books and advertising.

Although this approach is used by artists everyday without problem, it is still important to have an understanding of intellectual property rights before embarking on any project in which material produced by another party is referenced. Copyright principles are a complex body of understanding, but two basic rules should be kept in mind:

- It is wise to assume that any content, whether text or image, is protected by copyright, unless you can verify otherwise.

- The way you use the content affects the way it may or may not be protected.

The worst-case scenario of an artist running into problems by appropriating another's image can be seen in artist Robert Rauschenberg's experience. In a widely documented case, Rauschenberg used an original photograph made by a professional photographer in collage elements in several of his own works. When the photographer discovered the use of his work, he first sued but then settled out of court for a small amount and the right to be credited in any future catalogs that included the works in question.

To put the case in perspective, however, understand that Robert Rauschenberg is an immensely successful artist whose works demand high sums. Nevertheless Rauschenberg made no attempt to gain permission to use the photograph, which was created by a professional photographer who earns a living selling his images. Also, Rauschenberg used the photo in a form that left the image highly recognizable as belonging to its creator. Fortunately, this scenario is not one that teachers and students are likely to find themselves in.

To begin with, most classroom-use reference material will result in the creation of art that does not seek to present the work of others as belonging to the student—the first rule of thumb concerning student use of reference materials.

Simply translating an image from one medium to another does not necessarily guarantee that the creator of the original has no copyright on the derived image. However, it is also true that while a given photographer can own the rights to a specific image of a tree, for instance, that doesn't give the original artist the rights to images of trees in general. A work that bears only a superficial, passing resemblance (and represents the same subject in only a general manner) is not a reproduction. Good, fair-minded judgment is important here.

Many of the projects will be shared locally, within the classroom or school community only, and will not compete in the greater world with the creators of images that may be referenced. Bear in mind that sharing student work through publicly accessible Web sites can be construed as publishing, but that is not problematic if reference material is used properly.

The Pierce Law Center Web site states: "Copyright encourages the creative efforts of authors, artists, and others by securing the exclusive right to reproduce works and derive income from them." The projects outlined in this book will be produced for the purpose of education and not offered for sale. This point is important, as cases of copyright infringement most often involve commercial ventures that compromise the income of the rightful copyright holder.

- It is OK to use copyrighted material in the sense of Fair Use (see Fair Use box)

A number of authorities agree that copyrighted material may be used under the doctrine of Fair Use for purposes such as criticism, news reporting, research, parody, and teaching and scholarship. This is especially true if only a portion of the work in question is used and the originator is credited in any documentation that accompanies the presentation of the derived work.

Fair Use

Fair Use describes the guidelines that exempt educators and others from certain copyright restrictions. Fair use of educational materials allows some media products to be presented in a limited degree in the classroom. Individual school districts interpret Fair Use policy differently (taken from the PBS "My Journey Home" Media Literacy Glossary: www.pbs.org/weta/myjourneyhome/teachers/glossary.html).

- If, in the judgment of the teacher, copyright infringement is in question, an alternate approach may be taken. Permission to use the desired images may be requested from their creators by contacting them directly. Other images found on the Web may bear a statement about permission being granted without such a request or will give additional information about who may use the image and how. And finally, a wealth of images can be found on the Web that are specifically available free of copyright issues. Numerous repositories of such materials are available for educators and artists to use without the need to worry about property rights. The following are a few examples, and simple Web searches should turn up others. More sources are listed in chapter 4, "Getting Tooled Up."

  - The Morgue File: www.morguefile.com

  - bigfoto: www.bigfoto.com

  - Flickr Creative Commons area: www.flickr.com/creativecommons/

The principles described so far are only general, and if a project appears to be taking you deep into this area it might be wise to research it further. The Internet is a good place to begin the research. Furthermore, school districts are likely to have their own internal rules concerning the use of content, and it would be wise for teachers to familiarize themselves with such policies from the start of any project.

Web Resources

About.com: http://painting.about.com/cs/artistscopyright/f/copyrightfaq5.htm

Brad Templeton—10 Big Myths About Copyright Explained: www.templetons.com/brad/copymyths.html

Study Plans: www.studyplans.com/copyright_laws.htm

Springfield Township High School Virtual Library: www.sdst.org/shs/library/guidelines.html

Stanford University: http://fairuse.stanford.edu/

Pierce Law: www.piercelaw.edu/tfield/copyVis.htm#avoid

techLEARNING: http://halldavidson.net/TechLearningArticle.pdf

Tree of Life Web Project:
http://tolWeb.org/tree/learn/TreebuilderTools/trcopyright.html#ToLMaterials

U.S. Copyright Office: www.copyright.gov/fls/fl102.html

SECTION 2

Instructional Units

Table Top Still Lifes

Inspired by Paul Cézanne

What is real is not the external form, but the essence of things… it is impossible for anyone to express anything essentially real by imitating its exterior surface.

— CONSTANTIN BRANCUSI

Please see the sections "Using this Book" and "Assessing Digital Art Projects" for more information about these standards, the interaction between them, and connecting these standards to the lessons in this book.

STANDARDS

NETS•S

Although all or most of the NETS•S are touched on in this unit, the connection is strongest and easiest to see in the standards listed below:

1. a, b, d	4. b, c, d
2. a, b	5. a, b
3. a, b, c	6. a, b

National Standards for Arts Education (Visual Arts)

CS–1, AS–b

CS–2, AS–a, b

CS–3, AS–b

CS–5, AS–c

UNIT OBJECTIVES

Students will be challenged to:

- Research and learn about Paul Cézanne, an important artist who explored and helped define the art of still life painting.

- Analyze museum quality still lifes to see beneath the surface detail and discover the structure of the subject matter through understanding their basic shapes.

- Understand representation in painting and drawing within the context of its development throughout art history.

- Understand the relationship of basic shapes to the rendering of real life objects in two dimensions on a flat surface.

- Understand the decisions that still life artists like Cézanne make concerning the number of elements to include, as well as their size and placement within a picture.

- Apply these understandings in the creation of an original still life.

- Reflect on what they've learned and evaluate the quality of their own work and that of their peers.

CENTRAL IDEAS

The development of visual art can be seen as a continuum in which artists have, over millennia, worked through the mechanics of representation, striving toward pure design. This is an important concept for students to grasp if they are to understand the act of making art as one of making informed choices. By having my own students study, analyze, and reca- pitulate the work of Paul Cézanne they not only improved their drawing skills but developed an understanding of having an approach to making images, as opposed to simply attempting to represent subjects in a catch as catch can manner. I found that this understanding is the key to moving them away from the disempowering idea that only a lucky few are endowed with the talent to draw well.

In the still lifes of Paul Cézanne students can easily see how analyzing the real world in terms of the basics shapes from which it is constructed is a great aid to the act of representa- tion. They can also discover how this approach aids in the establishment of designs that are independent of references to real subjects.

Beyond having their eyes opened to an advantageous new approach to drawing objects, I observed a tremendous improvement in the students' understanding of composition, a key element in making art effectively.

By studying the work of Cézanne, an accomplished artist whose efforts embody the under- standing I want students to acquire, students were able to quickly see the fruits of Cézanne's hard-won discoveries.

TECHNOLOGY RATIONALE

In this project, technology enables students to do things quickly and easily that are ordinarily labor- and skill-intensive. For the particular set of operations needed, this is highly liberating, allowing them to overcome obstacles and disincentives that usually preclude learning some of the most essential and sophisticated aspects of picture making.

Specifically, by using an auto shapes drawing function, basic shapes such as circles, ovals, and rectangles can be created almost instantly, perfectly, and at will. Furthermore, these shapes may be adjusted in size and moved about the picture at will, facilitating experimentation and reinforcing the understanding that an effective artist chooses how large or small to draw the elements of a picture as well as their precise placement.

Having taught drawing to many hundreds of students, I know placement is one of the most challenging concepts for beginning artists to come to. Observing students draw, I've seen that their compositions (the arrangement of shapes on a page) often happen rather accidentally. The young artist begins in a random spot by chance, draws his shape a certain size or from a certain angle without considering the numerous possibilities he might have opted for, and finishes without adjusting size or placement.

Pointing out the need for continual experimentation and flexibility in a traditional art setting is often met with resistance. This is understandable, because trying out multiple varieties of size and placement is overwhelmingly labor intensive. And, of course, while students are devoting all that time and effort to making the kind of adjustments that come easy to professional artists, they are not experiencing the joy of expression and spontaneity that comes only after basic composition is mastered.

Likewise, understanding and using as a pictorial device the natural property of objects to overlap one another as they sit in space is difficult, as well. But because the auto shapes can be moved at will, and because the order function in the Draw menu makes placing objects in an approximation of real space simpler, understanding of this difficult concept is more easily acquired.

This project takes the labor and manual dexterity issues out of drawing so effectively that students are able to leap frog them and more quickly deal with the weightier issues of spatial perception and understanding. This challenge becomes far easier and is overcome earlier than if they had to struggle to meet it in the traditional manner. It is a good example of how technology is an empowering force for aspiring young artists.

Principal Technology Skills Addressed

- Internet research
- Digital drawing
- Printing
- Use of online blog/photo sharing

Technology Resources Needed

- Web access, browser, search engine(s)

- Drawing or painting program (manipulating the program with a mouse is sufficient for this project). The program selected should offer both auto shapes and freeform line functions.

- Black-and-white printer

- Storage (hard drive access or portable storage device)

WEB RESOURCES

WebMuseum Paris (Cézanne and the Art of Still Life)
www.ibiblio.org/wm/paint/auth/cezanne/sl/

Discover France (overview of life and art of Paul Cézanne)
www.discoverfrance.net/France/Art/Cezanne/Cezanne.shtml

NPR (National Public Radio Article—Touring Cézanne's Cultural Roots—
with accompanying audio file)
www.npr.org/templates/story/story.php?storyId=5132847

wikiHow (lesson on "how to draw an apple")
www.wikihow.com/Draw-an-Apple

Unit Conceptual and Pedagogical Overview

Deciding whether to follow one's instinct to faithfully represent observed reality or to indulge the impulse to create pure design is a classic challenge for artists—for students and professionals alike. All who would make art wrestle with this choice. Some artists find a balance between the two and produce wonderful works that have a foot in both worlds.

Paul Cézanne was a highly accomplished artist who spent a good deal of his career immersing himself in this dimension of drawing and painting. His still life paintings demonstrate a deep understanding that I've found invaluable for teaching. Students must all cope with the challenge of representation.

Cézanne's paintings allow the student viewer to see the relationship between accurately rendering real-world objects in two dimensions and their underlying structure as basic shapes, an approach that virtually guarantees a degree of success in this pursuit. This is a real eye-opener for young artists.

Students easily comprehend Cézanne's still life subject matter as basic shapes or conglomerates of basic shapes. They easily perceive apples and oranges as circles, grapes as ovals, pears as composites of circles (lower section) and ovals (upper section) that are blended together, and bottles as a melding of two cylinders (base and neck) with a circle between the two. But they may find it startling to see how these basic shapes underlie all realistically rendered subjects and how a master artist transforms them into real-world objects through the simple addition of color, shading, and small details.

This approach stands out in sharp contrast to a more common drawing method in which students attempt to *copy* the contours of a subject, without regard to its underlying structure. Students who haven't considered alternatives to this method, and to whom it may seem natural, generally get unsatisfactory and frustrating results. Understanding the approach that Cézanne took is often the first step toward success in drawing.

Most important, the project presented in this unit guides students to the understanding that Cézanne's achievement hinges not solely on his masterful technique, but how he applied it. His art is not just a series of demonstrations of mastery, but it is also his response to the challenge of balancing accurate representation with a celebration of pure design. Understanding this dual nature of the deceptively simple-looking paintings always turns on light bulbs over the heads of students learning to make art.

ACTIVITIES

DAY 1

1. **Research, analysis, and preparation**

    a. Have the students do Web searches to locate images of Cézanne's still lifes. Have them each select one work to analyze. The image should be printed as a hard copy, which may involve first saving it as a graphics file and then importing it into an intermediate program, such as Word, so that the size may be adjusted. Alternatively, the teacher may elect to do this step for the students and pass a supply of reproductions around the room and instruct students to take one for use in the next step.

    b. Direct the students to examine the subjects of their still life selections and analyze them for basic shapes beneath the surface appearances. Using the hard copy printout, have them next highlight or trace these basic shapes using a marker, crayons, or other classic drawing implement. Have the class discuss one another's discoveries and offer suggestions to each other about whether or not they found all the basic shapes, interpreted them properly, or missed any. The class's still life analyses can be put up as a grouping on a bulletin board or classroom wall or put in a portfolio to be spread out the next time the class meets.

    Note: Where available, an interactive whiteboard is a wonderful medium for this activity. The whiteboard would allow a photo to be projected and seen by all simultaneously. Analysis for underlying basic shapes can be traced in digital ink on top, and then the entire piece saved for future reference.

    Based on this analysis and the discoveries they make, the students will go on to create an original digital still life.

    Note: This project can be done based on the art of any still life artist whose work affords visual access to the basic shapes from which the subject matter is constructed.

DAY 2

2. **Creation of a still life**

    c. Have the students review the class's still life analyses and then choose three elements upon which they'd like to base an original still life of their own (apple, pear, box, bowl, orange, vase, grapes, bowl, etc.).

    d. Have the students use the auto shapes function of a simple drawing or painting program to create three preparatory studies for the larger, finished still life that they will produce. These studies should involve primarily the basic shapes of the subject matter. The important decisions that the student will make (besides which three elements to include) will be size and placement of the elements, as well as whether or not they will overlap one another or sit side by side. By concentrating on producing three approaches to the same still life, students will consider various aspects of composition and not simply involve themselves with problems of representation.

DAY 3-4

3. Refining and Experimentation

e. Have the students select what they feel is their most successful study. Next, have them use the copy or save as functions on the computer and bring up another and larger version of the selected study.

f. Have the students work the piece by adjusting the size of the objects, their placement in relation to one another and the picture as a whole, the color of the object (they may select various shades and tones from the software's color menu), and line weight. During this session, using the software's Line tools, the students may add details (stems, leaves, extra strokes, folds, tears, etc.) or light shading to the shapes (optional). Students use the save function when satisfied that the work is completed (or, perhaps, save two copies, which will allow the student to continue experimenting beyond the first level of satisfaction).

The piece may be finished at this point or you may allow students to experiment with other versions of their piece—some may be in color, some in black-and-white, some may use realistic color, some may take creative liberties with it, and so on. So long as additional experimentation is done on copies of the principal work, there is little to lose.

Note: As with all visual art projects, it is essential that teachers go through the exercise of completing this project themselves to verify that everything requested of students is possible and to generally inform themselves ahead of time of what the students' experience is likely to be.

Project Sample

Figure 1.1. Project Sample—Still life.

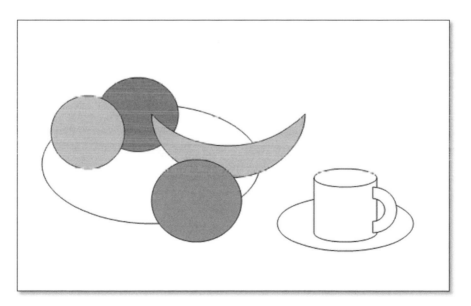

Process Used to Develop this Sample

Using the drawing functions of a word processing program (Word in this example) the artist drew the shapes needed to represent the desired subjects by using the auto shapes function of the program.

After he inserted all of the shapes into the picture, he used the size function to adjust their sizes relative to one another and the picture as a whole.

Next, he moved the shapes into a pleasing and interesting arrangement using the nudge function of the software.

Finally, he used the fill function to give the shapes colors. The order function was used to have the shapes overlap one another accurately, with the shape closer to the viewer covering those behind it.

Sharing the Work

This project lends itself well to a classic *art on the wall* style exhibit. After selecting the preferred finished version, each student's work can be mounted on mat or tag board and affixed to a wall with tape or push pins.

However, a more interesting approach, one that takes full advantage of the fact that a technology-rich process was used to create the drawings, would be a hybrid of a standard gallery show and an open portfolio exhibit. Because students used technology to produce a series of clearly defined and separately saved steps in the creation of the finished piece, a display showing all the the stages worked through can be presented as interesting and beautiful in its own right.

An interesting approach, then, would be to print out steps **c.** through **f.** and make an arrangement of all of them mounted together. Students would print the "finished" piece largest and then mount smaller versions of the other previous stages below that, with an eye toward the totality making up the final piece to hang on the wall.

Using Web 2.0 to Share the Work

Beyond the staging of a real-world exhibition, however, Web 2.0 resources offer numerous ways of staging effective and exiting virtual exhibitions. Blog- and Web-based photo sharing resources such as Google's Picasa can be used for a virtual exhibition. Picasa Web gallery (Fig. 1.2) can display the work of the entire group as a whole, as well as facilitate viewing each individual's work up close (clicking on a frame launches a much larger version). The captions function included in such online photo gallery resources allows for a modest, but valuable, amount of writing, reflection, and explanation from the students.

Note: School and district Internet Appropriate User Policies should always be consulted before student work is given a presence on the Web. The approach taken here does not violate the privacy and security concerns of typical IAUPs. See "Sharing Student Art with an Audience" for an overview of other possibilities.

Figure 1.2. Picasa gallery can display entire group's work, each individual's work up close, and a caption containing student reflection and explanation.

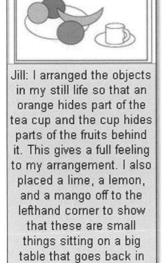

Jill: I arranged the objects in my still life so that an orange hides part of the tea cup and the cup hides parts of the fruits behind it. This gives a full feeling to my arrangement. I also placed a lime, a lemon, and a mango off to the lefthand corner to show that these are small things sitting on a big table that goes back in space.

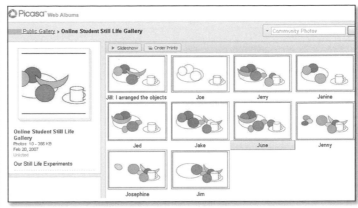

Assessment

Assessment for this project should center on the student's performance in applying the central concept of understanding the use of an underlying structure to realistically depicted subjects. When you review the finished still life, consider these questions: Are the basic shapes present beneath the details and surface textures? Does the work show a true understanding of the relationship of basic shapes and the subject matter? Other aspects of the project involve using the freedom that this understanding brings. For instance, has the student filled the space of the page purposefully and arranged the objects within so that they make a pleasing design?

Suggested General Assessment/Accountability Rubric for Unit 1

Project Components	Excellent	Proficient	Partially Proficient	Not Sufficiently Proficient or Incomplete
Completion of Project • Student replicates observed shapes with digital auto shapes • Shapes are arranged into a composition that represents a personal still life statement	All portions of the project are completed successfully at a high level.	Most portions of the project are completed successfully at a high or satisfactory level.	Some important (and other) portions of the project are completed successfully at a satisfactory level.	Few of the project portions are completed successfully at a satisfactory level.
Theme and Concept Learning • Student understands the concept of still life as an art genre • Student understands the method of analyzing subjects for basic shapes with which to represent them • Student understands that a finished still life reflects calculated decisions about composition	Fully understood the concepts and goals of the project. Understood the contextual background content. Understood how to apply the above in the creation of an original work.	Understood a good deal of the concepts and goals of the project. Understood the contextual background content to a high degree. Understood how to apply the above in the creation of an original work to a high degree.	Understood some of the concepts and goals of the project. Understood the contextual background content to a degree. Understood how to apply the above in the creation of an original work to a degree.	Did not adequately understand the concepts and goals of the project. Did not adequately understand the contextual background content. Did not adequately understand how to apply the above in the creation of an original work.
Technical Proficiency • Student utilizes shapes as design elements • Student varies shapes by size, tone, etc. • Student establishes pictorial space by overlapping and other devices • Student effectively arranges shapes and other design elements into a pleasing composition	Demonstrated a very high degree of understanding and mastery of the concepts and skills involved in the techniques required of the project.	Demonstrated a good degree of understanding and mastery of the concepts and skills involved in the techniques required of the project.	Demonstrated a satisfactory degree of understanding and mastery of the concepts and skills involved in the techniques required of the project.	Did not demonstrate an adequate degree of understanding and mastery of the concepts and skills involved in the techniques required of the project.
Technology Use • Student uses software drawing functions (auto shapes, fill, etc.) effectively • Student saves and manages files appropriately	Handled the technology portions of the project in a highly effective, insightful, and responsible fashion.	Handled the technology portions of the project very proficiently and in an effective, insightful, and responsible fashion.	Handled the technology portions of the project in a satisfactorily effective, insightful, and responsible fashion.	Did not handle the technology portions of the project in a satisfactorily effective, insightful, and responsible fashion.

(Continued)

Suggested General Assessment/Accountability Rubric for Unit 1 *(Continued)*

Project Components	Excellent	Proficient	Partially Proficient	Not Sufficiently Proficient or Incomplete
Creativity-Expression • Student develops a carefully crafted composition that reflects personal taste and takes advantage of resources and design possibilities	Conceived, developed, and executed a work of art that is highly original and that takes full advantage of the medium's possibilities.	To a good degree, conceived, developed, and executed a work of art that is original and that takes full advantage of the medium's possibilities.	To a satisfactory degree, conceived, developed, and executed a work of art that is somewhat original and that takes advantage of some of the medium's possibilities.	Did not well conceive and execute a work that is original or takes good advantage of the medium's possibilities.
Artistic Growth * • The student has used this activity as an opportunity to expand his or her understanding of art and how it is made • The variety and level of the work shows increased mastery of techniques and the ability to plan art works	To a high degree—compared to previous efforts—this work of art shows very significant growth.	To a good degree—compared to previous efforts—this work of art shows significant growth.	To a perceptible degree—compared to previous efforts—this work of art shows growth.	This work of art does not show much movement or growth.

* This criteria is not shown in other rubrics in this book.

Note: Refer to chapter 7, "Assessing Digital Art Projects" for an overview of assessing technology-supported student visual art projects.

Cross-Curricular Connection

Still Life and Language Arts

A representational still life can function in a variety of ways as a prompt for a writing assignment. One approach that will permit students to learn more about technology is to create a class blog for this purpose.

After each student's art work is uploaded to an online gallery (e.g., Picasa Web gallery), students can describe their work and explain the creative process they employed in working on it. Descriptive writing is an important skill with many useful applications.

Their blog entry can carry a link to the online gallery. Alternately, their comments, if brief enough, may be inserted directly below their work in the gallery. In this example, the full text of the comment appears in a window that opens when the cursor rolls over the art work.

Figure 1.3. Standard blog used to put students' reflective writing about their art work on the Web.

The blog entry in Figure 1.3 includes an embedded link to the Picasa Web gallery, giving a direct connection between the two. Links to both can be distributed easily within the school community, to parents and neighborhood acquaintances, and beyond.

UNIT **2**

Geometric Abstraction
Art as Pure Design

Great art picks up where nature ends.

— MARC CHAGALL

Please see the sections "Using this Book" and "Assessing Digital Art Projects" for more information about these standards, the interaction between them, and connecting these standards to the lessons in this book.

STANDARDS

NETS•S

Although all or most of the NETS•S are touched on in this unit, the connection is strongest and easiest to see and understand in the standards listed below:

1, a, b	4. a, b, c
2. a, b	5. a
3. b, c	6. a, b

Note: In this and other units, when students organize their art making to conduct focused experiments in which they systematically attempt a variety of solutions to a design problem (selecting one or more as the most appropriate and satisfactory finished product), they are *collecting and analyzing data to identify solutions and/or make informed decisions* (NETS•S 4.c).

National Standards for Arts Education (Visual Arts)

CS–1, AS–b

CS–2, AS–a, b, c

CS–3, AS–a

UNIT OBJECTIVES

Students will be challenged to:

- Discover the historical context for pure non-representational design as fine art.

- Understand the design elements and decisions that go into the creation of a non-representational design and, by extension, all design.

- Create their own composition based on the understandings they gain by examining and analyzing the work of Piet Mondrian.

CENTRAL IDEAS

Over the years I've observed with great interest the opinions and understandings about art that students bring with them to class. I've long noticed that abstract art is an area of particular interest and confusion for them.

In addition to wrestling with the idea that something generally regarded as easy to do could have great value, understanding the elements of design and how they function to make works of art powerful and effective is often something new to students. At best, they are just beginning to become aware of these deeper dimensions of the work that artists do.

Through projects like the one in this unit, students are freed from the challenges of technique and are allowed to concentrate on design alone. This is a highly valuable experience for students; one in which their growth recapitulates and parallels that of some of the great artists of the modern era.

20th-century artists such as Piet Mondrian worked their way to the creation of an art in which basic shapes and design elements can exist on their own—free from references to nature. Coming to this same understanding will enhance student appreciation for the work of abstract artists and will guide them in the creation of their own work.

Pictures composed of basic elements such as lines, shapes, and colors require the artist to make informed decisions about design. Not only will students be surprised at how challenging and satisfying this can be, but these understandings will spill over to other dimensions of their art making, exerting a positive influence on even their representational and realistic work.

TECHNOLOGY RATIONALE

The term drafting usually connotes a calculated, functional, mechanical variety of drawing, one that, in many ways, is the complete opposite of spontaneous and expressive fine art. However, in some examples—the work of Piet Mondrian for instance—drafting is used as a means to create fine art.

To do the project presented in this unit by traditional means would mean not only the need for teachers and students to acquire or create a variety of specialized tools, such as T-squares and triangles, but to acquire by a rather lengthy and frustrating process the skills and understanding needed to use them properly and with ease. All too often students find the latter to be off putting enough to severely compromise their art-making experience.

Creating a work like the end product of this project by drawing pencil lines and going over them with pen and marker, keeping the surface clean and the application of ink across it uniform, is beyond the reach of many students. Although I advocate appropriately challenging students, setting them up for certain frustration is something I've learned is counterproductive.

In this project, simple software is used to make the process easy enough so that the student is freed to concentrate on making the product through a truly unhampered creative process. Furthermore, he or she is assured a resulting product that exhibits a perfectly rendered surface, something that ordinarily would require taking great pains and would be possible for only those with great experience behind them.

Principle Technology Skills Addressed

- Internet research
- Digital drawing/painting

Technology Resources Needed

- Internet access/browser/search engine(s)
- Drawing or painting program

WEB RESOURCES

Abstract Art and Artists (examples of Mondrian's tree paintings):
http://abstractart.20m.com/trees.html

ArtCyclopedia (background of Mondrian and his work):
www.artcyclopedia.com/artists/mondrian_piet.html

Gallery Walk—Mondrian on Abstraction:
www.gallerywalk.org/PM_Mondrian.html

Museum of Fine Arts Houston (Mondrian work: *Composition in White, Black, and Red*):
www.mfah.org/exhibition.asp?par1=1&par2=1&par3=125&par6=3&par4=696&lgc-4&currentPage=2

Museum of Modern Art NYC (Mondrian work: *Composition with Red, Blue, Black, Yellow, and Gray*):
www.moma.org/collection/browse_results.php?criteria=O%3AAD%3AE%3A4057&page_number=5&template_id=1&sort_order=1

Wikipedia (overview of life and work of Piet Mondrian):
http://en.wikipedia.org/wiki/Piet_Mondrian

Unit Conceptual and Pedagogical Overview

Pure abstraction, design freed from any reference to the real world, was probably first hinted at in the later art of Gauguin. It was something he came to after long years of experimentation. Although it can be seen in small subsidiary portions of his paintings, he never produced works that weren't principally representational.

Abstraction was one of the great interests of artists who were members of the Modern Art movement of the late 19th century and on into the 20th century. However, it came about as part of a slow process of pictorial evolution, of a gradual moving away from realism to something else. It didn't happen in a single stroke overnight.

Piet Mondrian was one of the first artists to gain recognition for the exciting things he did with lines, areas, and colors that exist in a pure state. By following the evolution of his work students can see his vision's progression, from simplified representation to abstracted forms and on to pure design based in the rectilinear compositions that he became famous for. His 1942 painting *Broadway Boogie Woogie* is a well-known example of the realization of his explorations.

Mondrian, like many artists who would become involved with and known for non-representational painting, began his career as an artist doing traditional landscapes. Gradually, his personal search for a more personal and meaningful art led him to develop a style of painting that avoided reference to subjects in the real or natural world. This style was based on the use of a grid as a framework for his paintings. He experimented with the thickness of the lines that created the grid, as well as the primary colors that fill the shapes formed by it. His sophisticated "compositions" appear deceptively simple at first glance. However, they reveal many decisions about the number, character, and placement of the elements from which they are constructed.

Mondrian experimented with the function and identity of lines, and the distinction between line and shape, as line becomes heavier and takes on the quality of mass, is of particular interest in his work.

One can see the beginnings of Mondrian's method of breaking up the space of a picture with lines that define shapes (in the negative spaces) in his experimentations with simplified trees. The shape of a tree abstracted is a vertical line (the trunk) and a series of horizontal lines (the limbs). When grouped, these form a sort of grid. These pictures give a hint of how Mondrian may have bridged the world of representation and non-representation.

Once discovered through an interpretation of nature, the grid became an important platform on which effective art is made. It is a platform that is easy to establish and work with, and once understood, a logical choice to support the creation of student work. I have used the grid as the foundation for numerous student projects. It's a framework they understand and appreciate and is a useful in supporting them while they concentrate on the elements of design.

ACTIVITIES

In this unit students will create an original work based on the geometric elements of a grid. To accomplish this they will use the functions of a basic drawing or painting program.

DAY 1

1. Research and preparation

a. Engage the students in a discussion of Mondrian's later, non-representational works. A group review of museum Web sites supported with an LCD projector will greatly facilitate the discussion. Students should be guided to consider works based on simple geometric shapes as examples of a carefully considered and evolved approach to making art.

Alternately, direct the students to research the life and work of Piet Mondrian on the Web on their own. Give them the following research prompts, which may form the basis of focus questions for a follow-up whole-class discussion:

- *Broadway Boogie Woogie* was one of Mondrian's last works. Did he always make paintings with this type of image?

- Did other artists make this type of image before him?

- What decisions did Mondrian make when creating his paintings that influenced the way they looked when finished?

DAYS 2–4

2. Creation of a two-dimensional work

b. In a class discussion, have the students recall the discoveries they made about Mondrian's work in the previous session and have them list all the variables of design that an artist must consider in the creation of a grid-based rectilinear design (i.e., number and thickness of lines, number, size, and placement of the areas created by the intersection of lines, color, etc.). As a result of this brainstorming exercise, make a large chart that the class can refer to as it continues with this project.

Working at individual terminals, the students will create a two-dimensional work based on the elements listed in the chart and using the functions of a basic drawing or painting program (rectangle shape for design border, Line tool, line width adjustment, and fill function to fill the rectangles between the grid sections with color).

A good procedure would be to have the students create the spatial elements of the piece first: the number of lines, placement of lines, spaces between lines, and so on. Next, the width of the lines (and possibly their value and color) can be decided upon and adjusted. Third, the rectangles formed by the grid can be filled with color. The final step is to review and revise all of the three steps taken previously to adjust for the interplay of the various elements and their cumulative effect. Have students save the work.

Variation/Extension. As a result of the class discussion, have the group brainstorm a series of uniform design criteria on which all will produce a work (i.e., ten lines, three colors, three line thicknesses, etc.). Direct the students to each create their own individual works strictly following the group's criteria.

Ensure the students do these following a predetermined size and ratio (eight inches square will work well).

When the works are finished, students print two copies of each using a color laser or inkjet printer and use one for the culminating exercise (see Sharing the Work). The student may retain the other, which will serve for comparison between individual and combined versions.

Project Sample

Figure 2.1.
Project Sample—
Geometric
Abstraction.

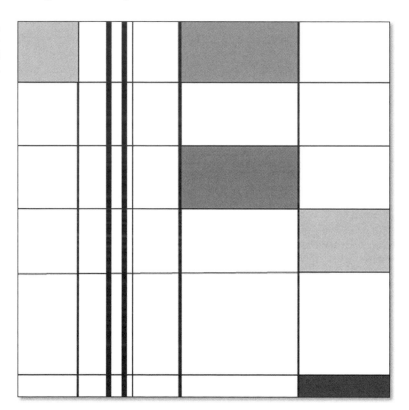

Process Used to Develop this Sample

Using the drawing functions of a word processing application (Word in this example, although any program that allows the drawing of lines and auto shapes will work), the artist first drew a six-inch square as a frame (picture plane) within which to place the composition.

Using the Line tool he divided the frame up into a variety of spaces of various sizes. He then adjusted these lines for visual variety using the line style function of the program.

Using the draw function (and selecting the Rectangle tool), he drew a rectangle within each space to be filled with color, then using the fill function selected a color to occupy that space.

Finally, in any places where the rectangle shape covers over the lines bordering it, he redrew lines over the original to reestablish a crisp line of uniform weight.

Sharing the Work

The individual works may be seen as modules, which when put together form a larger group work. By putting a loop of masking tape on the back of each, the group work can be temporarily placed on the wall as the group continues to work through the process of positioning and repositioning each within the whole until it is satisfied with the finished product. Discuss the implications of modular design by comparing the work produced and the experience of producing it among the individual works and the extended group compilation.

As the work is produced in digital form, a similar grouping of the class's work can be achieved directly in software. The advantage of this technique is that the work is archived for future exhibitions, an advantage over the hard copy exhibition, which may prove difficult to store and exhibit again after the first installation.

By importing the student modules directly into a slide show software (e.g., PowerPoint) or into an intermediary software that can later be imported into the slide show application, the experience of the group exhibition can be easily recreated by projecting the image on a wall.

Figure 2.2. Student pieces joined into a unified group piece.

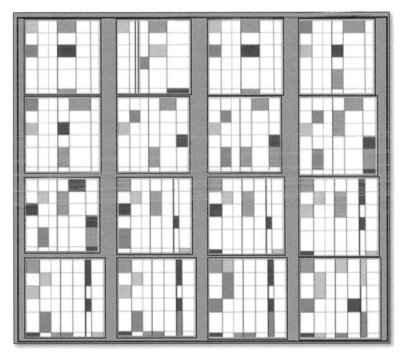

Note: See unit 18, "Sharing Student Art with an Audience" for a comprehensive overview of possibilities.

Assessment

An important aspect of the student performance is compliance with the directions regarding how to use the design elements discussed before work began and the way the student balances her own design sensibilities with them. Have the directions been followed? Has a successful, pleasing work been created?

This project may be a good one to have the student explain orally some of the many decisions made in making the work. Some focusing questions might be:

- Which aspect of the composition you created do you feel is most successful?

- Which part of the design would you like to change now and why?

- Are there design elements not on the list that you feel might have helped make a better or different composition? Which ones?

Suggested General Assessment/Accountability Rubric for Unit 2

Project Components	Excellent	Proficient	Partially Proficient	Not Sufficiently Proficient or Incomplete
Completion of Project • Student develops a design composed of rectangles of varying sizes and dimensions • Student introduces visual variety by using differing line weights and filling selected spaces with flat tone of varying value	All portions of the project are completed successfully at a high level.	Most portions of the project are completed successfully at a high or satisfactory level.	Some important (and other) portions of the project are completed successfully at a satisfactory level.	Few of the project portions are completed successfully at a satisfactory level.
Theme and Concept Learning • Student understands the concept and historical value of non-objective design as fine art • Student understands that abstract designs represent a series of carefully made decisions on the part of the artist	Fully understood the concepts and goals of the project. Understood the contextual background content. Understood how to apply the above in the creation of an original work.	Understood a good deal of the concepts and goals of the project. Understood the contextual background content to a high degree. Understood how to apply the above in the creation of an original work to a high degree.	Understood some of the concepts and goals of the project. Understood the contextual background content to a degree. Understood how to apply the above in the creation of an original work to a degree.	Did not adequately understand the concepts and goals of the project. Did not adequately understand the contextual background content. Did not adequately understand how to apply the above in the creation of an original work.
Technical Proficiency • Student executes design elements of line, shape, color field, and so on, effectively • Student organizes design elements into a well thought out, effective design	Demonstrated a very high degree of understanding and mastery of the concepts and skills involved in the techniques required of the project.	Demonstrated a good degree of understanding and mastery of the concepts and skills involved in the techniques required of the project.	Demonstrated a satisfactory degree of understanding and mastery of the concepts and skills involved in the techniques required of the project.	Did not demonstrate an adequate degree of understanding and mastery of the concepts and skills involved in the techniques required of the project.

(Continued)

Suggested General Assessment/Accountability Rubric for Unit 2 *(Continued)*

Project Components	Excellent	Proficient	Partially Proficient	Not Sufficiently Proficient or Incomplete
Technology Use • Student uses software appropriately to create and manipulate design elements • Student saves and manages files appropriately	Handled the technology portions of the project in a highly effective, insightful, and responsible fashion	Handled the technology portions of the project very proficiently and in an effective, insightful, and responsible fashion	Handled the technology portions of the project in a satisfactorily effective, insightful, and responsible fashion	Did not handle the technology portions of the project in a satisfactorily effective, insightful, and responsible fashion
Creativity-Expression • Student produces a unique, personal art work that reflects personal tastes and sensibilities	Conceived, developed, and executed a work of art that is highly original and that takes full advantage of the medium's possibilities	To a good degree, conceived, developed, and executed a work of art that is original and that takes full advantage of the medium's possibilities	To a satisfactory degree, conceived, developed, and executed a work of art that is somewhat original and that takes advantage of some of the medium's possibilities	Did not well conceive and execute a work that is original or takes good advantage of the medium's possibilities.

Note: Refer to chapter 7, "Assessing Digital Art Projects" for an overview of assessing technology-supported student visual art projects.

Cross-Curricular Connection

Geometric Abstraction and Language Arts

Narrative Procedure is an important form of writing that is commonly included in the language arts curriculum. It is also one of those writing tasks that have particular applicability across the curriculum in areas where sequential procedures are part of the course of study. Science, in particular, is an area in which procedures are often essential. Lab experiences in chemistry, field-based data collection projects, dissection activities, and the mounting of specimens are a few examples. In other areas, such as research processes in historical investigation, color mixing in fine art, and the setting up of equations in math, to name a few, procedures and the writing of narratives to define and record them are valuable and important.

An example of a formal integration of these ideas can be seen in the English/Language Arts Curriculum Standards approved by the Tennessee State Board of Education, which states

"…5.2.07 Write narrative accounts…

c.   Write with well-developed organizational structure, sequence of events, and details.

f.   Explain and/or illustrate key ideas…

5.2.08 Write frequently across all content areas.

a. Produce a variety of creative works utilizing knowledge from the content areas (e.g., journals, letters to the editor, historical fiction).

b. Compose and respond to original questions and/or problems from all content areas.

c. Explain procedures used to solve problems encountered in content areas (e.g., science experiments, math problems, and map and globe activities).

d. Investigate content specific topics to gather information and write.

e. Use experiences from the arts to write creatively and expressively..."

An interesting activity that uses the project discussed in this unit as a focus and that enhances and extends the learning acquired involves having the students write a narrative procedure that others could follow to replicate the design they created. After this is complete, have students choose a partner, switch procedures, and have the students attempt to follow the procedures. Observing the partner's progress and receiving feedback about instances where the procedure is inadequate to produce the desired result is a good way to gain insight into this type of writing.

An effective variation would be to break the class into groups of 4 or 5 students. Have the groups read through all group members' procedures, discuss them, and select one to represent the group. The groups then switch papers and attempt to replicate the design described in the narrative procedure they receive. As a culminating activity, the original is displayed for the whole group alongside the attempted replication, sparking a class discussion about the accuracy of the writing and the correctness of the interpretation, and determining whether the originator or the replicator group is the winner in this friendly competition.

Directions to Replicate My Design

1. Create a rectangular design that is six inches high and six inches wide.

2. Draw six lines from left to right dividing the picture into seven columns that run from left to right.

   The first line should be 1½ points thick, the second and third 6 points, the fourth 1½ points, the fifth 3 points, and the sixth 2¼ points.

   This first column running from left to right is one inch in width, the second is one half inch, the third one quarter, and the fourth one eighth. Also, the fifth is 1½ inches wide, the sixth 1⅞ inches wide, and the seventh 1½ inches wide.

3. Within the rectangle draw five lines from the top to the bottom creating six rows. Make all of these ¾ points thick.

4. Fill the top left hand segment created by the crossing of the lines with a light gray. In the far right column, count down to the fourth segment and fill that with light gray, too. Fill the bottom right hand segment with black.

5. Moving from left to right in the picture find the sixth column, which is the one next to the right hand column. Within the sixth column fill the top segment with medium gray tone. Moving down this column skip a segment and fill the next one you come to with medium gray, as well.

You are finished.

New Images from the
Floating World

What a society deems important is enshrined in its art.

— HARRY BROUDY

Please see the sections "Using this Book" and "Assessing Digital Art Projects" for more information about these standards, the interaction between them, and connecting these standards to the lessons in this book.

STANDARDS

NETS•S

Although all or most of the NETS•S are touched on in this unit, the connection is strongest and easiest to see and understand in standards listed below:

1. a, b	4. a, b, c
2. a, b	5. a
3. b, c, d	6. a, b

Note: In this unit and others, when students gather, analyze, select, and synthesize reference material from which they generate an original work of art, they are in effect *processing data from which an original work results* (NETS•S 3.d). Such works may be seen as alternative forms of a report.

National Standards for Arts Education (Visual Arts)

CS–1, AS b

CS–2, AS–a, b, c

CS–3, AS–a, b

CS–4, AS–a, b

CS–5, AS–b, c

CS–6, AS–a

UNIT OBJECTIVES

Students will be challenged to:

- Research and learn about Ukiyo-e, traditional Japanese woodblock prints.

- Understand the relationship of emerging technologies to the development of art forms that adopt and adapt them.

- Reflect on how the current technologies of print media and personal computing can be adapted to produce art works similar in spirit and intent to traditional Ukiyo-e.

- Produce an original edition of multiples that is a contemporary genre-based work of art and that taps a contemporary technology to enable the creation of images as editions of multiples.

CENTRAL IDEAS

Students love to tell stories with pictures, and I've often woven activities that capitalize on this into my work in the classroom. Students often respond particularly strongly to the use of details to support pictorial narrative. Furthermore, having them make certain that the details they choose to include in their work are visually and factually accurate is a brand of historical detective work they respond to favorably, as well. This natural affinity for narrative and historic art is a convenient entry point to projects based on genre, a facet of art history that can greatly enrich instruction across the curriculum.

Genre images, an important aspect of art, reveal much about the society that produces them. Ukiyo-e, traditional woodblock prints, is a genre that gives us a glimpse into the everyday life and values of the Japan of a bygone era.

A technology like traditional woodblock printing, or digital imaging today, has a strong influence on the design and aesthetic possibilities of the works produced with it. It also requires its own set of procedures and artistic understandings.

Today's students can tap technology to enable them to research images in the production of contemporary genre works, as well as to produce editions of prints that embody much the same spirit as traditional Ukiyo-e. I've found the project described in this unit to be one that accomplishes this in an easy and exciting manner.

TECHNOLOGY RATIONALE

There's nothing new about the art of collage or the role of line drawing in the creation of hand-crafted prints and other images. However, these forms carry their own special difficulties and challenges for student artists and can leave them frustrated and not well disposed toward tackling other areas of art making.

Encouragingly, it's been my experience that the project outlined here transforms the making of this type of art from an activity that would ordinarily resonate well for just a talented minority of students to something that any student can do well (and through which *all* can produce highly effective works of art). Furthermore, the facilitating dimensions of the technology used, as is the case in many of these projects, allow students to concentrate on the greater, cross-curricular concepts, rather than get stuck on technique and method.

Collage is not exceedingly challenging from the perspective of technique, although in the unskilled and inexperienced hands of students it can be difficult. The cutting and pasting processes of the traditional approach to collage can result in accidentally cutting off essential details, leaving extraneous material and the messiness of improper amounts of glue applied inexpertly. The technology used in this project will help students avoid all of those pitfalls. However, technology's greatest boon to student artists may be its assistance in locating the reference material required for projects such as this.

Going through perhaps hundreds of magazines and newspapers to find the elements needed to tell a story through collage is a daunting task and one for which the raw material needed is not likely to be on hand in the classroom. Using a search engine to find appropriate images makes access to the source material, and especially the difficult and tedious task of sorting through it, infinitely easier and more effective.

Furthermore, those who have made collage works know the extreme frustration of finding just the right image to include, but not being able to use it because of size problems, left to right orientation, light/dark contrast, color, and any number of other factors that must be accounted for in creating original art. Many downloaded images can be adjusted for all these factors, rendering what ordinarily would be useless images into perfect ones. Technology is the element that makes this possible.

In Ukiyo-e, images are presented as drawings developed from elegant contour lines, patterns, and areas of flat color. Shading is rarely seen and cast shadows practically never. Traditionally, this representation requires the skill and sophistication of highly accomplished and heavily experienced professional artists.

The informed and focused use of technology, though, makes the creation of such images something within the grasp of all students. Furthermore, by converting images produced with one set of aesthetic sensibilities to one with another, great insight into the act of representation is gained.

Principal Technology Skills Addressed

- Internet research/image mining

- Scanning of hard copy images and saving in a variety of file formats

- Image processing/retouching

Technology Resources Needed

- Internet-enabled computers/browser/search engine(s)

- Flatbed scanner

- Image processing/drawing-painting software

- Printer(s) (laser or inkjet with water-fast ink)

WEB RESOURCES

The Floating World of Ukiyo-e (comprehensive overview of Ukiyo-e):
www.loc.gov/exhibits/ukiyo-e/major.html

Japan Ukiyo-e Museum (background information on Ukiyo-e and
links to samples of master works):
www.ukiyo-e.co.jp/jum-e/

Jim Breen's Ukiyo-e Gallery (comprehensive meta listing of valuable Ukiyo-e resource links):
www.csse.monash.edu.au/~jwb/ukiyoe/ukiyoe.html

Kids Web Japan (illustrated explanations on Ukiyo-e for students):
http://web-japan.org/kidsweb/explore/culture/q2.html

Viewing Japanese Prints (illustrated essays on Japanese woodblock prints):
www.viewingjapaneseprints.net

Wikipedia—Ukiyo-e (overview of the history and making of Ukiyo-e plus external links):
http://en.wikipedia.org/wiki/Ukiyo-e

Unit Conceptual and Pedagogical Overview

Ukiyo-e, the traditional genre-themed woodblock prints of 17th- through 19th-century Japan are a wonderful jumping off place for learning a number of important concepts in art. These pictures were produced as editions of handmade images, featuring numerous colors and textures.

Ukiyo-e or "Images from the Floating World" were developed by a school of artists who merged a number of societal/cultural trends with artistic innovations and traditions to produce something so fresh and authentic that their work stands today as some of the most compelling and moving ever created.

Ukiyo-e illustrate an important movement by artists away from the accepted artistic dedication to representing official or courtly images to making images, not only of the common man's experience, but of an idealized notion held by commoners of fashion and luxury. Interestingly, they were not only depictions of the common people, but intended for consumption by them as well. Ukiyo-e were one of the first fine art techniques to be intentionally put within the reach of commoners and not made for institutional or royal purchasers.

Ukiyo-e portray worldly, simple pleasures, beauty reflected in casual and informal settings, and an ideal of the good life to be found in everyday settings. Fashionable women and their suitors, tasteful clothing and furnishings, and common household objects and their use are all typical of Ukiyo-e subject matter. Stylistically, they rely on informal poses of figures, and non-traditional and inventive composition and angles of view. Because artists produced them as editions of multiple images, great economy of representation and great inventiveness of depiction are often their hallmarks.

Ukiyo-e were much sought after by European modernists (such as the Impressionists and Post Impressionists) and their influence is strongly felt in the development of these movements. In fact, there are instances of unabashed copying of those movements by famous European artists.

Prominent among the pictorial aspects of Ukiyo-e that influenced Europeans are strong and elegant lines that define forms, an angle of view that lifts the picture plane toward the viewer while maintaining comfort with the scene presented, and flatness that is achieved by minimizing shading and refraining from the use of cast shadows.

Ukiyo-e were produced by master craftsmen who worked for or alongside the artists whose names they bear. The technique was laborious, involving the cutting of numerous blocks, printed one on top of the other for different colors and textures. The blocks were hand-colored, producing intense and personal tonal and color effects.

With the availability of digital technology, students can now make art similar in intent, content, finished product, and visual impact. Furthermore, by researching a traditional form to inform, inspire, and contextualize the creation of something new, with roots in the past, students are given a highly insightful experience. It's always been my experience that any project that encourages students to proudly define what's important to them in their world and show it off to others, is one that will be motivating, engaging, and satisfying. In this project students produce the type of art that I would fully expect them to keep into their adulthood.

ACTIVITIES

DAYS 1–3

1. **Research and preparation**

   a. Have students research Ukiyo-e through the Web as preparation for a short presentation to the class.

   Suggested focus questions:

   - How were Ukiyo-e made?

   - What subject matter do Ukiyo-e artists put in their pictures?

   - Do the materials and techniques used to make Ukiyo-e influence the way the images turn out?

   - Who were Ukiyo-e made for?

   b. Direct each student to download and print a personal favorite to be presented briefly to the group. These images can then be posted on a wall for class reference (or deposited into photo-gallery software and distributed as handy references while continuing work). Have the students discuss their discoveries about Ukiyo-e.

   c. Discuss genre images and have the class brainstorm the types of common pop-culture images that might constitute a modern-day corollary for the subjects and details depicted by Ukiyo-e masters.

   d. Students should next harvest examples of contemporary images that conform to their brainstormed ideas for use in the production of original works. Popular magazines and newspapers (both hard copy and online versions) as well as popular Web sites should prove fertile sources for these. Hard copy items can be scanned and saved as digital graphics files.

DAYS 4–6

2. **Production of original work**

   e. Direct the students to each select a number of the previously collected images that they feel work together to tell a story of an aspect of today's popular culture and the people who are part of it. *It may be convenient and effective for the students to deposit these images in a clearly named folder on their computer desktops for easy location.*

   f. Students start a new file for the creation of the work itself, which may be done in any word processing, drawing, painting, or photo processing program that allows for the importing of picture files.

   g. Once the students import the photos, they may move, enlarge, reduce, rotate, or overlap them as dictated by their taste, the needs of the story, or feeling they are attempting to convey. This (and step **e.**) are the principal steps in which the student artist makes a personal statement about the style and significance of our current culture and the manufactured items that shape it.

h. This step involves erasing the tonal material within and surrounding the selected photos and pasting them into the student's work file. This step is achieved by digitally using a paint or other software application that permits erasing the unwanted tonal material *or* by printing the student's work on a black-and-white printer and then using white-out to mask the tonal aspects. The object is to convert an image that is composed of a wide range of gray tones to a dark outline that has no gray tones inside or outside the image.

Note: If the hard copy approach is taken, the image should be either scanned or photocopied to render a clean image composed solely of lines. If done digitally, this step will not be necessary.

i. As a final step in the production of an edition, the student prints multiple copies of the work and then hand-colors them with either watercolor, watercolor marker, or colored pencil.

Note: For the final step it is advisable that a better-quality paper than ordinary 20 lb. printer paper be used. Consult the printer manufacturer's specifications to determine the limits of paper weight the printer (or photocopier) will handle. Also, encourage students to experiment with types of paper; some drawing or watercolor paper will be ideal for accepting ink and color.

FURTHER NOTES

Wet media will make the black ink used in many inkjet printers run. This problem can be avoided by using a laser printer, photocopier, or inkjet printer that takes ink specially prepared to be water-fast.

Using wet media to hand-color the prints also may wrinkle the paper. This situation can easily be remedied by carefully ironing the paper (as always, teacher experimentation is an essential part of ensuring that desired results are achieved with any given set of materials or procedures, especially before presenting them to students).

Project Sample

Process Used to Develop this Sample

After mining the Web for a body of raw reference material using a search engine (Google images was used here), the artist selected several images to communicate the piece's theme.

Using photo-editing software (Picasa, in this example) the artist converted the color photos to black-and-white images and then adjusted the contrast to eliminate as much middle tone (gray) as possible.

He then processed the photos in a way that gave them the look of a hard line drawing.

After importing the photos into a paint program (Paint, in this example) he eliminated the background tones by carefully tracing the contours with the application's thin virtual "brush" tip in white. Next, using progressively broader brush tips, the rest of the negative space was filled with white, as well. Then he traced important defining lines within the figure with the thin brush tip in black. Finally, using the software's Brush tool again (white tone selected), he covered the gray areas within the figure, leaving just the black outline.

Figure 3.1.
Project Sample—
Digital Ukiyo-e

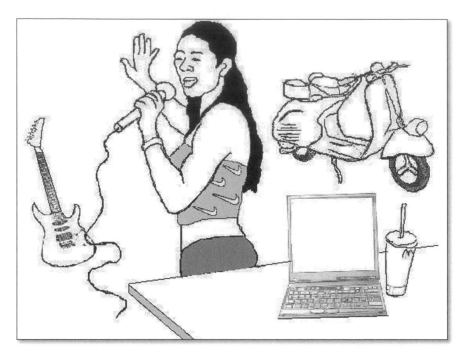

Using the Free-form Select tool, the images were freed from their background and placed within a new picture (document) in the painting program.

Using the fill function of the painting program, he filled selected areas with flat colors. Any spots left empty were colored in with the Brush tool.

Sharing the Work

Because these are works published as multiples, sharing may be accomplished by simply disseminating multiple copies of the paper version.

A more formal approach would be to hang the student prints in a traditional gallery style exhibition, or scan them a final time (after the process of hand-coloring), save them in graphics file format, and import them into either a slide show format (to be shown in a theater style setting) or into an online photo-sharing resource.

Note: See unit 18, "Sharing Student Art with an Audience" for an overview of other possibilities.

Assessment

The major thrust of assessing this project is to evaluate the student's understanding of how traditional Ukiyo-e imagery gives a glimpse into the culture that created it. Has the student built on that understanding by using modern techniques and technology, but in a way related to Ukiyo-e, in the creation of a work of his own? Additionally, has the student produced an image that clearly communicates ideas and that is pleasing enough to entice viewers to absorb the information that it presents?

Suggested General Assessment/Accountability Rubric for Unit 3

Project Components	Excellent	Proficient	Partially Proficient	Not Sufficiently Proficient or Incomplete
Completion of Project • Student uses paint program to transform selected reference images to black-and-white line drawings • Student digitally pastes images into picture, sizing and positioning them appropriately • Student digitally fills selected areas with flat fields of color	All portions of the project are completed successfully at a high level.	Most portions of the project are completed successfully at a high or satisfactory level.	Some important (and other) portions of the project are completed successfully at a satisfactory level.	Few of the project portions are completed success-fully at a satisfactory level.
Research and Preparation • Student researches and mines the Web for reference images • A small body of images are selected to tell the story of the identified theme	Conducted the needed research/ preparation in a way that allows for a full level of participation in the project.	Conducted the needed research/ preparation in a way that allows for a high level of participation in the project.	Conducted the needed research/ preparation in a way that allows for a satisfactory level of participation in the project.	Conducted the needed research/prep-aration in a way that allows for a minimal level of participation in the project.
Theme and Concept Learning • Student understands the historical, social, and aesthetic significance of Ukiyo-e and other forms of genre art • Student understands how to develop his own genre piece taking advantage of charac-teristics and approaches of Ukiyo-e	Fully understood the concepts and goals of the project. Understood the contextual back-ground content. Understood how to apply the above in the creation of an original work.	Understood a good deal of the concepts and goals of the project. Understood the contextual background content to a high degree. Understood how to apply the above in the creation of an original work to a high degree.	Understood some of the concepts and goals of the project. Understood the contextual back-ground content to a degree. Understood how to apply the above in the creation of an original work to a degree.	Did not adequately understand the concepts and goals of the project. Did not adequately under-stand the contextual background content. Did not adequately understand how to apply the above in the creation of an original work.

(Continued)

Suggested General Assessment/Accountability Rubric for Unit 3 *(Continued)*

Project Components	Excellent	Proficient	Partially Proficient	Not Sufficiently Proficient or Incomplete
Technical Proficiency • Student produces graphic elements with effective line quality • Student integrates separate elements into a visually interesting, harmonious composition that communicates information as intended	Demonstrated a very high degree of understanding and mastery of the concepts and skills involved in the techniques required of the project.	Demonstrated a good degree of understanding and mastery of the concepts and skills involved in the techniques required of the project.	Demonstrated a satisfactory degree of understanding and mastery of the concepts and skills involved in the techniques required of the project.	Did not demonstrate an adequate degree of understanding and mastery of the concepts and skills involved in the techniques required of the project.
Technology Use • Student uses image search engines appropriately • Student uses paint software to transform the raw graphic to line drawing • Student uses crop, import, size, move, and fill functions to place elements in composition	Handled the technology portions of the project in a highly effective, insightful, and responsible fashion.	Handled the technology portions of the project very proficiently and in an effective, insightful, and responsible fashion.	Handled the technology portions of the project in a satisfactorily effective, insightful, and responsible fashion.	Did not handle the technology portions of the project in a satisfactorily effective, insightful, and responsible fashion.
Creativity-Expression • Student uses the project as an opportunity to communicate a personal understanding of the world • Student uses design sense to take advantage of unique possibilities presented by raw graphics • Student produces a visually interesting and compelling work of art	Conceived, developed, and executed a work of art that is highly original and that takes full advantage of the medium's possibilities.	To a good degree, conceived, developed, and executed a work of art that is original and that takes full advantage of the medium's possibilities.	To a satisfactory degree, conceived, developed, and executed a work of art that is somewhat original and that takes advantage of some of the medium's possibilities.	Did not well conceive and execute a work that is original or takes good advantage of the medium's possibilities.
Graphic Relevance* All graphic elements are easy to "read," the purpose in their inclusion is clear, and they add to the visual impact and help tell the story of the piece.	Graphic elements clearly relate to the theme and help carry the message of this work.	Graphic elements generally relate and contribute to a identifiable theme for the work.	Graphic elements are somewhat clear in purpose.	It is not clear how the graphic elements employed relate or contribute to the theme of the work.

* The criteria expressed in this row is not included in rubrics for other projects in this book.

Note: Refer to chapter 7, "Assessing Digital Art Projects" for an overview of assessing technology-supported student visual art projects.

Cross-Curricular Connection

Digital Ukiyo-e and Social Studies

Ukiyo-e is a good example of genre art, a form that gives a slice of life view into the world of those who created and consumed it. In Ukiyo-e we find graphic evidence in artifacts, in the gestures and actions of figures, and in details of the environments in which we find them. These tell us about the manner and spirit of life in bygone Japan. All of these qualities are expressed clearly and economically in ways accessible to students.

After a brief discussion about Ukiyo-e that outlines its history, principles, and aesthetic characteristics, the following simple activity will enable students to use it as a focus for studying Japan.

1. Locate a Ukiyo-e work that you find interesting and that promises to provide information about the place and time in which it was created.

2. State the name and date of the work. Can you identify items and the actions of figures within it that correlate to the name? The date?

3. What can you find depicted in the picture that gives information about the life of the people of Japan?

The history of pictorial art is full of other examples of genre art—Jacob Lawrence's depictions of the lives of African Americans, the peasant scenes of Pieter Brueghel the Elder, and the nightclub drawings of Toulouse Lautrec, to name a few. After having studied Ukiyo-e, assign the following activity for a period in history during which genre art was produced.

1. Locate a work of art that is emblematic of _____.

2. How would you characterize this type of genre art? What can you discover about the artist who produced it? Which members of the society that produced it would have had access to it? Contrast it to Ukiyo-e.

3. How does the title relate to what is depicted and the time frame in which it was created?

4. List some of the items, figures, or actions depicted that give information about the society this work of art comes from?

By creating a technology-supported version of modern day Ukiyo-e, students are afforded an approach and artistic medium that can serve as a focus, motivator, and platform with which to research, understand, and report on their findings about any culture assigned to them.

Based on the project described in this unit, assign the students to create a "digital Ukiyo-e" of an historical period studied in class.

UNIT **4**

Holiday Surprise Calendar
Digital Image Album

Imagination will often carry us to worlds that never were.
But without it, we go nowhere.

— CARL SAGAN

Please see the sections "Using this Book" and "Assessing Digital Art Projects" for more information about these standards, the interaction between them, and connecting these standards to the lessons in this book.

STANDARDS

NETS•S

Although all or most of the NETS•S are touched on in this unit, the connection is strongest and easiest to see and understand in the standards listed below:

1. a, b	4. b, c
2. a, b, d	5. b, c
3. a, c	6. d

Note: In this unit and others, when students genuinely rise to the challenge set before them to identify a personal area of exploration in order to produce a work that will be part of a group effort that carries its own theme and criteria for relevance, they are *demonstrating personal responsibility for lifelong learning* (NETS•S 5.c)

National Standards for Arts Education (Visual Arts)

CS–1, AS–b

CS–2, AS–a, b, c

CS–3, AS–a, b

CS–4, AS–a

CS–5, AS–b, c

UNIT OBJECTIVES

Students will be challenged to:

- Understand the relationship of technology to the presentation of art content.

- Produce images that perform functions as well as embody design.

- Use technology to accomplish a series of steps in the production of an interactive art product.

CENTRAL IDEAS

Art products made for mass consumption occasionally establish a pictorial tradition that is culturally and artistically significant. The Holiday Surprise calendar (advent calendar) is a good example of this type of popular art.

In presenting this art form to my students as the basis for a project, I found that the same qualities that have made it so popular over the years ensured they would respond to it enthusiastically. Students appreciate making their contribution to a long-standing artistic tradition, especially one that is so easy to understand culturally, functionally, and aesthetically.

Traditional forms such as this one are made fresh again by their translation into a digital format, something that opens up many new possibilities.

The project presented in this unit offers the opportunity for reflection on communicating ideas through images and their relationships to one another. It also gives a focus for experimentation with new methods for presenting images in a digitally navigated format.

It is a given that students will produce holiday-themed art at numerous times during their school careers. This is often seen, however, as a traditional part of school culture, but not necessarily an essential learning activity. In developing this project, therefore, I seized a teachable moment to give students the opportunity to learn new and important ideas and skills through a classic activity, the instructional value of which is often overlooked.

TECHNOLOGY RATIONALE

The greatest impact technology gives to this project is in the way it presents art to the viewer. As the title suggests, there is a surprise to be promised and delivered. By hiding a portion of the student's work and delivering it when it is requested by the curious viewer, both needs are satisfied. This is done effectively through the use of a hyperlink, a digital device that has already become a highly accepted part of visual and literary publishing.

The finished product to be achieved through this project is a collaborative document (calendar) that is made viewable through a browser. Thus, the use of technology incorporates the work of many students into a single group work, the success of which is dependent on the participation of all and which displays the work of all equally. This is a powerful way to model collaborative projects, a highly prized work mode in the evolving workplace and an important 21st-century skill and educational goal.

The individual drawings the students do in this project may be done with traditional materials and later scanned to save them as graphics files, or they may be done in drawing/painting software that yields a document saved in graphic format from the beginning.

Principal Technology Skills Addressed

- Digital drawing/painting
- Hyperlinking digital content

Technology Resources Needed

- Drawing/painting program
- Multimedia program (that permits hyperlinking)

WEB RESOURCES

Online Advent Calendar (related example of digital surprise calendar):
www.smmp.com/Advent/Advent.htm

Woodlands Junior School (school-made examples of digital surprise calendars):
www.woodlands-junior.kent.sch.uk/customs/Xmas/calendar/

Holidays on the Net (related example):
www.holidays.net/adventcalendar/

Tate, the Cat Who Laughed (related examples):
www.advent-calendars.com
www.advent-calendars.com/previous.html

History of the Advent Calendar and Museum (overview and history with examples):
www.sellmer-verlag.de/history.htm

Whitney Museum—Create a Visual Narrative (how-to basics on simple hyperlinked student projects):
www.whitney.org/jacoblawrence/tell/narrative_links.html

Unit Conceptual and Pedagogical Overview

Sometimes the format of a work of art can be as interesting, thought provoking, and fun as its theme or message. People, young ones especially, love surprises, and an art format that is calculated to deliver surprises as its primary punch wins over the hearts of viewers and artists alike.

A much-loved and looked-forward-to art object, one that has a long tradition in Europe (where it originated), is the Christmastime advent calendar. While a religious theme is not appropriate in public school settings, the format that has evolved from the advent calendar is one that can be employed to lovely effect in a wide variety of school settings. This format can easily be re-contextualized into a Holiday Surprise calendar or Digital Image Surprise Album, as it lends itself to a wide variety of themes to be explored in connection with it.

Part of the charm of this format is the small, personal scale. Advent calendars were often given as Christmas cards or small seasonal decorations that encouraged viewers to manipulate them personally, one-on-one, and display them afterward for close up inspection by family, friends, and visitors.

In this regard, the small, personal, and close-up one-on-one nature of a computer screen becomes a perfect digital-age corollary.

Another dimension of the advent calendar format that begs adaptation as an art project is that the windows the viewer opens all reveal a surprise image. A different image resides in each window, but they are all related to a common theme.

Teachers new to the creation of art with students can inadvertently steer themselves and their students into frustration by failing to set clear goals, expectations, and parameters on the art works their students will make. Parameters, as many artists will agree, don't squelch creativity, but in fact often release it as each personality tackles the task of fulfilling a specific goal in its own individual and personal way. For example, how many ways are there to represent an evergreen tree: close-up, from a distance, in a group or forest? Should the focus be on the pattern of the needles or the cone? Should the tree be depicted as a simplified triangle, or in detail showing every knot in the bark? The possibilities are endless, and a class project that involves individual interpretations of such a unified theme benefits greatly from the criteria that hold it together.

Having students reflect on the mechanics of presentation in this project format, the parameters needed to make it work, as well as the overall concept, theme, and form, make it a rich and enlightening experience for young artists.

ACTIVITIES

The format of this project in particular requires a good understanding of the finished product before work begins. The way the parts fit the finished whole is essential and must be known before it can be produced.

DAY 1

1. Background and preparation

a. The teacher should present some examples of holiday surprise calendars (or similar small-scale products that involve the hiding of images and inviting viewers to discover them). Examples can be found on the Web (see Web Resources section). A discussion about why people enjoy this format, shared anecdotes of the students' personal experiences, and ideas about how to make surprise calendars (or similar art items) more effective, would all be good focusing and motivating exercises.

b. The discussion should end with the class deciding on a specific theme on which they will base their work (i.e., winter in the city, holidays in the tropics, New Year's wishes for the world, etc.)

2. The project

Once the teacher or class has selected the theme, the next step will be to produce the individual images in the windows. Traditional holiday surprise calendars (advent calendars) contain hidden images, one to be opened each day during the season leading up to Christmas. This is easily adapted to the number of days preceding school winter break (or any other day marking a celebration or seasonal milestone). Using January 1st, New Year's Day, as the culminating date for the calendar works well, as the 31 days in the month of December preceding it necessitates the production of 32 windows/drawings in all. This number is close to the average number of students in most public school classes. It is an easy matter to have the class generate a couple extra drawings, as it is to include a bonus window somewhere in the event of a larger than typical class.

Alternately, this may be an opportunity for a rather extensive individual project. Or the class could be divided into six or eight groups, each one producing its own calendar, which will call on each group member to produce several images.

The technology applications that make this project work are hyperlinks from one document to another. The project can be made to work on a simple level by using thumbnail gallery software (provided it's a variety that allows for the proper number of thumbnails to be placed on the page). Or the thumbnails can be created from scratch (a worthwhile exercise that will give students greater insight into Web graphics) by creating pairs of images, one a small image and the other full screen, and then in a Web authoring program, hyperlinking from the small to the large image.

In this project the element of surprise is key. The small image would be the set-up image, giving at best a hint of what clicking the link will open.

A suggested approach might be a collection of ornaments to make up the calendar view. When each ornament is "clicked" the viewer is taken to a surprise, full-screen message or image.

DAYS 2–4

3. Making original art

c. Students create images in pairs:

One image is an introductory, or cover, image that is both attractive and inviting, but that is also somewhat expected and even familiar. In the case of a "Winter in the City" calendar, the cover image might be the exterior of a building (with each student creating his or her own such image) or a window in a building (again, with each student creating his or her own). In the case of a "New Year's Resolutions" calendar, the cover might be an ornamental number one (to symbolize the first day of the New Year) with each student producing his own version.

The second image is the inside surprise image or message, which should relate to the group theme. This one calls on the unique personality, creativity, and sensibility of each student to come up with something imaginative, startling, or thought-provoking while relating to the theme.

Note: The images can be created as conventional drawings with conventional materials and then scanned and saved as (low density) graphics files (be careful not to use a paper that is too large for the scanner bed) or can done with digital drawing and painting software.

4. Assembling the finished piece

d. This project relies on technology more as a vehicle to present images powerfully, t han as a vehicle to create them. Assembling the finished piece is a separate, second step. Some teachers may opt to assemble the finished piece themselves out of the many pieces created by the students.

Or *(recommended where appropriate)*

Depending on ability levels and the availability of technology, a further portion of the project may be undertaken in which the students create the finished project, in addition to the individual images to be placed within it. Because the finished piece will be done on a computer using graphics files of the art produced by the students, the image can be copied so that any given image may be incorporated into any number of finished works.

It may be most effective to have this part of the project completed by small, collaborative groups of students, with three to five students working on the finished digital calendars together.

The technique is relatively simple. Each of the small cover images is imported into a single document or into a page within a multimedia program that allows for the creation of hyperlinks to other pages. Each of these can be placed as a rectangle (with or without a border, depending on the artist's taste and the capabilities of the chosen program) with a link established to the larger, surprise image, which resides on its own page.

Programs to make this work can be simple multimedia software, such as MediaBlender, or Web authoring applications, like Dreamweaver, that use standard navigational features such as those found in word processing applications. PowerPoint can also be used to finish the project. Use the Help function for information on creating hyperlinks between graphics located within the slide show.

Note: Alternately, an intermediate step may be taken: the artist can insert the individual images into a "table" in any program that performs this function (Word, Dreamweaver, etc.), then save the table as a JPEG file. The student can then import this table graphic into the Web or multimedia authoring program and add the buttons and links from the table to the separate pages.

Project Sample

Figure 4.1. Project Sample—Hyperlinked Holiday Calendar

Process Used to Develop this Sample

The students each executed an individual work within the parameters of theme, size, and medium that were set by the group under the guidance of the teacher at the start of the project. They used paper, pencil, and colored pencils. The images were scanned and saved in a graphics format (JPEG files, in this case).

The teacher then imported the scanned files into a table opened in Word, to produce a group work showing each individual's effort. Then the Word file was grabbed as a screen capture and saved as a JPEG file.

In WebBlender a button was put in the lower right hand corner of each drawing. These were hyperlinked to separate pages of the students' holiday Haiku poems.

Figure 4.2. Working on the project in WebBlender, a user-friendly Web authoring software for students

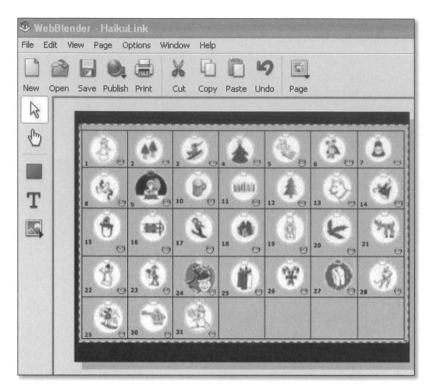

Figure 4.3. Haiku page linked from "candles" decoration (December 11th) on the calendar.

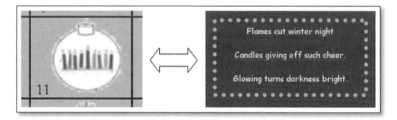

The viewer sees the entire calendar in the computer browser. By clicking on the button in the lower right corner of each day (Fig. 4.2), the viewer is taken to a full screen version of the corresponding student artist's poem (Fig. 4.3).

Sharing the Work

This project lends itself well to a digital presentation. If done in multimedia or presentation software (WebBlender or PowerPoint) it may be exhibited by offering it in a public place with a computer (set up as a kiosk) running the project. Additionally, the finished calendar would work well as a Web page, something that can either be uploaded to the Web or distributed on disk and viewed on a personal computer through a Web browser.

Note: If completed in multimedia software, converting to Web format should be researched ahead of time, although much of this type of software allows this to be accomplished easily.

Note: See unit 18, "Sharing Student Art with an Audience" for an overview of other possibilities.

Assessment

As each student produces his or her own individual images as a contribution to the group work, assessment of that portion of the project can be handled and facilitated with the use of a rubric (see below). However, aspects of the work in this project involve collaboration, a dimension that will require additional steps and criteria if it is to be included in the grade (see rubric for collaboration elsewhere in this book).

Suggested General Assessment/Accountability Rubric for Unit 4

Project Components	Excellent	Proficient	Partially Proficient	Not Sufficiently Proficient or Incomplete
Completion of Project • Student creates a pair of related drawings or drawing and related work • Drawings are scanned and saved in graphics format (If student is assigned this portion)	All portions of the project are completed successfully at a high level.	Most portions of the project are completed successfully at a high or satisfactory level.	Some important (and other) portions of the project are completed successfully at a satisfactory level.	Few of the project portions are completed successfully at a satisfactory level.
Research and Preparation • Student conceives an original work that will be a contribution to a group work	Conducted the needed research/ preparation in a way that allows for a full level of participation in the project.	Conducted the needed research/ preparation in a way that allows for a high level of participation in the project.	Conducted the needed research/ preparation in a way that allows for a satisfactory level of participation in the project.	Conducted the needed research/ preparation in a way that allows for a minimal level of participation in the project.
Theme and Concept Learning • Student understands the idea of an advent calendar–style work of art • Student understands the concept of hyperlinked documents	Fully understood the concepts and goals of the project. Understood the contextual background content. Understood how to apply the above in the creation of an original work.	Understood a good deal of the concepts and goals of the project. Understood the contextual background content to a high degree. Understood how to apply the above in the creation of an original work to a high degree.	Understood some of the concepts and goals of the project. Understood the contextual background content to a degree. Understood how to apply the above in the creation of an original work to a degree.	Did not adequately understand the concepts and goals of the project. Did not adequately understand the contextual background content. Did not adequately understand how to apply the above in the creation of an original work.
Technical Proficiency • Student uses drawing techniques and design elements to create an attractive piece that conforms to the theme	Demonstrated a high degree of understanding and mastery of the concepts and skills involved in the techniques required of the project.	Demonstrated a good degree of understanding and mastery of the concepts and skills involved in the techniques required of the project.	Demonstrated a satisfactory degree of understanding and mastery of the concepts and skills involved in the techniques required of the project.	Did not demonstrate an adequate degree of understanding and mastery of the concepts and skills involved in the techniques required of the project.

(Continued)

Suggested General Assessment/Accountability Rubric for Unit 4 *(Continued)*

Project Components	Excellent	Proficient	Partially Proficient	Not Sufficiently Proficient or Incomplete
Technology Use • Student scans drawings and saves scans in graphic file format (if appropriate)	Handled the technology portions of the project in a highly effective, insightful, and responsible fashion.	Handled the technology portions of the project very proficiently and in an effective, insightful, and responsible fashion.	Handled the technology portions of the project in a satisfactorily effective, insightful, and responsible fashion.	Did not handle the technology portions of the project in a satisfactorily effective, insightful, and responsible fashion.
Creativity-Expression • Student creates an original work of art that reflects personal taste and sensibilities, takes advantage of design possibilities presented by materials, while conforming to the standards set for the group effort	Conceived, developed, and executed a work of art that is highly original and that takes full advantage of the medium's possibilities.	To a good degree, conceived, developed, and executed a work of art that is original and that takes full advantage of the medium's possibilities.	To a satisfactory degree, conceived, developed, and executed a work of art that is somewhat original and that takes advantage of some of the medium's possibilities.	Did not well conceive and execute a work that is original or takes good advantage of the medium's possibilities.

Note: *Refer to chapter 7, "Assessing Digital Art Projects" for an overview of assessing technology-supported student visual art projects.*

Cross-Curricular Connection

Digital Calendars and Social Studies

The format of this project can be adapted to produce a wide variety of worthwhile technology-supported, art-centered projects across the curriculum. The basic premise of having each student produce two related items that are hyperlinked, one to entice the viewer and the other to reward him with a surprise, can be adapted beyond the format of a calendar to any class body of work presented as a hyperlinked chart.

However, the calendar is a familiar functional and cultural mechanism that can serve as the basis for many class activities. Because the number of days in a month is close to the number of students in a class, the collaborative nature of the project works well with the calendar approach.

National Women's History Month, for instance, would serve as a powerful curricular alignment for the project shown here. In this variation each student designs and illustrates a pair of images. The teaser image grabs the attention of the viewer with a question such as, "I am a physician, professor, and researcher. I am famous for being a NASA astronaut. Who am I?" The pay-off image provides an illustrated answer: "My name is Mae Jemison, and in 1992 I flew a mission aboard the Space Shuttle Endeavour."

Each student would create a pair of illustrated pages that would be incorporated into the class's hyperlinked calendar project. There are many possible adaptations for a class calendar project that celebrates cultural phenomena of significance: Disability Awareness Month (October), Black History Month (February), National Poetry Month (April), Luzo Brazilian Month (June), to cite a few.

UNIT 5

Time Warp Photo Portraits

> I really believe there are things nobody would see
> if I didn't photograph them.
>
> — DIANE ARBUS

Please see the sections "Using this Book" and "Assessing Digital Art Projects" for more information about these standards, the interaction between them, and connecting these standards to the lessons in this book.

STANDARDS

NETS•S

Although all or most of the NETS•S are touched on in this unit, the connection is strongest and easiest to see and understand in the standards listed below:

1. a, b, d	4. a, b, c, d
2. a, b, d	5. a, b, c
3. a, b, c, d	6. a, b, d

Note: In this unit and others, when students are configured in small and large work groups in order to share materials, assist one another, produce group projects and exhibitions, or other group approaches to sharing their art works, they are working to *contribute to project teams to produce original works or solve problems* (NETS•S 2.d).

National Standards for Arts Education (Visual Arts)

CS–1, AS–a, b

CS–2, AS–a, b, c

CS–3, AS–a, b

CS–4, AS–a, b, c

CS–5, AS–a, b, c

CS–6, AS–a, b

UNIT OBJECTIVES

Students will be challenged to:

- Understand the portrait as one of the principle forms of artistic expression.

- Comprehend the fine art aspect of photography as opposed to its casual or functional existence.

- Produce an original photograph with the qualities of a work of art.

- Consider the qualities of monochromatic works as opposed to full color representation.

CENTRAL IDEAS

Photography, often seen as a casual pastime that produces a common product, can be a medium used to produce works of truly fine art. However, this concept can leave many students struggling. Perhaps this shouldn't be surprising, as it's an understanding about a dimension of art that escapes much of the adult population, too.

One particular aspect of photography's range of possibilities is its remarkable suitability for portraiture. Through studying photography as portrait art, I've found that its role as an art-making medium becomes easier for students to comprehend. Furthermore, by studying historic portrait photographers, the approaches and design factors developed within this medium can give great insight into the art-making process in general.

Students can tap technology to produce effective photographs within the context of classic fine art photography, particularly within the field of portraiture.

TECHNOLOGY RATIONALE

Through the project presented in this unit, students will come to a greater understanding about the art of photography. Not only will they produce an original photo portrait, but they will attempt to create one that can sit as an equal alongside another from an historical period.

To create such an image, one that gives the appearance of great age, would be difficult if it were not for the availability of low-cost or free, easy-to-use software. Such resources are widely available, many of them downloadable from the Web.

This project employs technology to create an original image, to process it as a work of art using standard photo-editing effects, and to create a customized effect of aging, making it look like an antique photo.

Additionally, the research needed to gain insight into the processes to accomplish this is made possible by Web-based search engines, particularly those that primarily ferret out images.

Principal Technology Skills Addressed

- Web research/image mining

- Digital photography

- Image processing

Technology Resources Needed
- Digital cameras
- Printer(s)
- Photo/image processing software
- Digital photo organizer

WEB RESOURCES

American Museum of Photography (collections of related daguerreotypes):
www.photography-museum.com/sandh1.html

About.com (timeline of photography, film, and cameras):
http://inventors.about.com/od/pstartinventions/a/Photography.htm

Library of Congress (comprehensive resource of Civil War photographs):
www.lib.lsu.edu/cwc/links/photo.htm

TreasureNet (classic examples of Civil War photos):
www.treasurenet.com/cgi-bin/treasure/images.pl/Search?search=+"Civil War" +"Georgia"

Indiana State Library (Civil War Soldier Photograph Exhibit):
www.statelib.lib.in.us/www/isl/indiana/civilwarex/civilwarindex.htm

PhotographyTips.com (general how-to basics of portrait photography):
http://photographytips.com/page.cfm/368

Unit Conceptual and Pedagogical Overview

Photography as a visual art form is a fruitful area for students to explore. Today's digital cameras automatically handle many of the technical aspects of focus, lighting, and exposure, and other variables for the photographer. Consequently, students are freed from the difficult aspects of mastering technique, a factor that dominates freehand drawing and painting exercises, and can make personal, compelling, and original images with confidence. Furthermore, because there is no monetary expenditure on film or processing, young photographers are freed to experiment without limiting the number of ideas and approaches they'd like to try.

However, because pointing and clicking in almost any direction, even at random, can produce a somewhat acceptable image, design and project parameters must be imposed on student photography projects in order to give them full meaning and bring them into the realm of true discipline.

The study of famous photographers is a good jumping-off place for students to understand the art of photography before they begin to practice it themselves. This will help them distinguish between casual household photographs and serious fine art photography, a distinction they may not have discovered prior to this unit, and one they may have some difficulty comprehending. As is often the case with newcomers to the study of art, the notion of difficulty in the execution of images and their value as aesthetic objects can be confused.

A Web search on fine art photographers will turn up the names Stieglitz, Brady, Adams, Abbott, and others who applied many classic design principles to photography. A study of their work will reveal much in common with master painters who worked in the areas of portraiture, still life, landscape, and other classic formats.

Viewing art photography in an historical context will prove highly fruitful as well. Civil War photographs are sufficiently removed from most of what, in our experience, would be categorized as familiar and therefore offer a good opportunity to view photography afresh. Many compelling and moving art photographs of this era can be found on the Web for the inspection, reflection, illumination, and inspiration of young artists.

Mathew Brady is but one good example of a latter 19th-Century photographer of high achievement. Studying his work will help establish a unit focus. Research will turn up others, as well.

It's interesting to note that Civil War photographs easily sort themselves out into a limited number of clearly identifiable genres. There are battlefield scenes; photos of buildings that served as important headquarters, command posts, and meeting places; group portraits of regiments, platoons, and battalions; portraits of officers and politicians; and several other categories. This is likely the case because photography was generally not considered a casual undertaking at the time. Photographs were made on a regular basis, but with some pains in preparation and processing. Photography was generally undertaken with a set and easily definable purpose in mind. These aspects make it easy to study and discuss Civil War photography with students.

One popular photographic genre of that time was the seated portrait, which offers a fine exercise for student photographers. This project can be done in the classroom and offers all students the opportunity to participate as both a photographer and as a model. Another genre is the standing group photo, which offers another and related possibility. The relationship between the studied, historical photographs and the creation of similar but updated works by the students can establish a context that supports the kind of control in the classroom situation that will aide the teacher in supervising and assuring that the ease of photography doesn't allow the exercise to lose its meaning.

Again, because acceptable images are so easy to produce by digital photography, expanding the scenario beyond the simple production of singleton photos enriches the learning experience greatly. The production of a cohesive, comprehensive body of products is the perfect approach for this.

An exhibition, virtual or real world, and the publishing of a catalog or album offer great possibilities for class projects such as this one. In this case the album takes on the role of organizing and planning rather than serving as the culminating product or activity.

ACTIVITIES

DAY 1

1. **Research and preparation**

   a. Introduce the project by passing around a reproduction (digital copy) of a 19th-century photograph, and engage the students in a discussion about its probable place in the history of image making.

   Suggested focus questions:

   - How old is the art of photography?

   - How has it changed since its inception? How has access to the tools of photography changed over the years?

   - For what purposes did people primarily use photography in its early days? What were the alternatives to photography then?

   - Looking at photographs from the 19th century, describe their look and characteristics as images.

   As a follow-up, you may wish to assign the students to research both the history of photography and photography as fine art. Have a class follow-up discussion in which the students report and reflect on their Web-based research.

   b. Direct the students to find and print examples of Civil War-era photographic portraits. These can be saved individually and/or put up together (temporarily) on a wall or bulletin board for reference as the group works on this project.

   c. Inform the students that they will be posing for and taking photographs in the spirit of Mathew Brady's portraits the next time the class meets and they may wish to alter their dress accordingly.

   Note: The inclusion of time-identifying objects in the photo can take this project in interesting directions. This project can be done as a contemporary portrait that embraces the aesthetics of a bygone era, a mock photo from the past with students dressing the part, or an intentionally contradictory blend of both approaches.

   Additional focus questions that will inform the project might include:

   - What sort of camera angle is most commonly used in classic 19th-century portrait photos? (Eye level? Bird's eye? Worm's eye?)

   - Do the photos appear to have used available light, available light with fill-in flash, or artificial light?

   - What sorts of instructions might the photographer have given his subjects?

DAY 2

2. **Making original photographs**

    d. Split the class into small collaborative groups (three to five students). Each group will share a digital camera and assist one another in production of original photos. Within the work schedule of each group, each student will:

- Take at least one individual portrait of one of the other group members.

- Take at least one group photo of all of the other group members.

- Have at least one individual photo taken of himself by one of the other group members.

- Be part of at least one group photo that includes all of the other group members except for the photographer of that shot.

A simple cyclic shooting schedule can be worked out by the members, rotating and taking turns posing and acting as photographer. The group can experiment beforehand with how to take advantage of available light for effective exposures, the use of fill-in flash, backgrounds, and so on.

Save the photos for the next session.

DAY 3

3. **Processing images**

    e. The next phase of the project involves students working either individually or in pairs or small groups to process their photos. Students are directed to select a single portrait and group portrait that they took and process it to give it the effect of a Civil War-era photograph. Image-processing software that offers a variety of useful effects is common; many varieties are free and downloadable or are provided with the purchase of a digital camera. Various functions will render an image as black-and-white, sepia, or other monochromatic finishes, and vignetting or other edge effects can assist in aging the image, as well.

The finished "antique" photos can be saved as a digital graphics file and/or printed out.

Project Samples

Process Used to Develop this Sample

The technology involved in this project is simple yet effective.

By studying authentic photos that date from a distant period and comparing them to contemporary photos, a number of characteristic differences were easy to observe.

In addition to the black-and-white aspect, early photos have a yellowish or sepia tone. Photos, even though they are in focus, may have fuzziness as a result of the different types and

Figure 5.1. Project Sample—Time Warp Photographs

Figure 5.2. Archival Reference Photo

quality of lenses, as well as the photographic processing of bygone times. Shadows, too, are somewhat different. Because of the long exposures used to create these images, the lighting effect is similar to a somewhat diffused light, even if taken in brilliant sunlight.

Another distinct characteristic of historic images includes vignetting—the use of a soft edge surrounding pictures that tapers off into the white of blank paper. And of course, the wear and tear experienced over time may have produced cracks, tears, deterioration of the surface, and other gross indications of great age.

All of these elements were taken into account when planning this project and the approach taken to create its visual end products.

Modern-day digital photos are generally clear, sharp, and flooded with intense light. Through the use of readily available software though, they can be transformed to look like their predecessors from the long-distant past of early photography. Photo-editing software, some of it available as free or low-cost downloads, will transform contemporary photos to close facsimiles of antique photos. Applications such as Picasa, for instance, will convert color to black-and-white or sepia monotone. They can also allow the image to be made fuzzy or out of focus and for shadows and highlights to be minimized. A palette of effects can be applied nearly instantly for this kind of purpose. In this particular case, all of the effects were employed using Picasa.

Additionally, by importing the photo into a paint program, cracks and other effects of extreme aging can be added to the photo. By doing some Web image mining, examples of antique photos were acquired for the purpose of visually studying the appearance of such features. A few of these were selected and reproduced to fake indications of age (i.e., cracks, age pitting in the surface, and a burn pattern).

In addition to their technical and aesthetic "fingerprints," the style and fashion of 19th-century photos gives away their age. In addition to the details of photos, clothing, architecture, machines, and so on, there is the manner of pose and composition. Taken before candid photos were commonplace, 19th-century photos generally are still and contrived. Portraits are clearly posed. Almost everything is shot frontally and in full length. While the photos are composed, there is little evidence of pre-cropping in the composition at the time of shooting, or cropping during final processing in terms of offering segments of the whole figure or tableau. This approach was used in Figure 5.2.

Overall, the sensibilities about how a photo should be crafted and what makes a good photo are entirely different now from what they were a hundred or more years back. Photography in the past warranted much more effort, resources, cost, and time, resulting in photographers taking a much more formal, predictable, and risk-averse approach. Without the luxury of being able to shoot many photos casually, the result was an entirely different photographic product. By adopting the attitudes and approaches of these long-ago photographers, a facsimile photo was produced similar to those shot in the past.

Sharing the Work

Ways to share this work with an audience might include:

- A traditional exhibition of hard copy printouts of the student photos
- A kiosk-based digital exhibition using photo-gallery software
- A PowerPoint presentation of the class's body of work on this project
- A Web site carrying a photo gallery version of the work

An interesting and amusing variation on the project can be had by displaying the preparatory image research the students did alongside their finished facsimile photos. The effect of both is enhanced this way as the authentic historical photos establish a context for the student work and the facsimiles speak to a continuing tradition. The synergy created by displaying them together speaks of student work that is not only imaginative and creative, but authoritative, reflecting knowledge of how one's work extends that of those who came before.

Note: See unit 18, "Sharing Student Art with an Audience" for an overview of other possibilities.

Assessment

This project calls on students to process digital photos in order to give them the look of antique photos. Although the goal of the assignment is given, there is no precise approach or method stipulated in how to achieve this. Accomplishing the goal will require drawing conclusions through comparisons as well as experimentation and insight based on comprehension of the background information (discussed at the beginning of the unit).

Suggested General Assessment/Accountability Rubric for Unit 5

Project Components	Excellent	Proficient	Partially Proficient	Not Sufficiently Proficient or Incomplete
Completion of Project • Student shoots original digital photos • Student transforms the original to a facsimile of an antique photo	All portions of the project are completed successfully at a high level.	Most portions of the project are completed successfully at a high or satisfactory level.	Some important (and other) portions of the project are completed successfully at a satisfactory level.	Few of the project portions are completed successfully at a satisfactory level.
Research and Preparation • Student researches style and appearance of historical photos • Student researches and acquires artifacts with which to pose figures	Conducted the needed research/ preparation in a way that allows for a full level of participation in the project.	Conducted the needed research/ preparation in a way that allows for a high level of participation in the project.	Conducted the needed research/ preparation in a way that allows for a satisfactory level of participation in the project.	Conducted the needed research/ preparation in a way that allows for a minimal level of participation in the project.
Theme and Concept Learning • Student understands the history of photography and what can be learned from historical photos • Student understands the concept of artistic media, aesthetics, and techniques relate to history	Fully understood the concepts and goals of the project. Understood the contextual background content. Understood how to apply the above in the creation of an original work.	Understood a good deal of the concepts and goals of the project. Understood the contextual background content to a high degree. Understood how to apply the above in the creation of an original work to a high degree.	Understood some of the concepts and goals of the project. Understood the contextual background content to a degree. Understood how to apply the above in the creation of an original work to a degree.	Did not adequately understand the concepts and goals of the project. Did not adequately understand the contextual background content. Did not adequately understand how to apply the above in the creation of an original work.
Technical Proficiency • Student uses design elements to produce a facsimile historical photo that is effective, convincing, and communicates appropriate information	Demonstrated a very high degree of understanding and mastery of the concepts and skills involved in the techniques required of the project.	Demonstrated a good degree of understanding and mastery of the concepts and skills involved in the techniques required of the project.	Demonstrated a satisfactory degree of understanding and mastery of the concepts and skills involved in the techniques required of the project.	Did not demonstrate an adequate degree of understanding and mastery of the concepts and skills involved in the techniques required of the project.

(Continued)

Suggested General Assessment/Accountability Rubric for Unit 5 *(Continued)*

Project Components	Excellent	Proficient	Partially Proficient	Not Sufficiently Proficient or Incomplete
Technology Use • Student uses digital camera and photo-editing software effectively • Student retouches digital photos effectively in paint (or other) program	Handled the technology portions of the project in a highly effective, insightful, and responsible fashion.	Handled the technology portions of the project very proficiently and in an effective, insightful, and responsible fashion.	Handled the technology portions of the project in a satisfactorily effective, insightful, and responsible fashion.	Did not handle the technology portions of the project in a satisfactorily effective, insightful, and responsible fashion.
Creativity-Expression • Student produces an original work that reflects his or her personal sensibilities and that effectively communicates information and affect about chosen subject	Conceived, developed, and executed a work of art that is highly original and that takes full advantage of the medium's possibilities.	To a good degree, developed, and executed a work of art that is original and that takes full advantage of the medium's possibilities.	To a satisfactory degree, conceived developed, and executed a work of art that is somewhat original and that takes advantage of some of the medium's possibilities.	Did not well conceive and execute a work that is original or takes good advantage of the medium's possibilities.

Requiring the student to explain the process followed and the decisions made will greatly enrich the assessment. The chart below is designed to help facilitate this aspect of assessment.

Explains the Art Work Produced through Participation in the Project

Prompt	Exemplary	Satisfactory	Unclear
How does the way you posed the photograph cue the viewers to the time and place you would like them to perceive?			
What objects, backgrounds, or other information-giving elements did you include in your photo to place it in an historical context?			
What photographic qualities did you give the photo to date it?			
What aspects of the photograph as a physical object did you add to make it appear authentic to the time and place you selected?			
Please give examples of authentic photos upon which you modeled yours.			

Note: Refer to chapter 7, "Assessing Digital Art Projects" for an overview of assessing technology-supported student visual art projects.

Cross-Curricular Connection

Historical Photos in Social Studies

This project lends itself well to adaptation as a research-centered project done within the Social Studies area.

Attention to the details of the physical makeup of the historical world portrayed is what makes this project work. Items such as clothing, tools, weapons, transportation, signage, and architectural features all give visual cues to the era captured within the photograph. The teacher can capitalize on this in a number of ways to establish a worthwhile and engaging Social Studies research project.

A good approach would be to create a list of criteria for things the student should include within the project. By requiring, for instance, the inclusion of at least one piece of advertising from the era portrayed (e.g., a hat, a mock (or authentic, if possible) newspaper or other publication, or other historical artifacts), an interesting challenge is presented. Students, after identifying examples of the elements to include, would either acquire them directly or make facsimiles for use in their photo projects. At the presentation of the photo to the class (an enjoyable and engaging activity in and of itself) the student would defend his or her choices as authentic and valid items to establish the given time period.

An interesting twist to put on this project would be the intentional inclusion of an element of anachronism in the photos. For instance, a laptop computer in a Civil War scene or a skateboard in a Roaring Twenties scene. Such inclusions spark amusing and worthwhile discussions and reinforce the concepts associated with the study of history and the role that graphic images, particularly photography, play in it. Taking this idea even further, a highly amusing variation of the project involves creating antique photos from periods before the invention of photography, for instance photographic evidence of the building of Mayan temples.

"Devolving" Drawings
An Animal Study Series

The object of art is not to reproduce reality,
but to create a reality of the same intensity.

— ALBERTO GIACOMETTI

Please see the sections "Using this Book" and "Assessing Digital Art Projects" for more information about these standards, the interaction between them, and connecting these standards to the lessons in this book.

STANDARDS

NETS•S

Although all or most of the NETS•S are touched on in this unit, the connection is strongest and easiest to see and understand in the standards listed below:

1. a, b, c, d	4. a, b, c, d
2. a	5. a, c
3. a, b, c	6. a, b

Note: In this unit and others, when students analyze and/or use graphic systems of representation of real world objects, they are *using models and simulations to explore complex systems and issues* (NETS•S 1.c)

National Standards for Arts Education (Visual Arts)

CS–1, AS–b

CS–2, AS–a, b, c

CS–3, AS–a, b

CS–4, AS–a

CS–5, AS–a, b, c

CS–6, AS–a

UNIT OBJECTIVES

Students will be challenged to:

- Develop an understanding of drawing figures (animals) by analyzing them for the basic shapes in their construction.

- Understand the development of images as the result of a sequentially evolved process.

- Develop an understanding of the evolution of design through the process of reduction, abstraction, and invention.

- Create an original work in line only.

CENTRAL IDEAS

Although an important part of art making involves referring to or representing a real-world subject, great diversity is found in the universe of approaches artists take in constructing such images. Young artists rarely reflect on this breadth of diversity.

In working with a great many students over the years, it's been my experience that they don't easily comprehend the difference between and significance of styles and levels of representation. A cartoon-type drawing of a bunny may draw their attention as thoroughly as a photo-realistic one of the same subject, so long as it is well executed. Students tend to gravitate toward a style that is easy to understand or is familiar to them. I find that guiding them through the experience of producing multiple varieties of representational images on a theme enlightens the students and ultimately provides them with choices, an empowering enhancement to their experience as artists.

One significant understanding of representational art is to see styles and approaches as a continuum that runs from the realistic to the loosely referential and inventive. Many artists have explored this continuum through a process of progressive abstraction, one that moves images from highly detailed representations toward basic shapes that relate to the underlying structure of their subjects.

Another observation I've shared with many colleagues is that students tend to view drawing in terms of an end result rather than as a valuable *process* that produces the end product. Guiding them through the creation of drawings in series fosters their understanding of this process. They often benefit greatly from the opportunity to experience representation as an ongoing exploration, as opposed to a method directed solely at the production of a precon-ceived finished work.

TECHNOLOGY RATIONALE

This use of technology in this project combines a number of approaches and techniques that are also used in other projects appearing in this book. This is so because the finished piece is at once a continuum of an evolving image, one that goes through a variety of changes and transformations and then assumes yet another identity as all its phases are embraced in an inclusive compilation that is a work of art in its own right.

This continuum begins with a search for an appropriate starting-point reference photo. In the next phase, photo-editing produces an image with some of the characteristics of a photograph and some of a flat drawing. The journey from photo to line drawing is finished by using black outlining in a paint program and eliminating all middle tones.

Our image continues its journey from contour line drawing to an analysis of the complex form of the subject as a collection of simple shapes. And finally, once it has been broken down into simple shapes, they are moved, manipulated, and rearranged in pure design.

Such an extended and complex process could only be attempted by a master artist, such as Picasso, and that over a lengthy period of time. Through the use of technology, a straight-forward approach that allows students to comprehend this pictorial process while executing stages in a predictable and easy-to-achieve fashion will result in a high degree of success.

One of the great advantages of completing this type of project on a computer is that one image can be drawn right over another. The artists can work from a saved set of information taken from a previous version (i.e., size, placement, line quality, etc.). It also makes infinitely easier and more feasible the logistics of working on, tracking, saving, and above all, picking up the thread of a work session precisely where it was left off.

Finally, in a complex process such as the one described here, the technology establishes parameters that keep all students and their work on the same page. When having discussions about the work is part of the learning process, sharing and assessing the work in an exhibit (whether virtual or real-world) provides a unifying and technology-based structure to the project.

Principal Technology Skills Addressed

- Web research/image mining
- Image processing
- Digital drawing

Technology Resources Needed

- Internet access/browser/search engine(s)
- Photo/image processing software
- Drawing program

WEB RESOURCES

Inuit Art

Carleton University Art Gallery—Transformation:
www.carleton.ca/gallery/Creature/trans.html

Picasso Bulls

Art Experts, Inc. (scroll down to Linear Bull Study):
www.artexpertswebsite.com/pages/artists/picasso.php

Impressionism & the Making of Modern Art—Picasso's Bulls:
http://blogs.princeton.edu/wri152-3/nbisaria/archives/001985.html

Moors Magazine (single image of Picasso bull):
www.moorsmagazine.com/images/bull3.jpg

Animals in African Art

Hamill Gallery of African Art—Animals in African Art:
www.hamillgallery.com/SITE/Animals.html

African Rock Art

The Rock Art Foundation—Rock Art Gallery:
www.rockart.org/gallery

Imagery in African Art

National Museum of African Art/Smithsonian Institution—Imagery in African Art
(interactive tool to search for images):
http://africa.si.edu/collections/imgrypg.asp

Unit Conceptual and Pedagogical Overview

In his various studies of the bull, Picasso demonstrates a variety of creative processes that are central to his consistent making of great art. First is the identification of a motif that holds particular fascination for the artist. Picasso chose the bull, an animal that looms large in the iconography of his native culture. It is both personal and universal for Spaniards.

In the bull, Picasso found a simple, yet wide platform upon which he could experiment and learn from during the course of a lifetime of art making. He would return to this motif again and again, each time coming at it from a different angle, and finding it to be a perfect home base from which to launch renewed forays into the world of image making. One of the great opportunities for students in the following activity is for them to personalize this approach by identifying their own subject, one they will handle in the traditional way described here.

We see this loyalty to a basic, central motif in artists other than Picasso. Dali had elongated architectural figures in profile, Trova used the Fallen Man, Wayne Thiebaud glazed pastries, Warhol had the soup can, Monet came back to water lilies, and the list goes on. What is especially interesting about this approach to making art is the way these icons aid in the creation of a personal language and how both icon and language evolve in tandem over the course of time.

It is especially revealing to see how an artist, while concentrating on a set motif, will change, refine, and evolve it over a series of steps in a process that begins with the familiar and ends wherever the artist's imagination and design sensibilities take it. This is an important dimension to art making, not only in the overall development of the field of modern art, but also in the development of the visual language of specific artists. The process undertaken involves the evolution of a series of approaches to portraying a subject. In the beginning we often see a somewhat traditional rendering of the reality of the subject. This later gives way to the use of the subject as a launching pad for explorations into invention and fancy that leaves mere representation behind and drifts off in new directions.

Animal imagery in African art demonstrates a similar fanciful and expressive design based on the broad truths that underlie the structure of animal bodies. African art provides a useful and thought-provoking counterpoint to modern art, and it is an informative and fruitful focus for students as they work on this and similar projects. Many European modern artists slowly evolved their image making from a realistic representational approach to the kind of invention of fanciful images that loosely refer to their subjects that we see in African art. These European artists studied African art and found much to admire in the simplicity and freedom with which traditional African artists worked. Today's students can benefit as well by making and studying this connection.

This project will call on students to create a series of images of a basic subject. The students' images will progress from imitation to representation through analysis, to simplification and abstraction, ending up with the nonobjective or near nonobjective use of design elements that will assume a visual identify of their own.

It is only by experimenting with a variety of styles and approaches to representation and abstraction that a developing artist can begin to decide which is his own personal signature style. The activity presented in this unit not only involves the students in that process directly, but has them reflect on the concept behind it as well, showing how struggles fit within the context of the great history of art. I have observed many light bulbs go off over young artists' heads as they work through this process.

ACTIVITIES

DAY 1

1. **Research, analysis, and preparation**

    a. Instruct the students to mine the Web for large photographs of animals. Alternately, you may wish to have the students shoot their own photos of pets or zoo animals and share them for use in this project. Images that show the entire figure and display its parts in an easily identifiable manner will work best. The images selected must fill most of an 8.5 x 11 inch piece of paper or be of sufficient resolution to enlarge to fill this space while remaining clear enough to identify the subject. After collecting several images, the students should select one on which to base this project.

    The students should save the selected photographs as graphics files that they can import into a photo processing or painting program.

DAY 2

2. **Transform a photograph**

    b. Save the chosen photo as version 1.

    c. Perform the following steps to transform the photograph into a line drawing:

    -   In a photo-editing program (e.g., Picasa, Adobe Photoshop Elements) manipulate the contrast of the photo to enhance the visibility and prominence of the outlines within and without the figure. Save and label the file as version 2 (or, depending on how the raw photo influences the results, go directly to the next step).

    -   In a painting program, trace the outlines of the figure and the identifiable shapes within using the drawing tool.

    -   With the eraser tool for large areas, and with the drawing tool again (but with a white tone selected), erase the toned material from within and outside of the figure. This process may go on for some time, switching between black line to define the basic shapes from which the figure is composed and erasing unwanted lines and toned material. This process is complete when the figure is composed entirely of black lines on a white background and is broken into a series of basic shapes (circles, ellipses, peanut or sausage shapes, triangles, etc.) from which the still-recognizable figure of the animal subject is composed. Have students save this as version 3.

DAY 3

3. **Transform a line drawing**

    d. In a drawing program that allows for the creation of groupings of auto shapes, place version 3 to the left side in a new file (select landscape mode for the page setup). Next to it, on the right side of the page, copy the line drawing by choosing an ellipse, triangle, or other auto shape for each shape outlined in version 3. Group these together until an approximation of the original line drawing is achieved. Save the grouping as version 4.

e. By dragging and dropping the basic shapes that still represent the original animal figure, create a new composition that is a non-representational design. Shapes should be moved until a pleasing design is achieved. Save the new image and label it as version 5.

f. The finished project shows the progress of the design in its sequential steps, all versions working together to create a whole work. Lay the images out in the order completed, from left to right. Students may accomplish this in the following ways:

- A hard copy piece that is a series of drawings affixed to one another in a horizontal band, with the earlier drawings to the left and the latter drawings to the right.

- A virtual piece that reduces all of the images and imports them into a single page/screen of a multimedia or Web-authoring program. Set them as a single band running from left to right. Each drawing should also exist as a full-screen version on its own. Have the artist create a hyperlink from each of the small pictures to the larger version's page.

Project Sample 1

Process Used to Develop this Sample

In this sample we see six progressive responses to an ordinary photograph of a cat. In the first (top left) the artist processed the photo using the free Google resource Picasa to increase the contrast and flatten the image to something in which lines and shapes are easy to identify.

Figure 6.1. Project Sample—Hard copy composite of the drawing series.

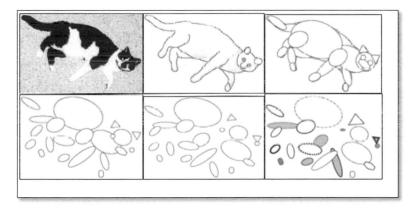

Moving from left to right (top row), the middle image is a transformation of the first, accomplished with the program Paint by erasing or going over all of the areas in white and heightening the lines in black (this is made easier by selecting a view of the image several times normal size, allowing manipulation of the mouse with greater control).

The artist then imported the resulting image into a word processing program (Word in this case, but any program that allows drawing with auto shapes will work) and drew shapes directly over the outline of the cat using the auto shapes, nudge, size, and free rotate functions.

The fourth (bottom left) image is produced by highlighting and deleting the outline below the shapes and then nudging them into new positions.

The fifth image is a continuation of this process. Creating the sixth image (bottom right) involved further moving the shapes and then selecting and treating them with the program's line weight and quality functions and filling them with a tone.

During the entire process the artist kept one copy of each version in its original state as he worked on and transformed a second copy as described above.

All six versions were combined to produce a single work in sequence. The artist accomplished this by inserting them into the word processing program, adjusting their sizes, and nudging them to form the final configuration. He employed a heavy black line border around each of the images to tie the composite together visually.

Project Sample 2

In this version, seven Web pages are used to display the completed piece—one for the composite piece and one for each of the six images. The image sections of the composite are each hyperlinked to another page on which their corresponding individual image fills the entire page. In this way, with the click of a mouse, the viewer can toggle between a view of the entire piece and any one of its constituent parts.

Figure 6.2.
Project Sample—link to a larger version of a drawing in the series

Process Used to Develop this Sample

The artist saved the entire composite image as a JPEG file (in this case, after highlighting all images by using the select all function), and then copied and pasted them into PowerPoint, which permits documents to be saved in graphic format. These images were imported into a Web authoring software (Dreamweaver, in this example) and a Web page that presents the six-image composite as a full screen was created. Next, he followed the same procedure to create a full-page version of each of the individual images, which he had also separately saved as JPEG files. Using the image mapping function of the software, each of the segments of the composite were hyperlinked to their corresponding large image page. To view the piece, it must be opened in a browser or other link-enabling software.

Sharing the Work

The hard copy version can be hung in a conventional gallery style exhibit. The digital version can be reproduced on CDs and distributed in quantity. The recipients can load them into the computers to view. This version might also be attached to an e-mail and distributed that way. Of course, the Web pages could also be uploaded to an available server to share through a Web site, provided the school has that capability.

Note: See unit 18, "Sharing Student Art with an Audience" for an overview of other possibilities.

Assessment

This project has a starting and finishing point, which should be clear from its graphic style. It is important that students work through the various intermediate stages of the progression of images in order to arrive at the final stage. Assessment, therefore, should consider each of the stages individually, as well as the cumulative end result.

Suggested General Assessment/Accountability Rubric for Unit 6

Project Components	Excellent	Proficient	Partially Proficient	Not Sufficiently Proficient or Incomplete
Completion of Project • Student creates six individual images that clearly progress in increments from close representation to total abstraction • Student incorporates the six images into an effective final collective image	All portions of the project are completed successfully at a high level.	Most portions of the project are completed successfully at a high or satisfactory level.	Some important (and other) portions of the project are completed successfully at a satisfactory level.	Few of the project portions are completed successfully at a satisfactory level.
Research and Preparation • Student locates an appropriate reference image on which to base the project	Conducted the needed research/ preparation in a way that allows for a full level of participation in the project.	Conducted the needed research/ preparation in a way that allows for a high level of participation in the project.	Conducted the needed research/ preparation in a way that allows for a satisfactory level of participation in the project.	Conducted the needed research/ preparation in a way that allows for a minimal level of participation in the project.
Theme and Concept Learning • Student understands the concept of analyzing realistic images for underlying structure/basic shapes • Student understands the concept of a continuum of representational styles, from realistic to abstract	Fully understood the concepts and goals of the project. Understood the contextual background content. Understood how to apply the above in the creation of an original work.	Understood a good deal of the concepts and goals of the project. Understood the contextual background content to a high degree. Understood how to apply the above in the creation of an original work to a high degree.	Understood some of the concepts and goals of the project. Understood the contextual background content to a degree. Understood how to apply the above in the creation of an original work to a degree.	Did not adequately understand the concepts and goals of the project. Did not adequately understand the contextual background content. Did not adequately understand how to apply the above in the creation of an original work.
Technical Proficiency • Student produces outline contour drawing effectively • Student uses auto shapes appropriately to translate the image into components • Student produces effective arrangements of shapes as the image progresses toward abstraction • Student makes sufficient, appropriate, and effective choices of line quality and tone/color	Demonstrated a very high degree of understanding and mastery of the concepts and skills involved in the techniques required of the project.	Demonstrated a good degree of understanding and mastery of the concepts and skills involved in the techniques required of the project.	Demonstrated a satisfactory degree of understanding and mastery of the concepts and skills involved in the techniques required of the project.	Did not demonstrate an adequate degree of understanding and mastery of the concepts and skills involved in the techniques required of the project.

(Continued)

Suggested General Assessment/Accountability Rubric for Unit 6 (Continued)

Project Components	Excellent	Proficient	Partially Proficient	Not Sufficiently Proficient or Incomplete
Technology Use • Student uses painting/drawing functions of software appropriately • Student imports, saves, and manages files appropriately to support participation	Handled the technology portions of the project in a highly effective, insightful, and responsible fashion.	Handled the technology portions of the project very proficiently and in an effective, insightful, and responsible fashion.	Handled the technology portions of the project in a satisfactorily effective, insightful, and responsible fashion.	Did not handle the technology portions of the project in a satisfactorily effective, insightful, and responsible fashion.
Creativity-Expression • Student produces work that is original and interesting, expressing personal taste and design preferences	Conceived, developed, and executed a work of art that is highly original and that takes full advantage of the medium's possibilities.	To a good degree, conceived, developed, and executed a work of art that is original and that takes full advantage of the medium's possibilities.	To a satisfactory degree, conceived, developed, and executed a work of art that is somewhat original and that takes advantage of some of the medium's possibilities.	Did not well conceive and execute a work that is original or takes good advantage of the medium's possibilities.

Note: Refer to chapter 7, "Assessing Digital Art Projects" for an overview of assessing technology-supported student visual art projects.

Cross-Curricular Connection

Devolving Drawings in Language Arts

This project involves the gradual transformation of a recognizable subject to an abstract design. The result is an image that can no longer be seen as representation. The challenge this project offers can serve as an effective prompt and focus for learning a number of important skills across the curriculum.

In the area of language arts, a number of writing skills and activities are easily aligned with this project—description of an observed phenomenon and comparing and contrasting are chief among them. These techniques can be accomplished through the implementation of several gamelike activities that use the student art works and their constituent parts.

In one variation, the finished product, which is composed of six versions of the subject, is cut into six individual cards. Each student would present the cards (stacked one on top of another) to a partner in the class, with the last version in the series face up. If the project has been done by several classes in the same school, it may be more effective to swap cards between classes to ensure the recipient is not at all familiar with the work to be examined.

When each student in the class has received a stack of cards, the following directions are given to the class by the teacher:

- When directed to begin, you will turn over the top card in the stack in front of you and examine it visually. Do not turn over the next card until directed.

- You will write a short piece after looking at each card.

- Looking at the top image only, which is the last in a series of images produced by your partner, write a description of what you see.

- Turn over the next card in the stack, examine it, and describe what you see. Then place it face up next to the previous card and write another short piece that compares and contrasts the two images. How are they the same and how do they differ?

- At a certain point in this activity you will believe you know what the realistic subject of the stack of cards is. In addition to the description and the comparison, write down what you think the subject is when you feel you know it. You may change your mind after a subsequent card, but do not go back and change what you have already written.

- Continue as instructed until all cards have been processed, and you have written descriptions for all six images.

When all students have finished their writing assignments, distribute the full version of the sequence of images to each. At this point, conduct a class discussion in which the students are invited to share their experiences and discoveries.

An interesting variation on the preceding activity would be to simply give each student a stack of the six cards and ask them to attempt to reconstruct the order in which they were created. After the students are finished, a copy of the full original is given to them and they are directed to report on their experience. As part of this, they might be invited to share (in writing) how they might have handled the creation of the piece differently than the student artist whose work they have been analyzing.

UNIT 7

Surrealist Landscape in **Mixed Media**

To become truly immortal, a work of art must escape all human limits: logic and common sense will only interfere. But once these barriers are broken, it will enter the realms of childhood visions and dreams.

— GIORGIO DE CHIRICO

Art is not what you see, but what you make others see.

— EDGAR DEGAS

Please see the sections "Using this Book" and "Assessing Digital Art Projects" for more information about these standards, the interaction between them, and connecting these standards to the lessons in this book.

STANDARDS

NETS•S

Although all or most of the NETS•S are touched on in this unit, the connection is strongest and easiest to see and understand in the standards listed below:

1. a, b   4. a, b, c, d
2. b   5. a, c
3. a, b, c, d   6. a, b

Note: In this unit and others, when students appropriately search for and use reference material gathered from the Web to support them in the creation of an original work, diligently avoiding infringement on the intellectual property rights of others, they are *advocating and practicing safe, legal, and responsible use of information and technology* (NETS•S 5.c).

National Standards for Arts Education (Visual Arts)

CS–1, AS–a, b

CS–2, AS–a, b, c

CS–3, AS–a, b

CS–4, AS–a

CS–5, AS–b

UNIT OBJECTIVES

Students will be challenged to:

- Understand the ideas and context central to Surrealism.

- Understand the principles of pictorial landscape.

- Apply these understandings to create an effective original landscape work in the surrealist idiom.

- Evaluate their own work and defend their criticism of peers' work done in the same genre.

CENTRAL IDEAS

Imaginative, fantastic, and playful, Surrealism is an art movement that has always captured the fancy and attention of the students to whom I present it. Once aware of its impact, they are motivated to analyze and understand its nuances in preparation for making this variety of art themselves.

Much of the Surrealists' art involved giving easily identifiable, common subjects a fantastic dimension through the addition of impossible details or by placing them in an impossible setting. Surrealists also made landscapes dreamlike through the improbable relationships of their environmental features and the subjects they set within them. I've found these approaches to picture making to be liberating for students, freeing them to concentrate on communicating ideas without having to wrestle with the laws of realistic representation.

The creation of fantastic pictures was further facilitated by some Surrealists through the then-new technique of photo collage—the appropriation of mass published images and inserting them into their paintings and drawings. This is another dimension I've found to be liberating for students, eliminating the struggle to personally generate all the elements they wish to include in their pictures.

Through the use of technology, today's artists can accomplish even more with the technique of collage than those of the pre-World War II Surrealists. Far more mass-published images are available now than ever before and many can be located easily through image searches on the Internet.

Even though products of mass-publishing technology are tapped to aid in the creation of these Surrealist landscapes, in the project presented in this unit student work assumes a hand-made character by an approach that combines traditional art-making techniques with newer digital ones. The results of this combination are highly effective works of art, and ones from which young artists will gain great satisfaction as well as acquire new skills and background knowledge.

TECHNOLOGY RATIONALE

Like the Ukiyo-e project (covered in unit 3), this project employs much of the body of techniques associated with collage or photo montage. It's also a project that illustrates the advantages of digital images for this type of work over the traditional ones that artists clip from magazines or other hard copy published materials, trim to suit their needs, and then paste into place.

With digital images several things are achieved. First, the source material can be altered in a paint program in ways that make it difficult for the viewer to perceive them as artist-made changes: they appear to be original. In the project sample (Fig. 7.1), the masonry of the monk's robe was drawn over a photo, resulting in a convincing, seamless look.

More important, the student artist can produce many different versions of the original image. These can be made in a variety of sizes, although identical in appearance otherwise. This technique offers far greater picture-making opportunities for collagists who, by traditional means, generally have access to just one copy of an image however large or small.

Using a paint program in which all aspects of an image, no matter its source or origin, are created equally from pixels, the artist can create a visual context in which to paste them seamlessly. This results in a uniform surface on which drawing and collage blend to produce a single image of uniform character.

Principal Technology Skills Addressed

- Web research/image mining

- Scanning and printing

- Image manipulation (sizing)

Technology Resources Needed

- Internet access/browser/search engine(s)

- Scanner

- Software that allows images to be "sized"

WEB RESOURCES

Museum of Modern Art NYC (examples of Dali works, including landscapes)
www.moma.org/collection/browse_results.php?criteria=O:AD:
E:1364&page_number=1&template_id=6&sort_order-1

Art Institute of Chicago (examples of Salvador Dali works, including landscapes)
www.artic.edu/aic/collections/citi/search?keyword=&artist=dali&title=&mainrefnum=
&Search=Search

Magritte La Golconde (famous Magritte landscape painting)
http://i3.photobucket.com/albums/y89/daniladiav/magritte-rene-golconde-3100609.jpg

Smithsonian Education (principles of landscape)
www.smithsonianeducation.org/educators/lesson_plans/landscape_painting/creating_
illusions.html

Unit Conceptual and Pedagogical Overview

The surrealists used several approaches to picture making that can be employed as the basis for an interesting and worthwhile project for students. In one approach, everyday objects are transformed (e.g., clocks melt, statues have drawers in their bodies, rocks burn, etc.). Likewise, in the work of the Surrealists, we often find ordinary objects assuming an aspect of the fantastic by virtue of their behavior or their relationship to other common things (e.g., stones float in the air or an evening scene takes place under a brightly lit sky) both of these approaches, as well as a combination of the two, will offer students the opportunity to stretch their imaginations, tackle the problems of communicating their ideas pictorially, and learn about important aspects of art making.

In this unit, students create a landscape in which they place transformed subjects. These may be objects, people, animals, or a combination of these elements. Although the objects may be fantastic, their placement establishes a convincing traditional landscape through the use of the pictorial conventions of that form.

ACTIVITIES

The technology employed to make this project involves Internet image searches, sizing and printing of graphics, and scanning. This project offers a hybrid approach between the use of technology-supported and traditional materials and techniques for making art. This, in and of itself, is a worthwhile concept to model for students. The flow between technology and traditional modes is as follows:

1. The student artist searches the Web for images to use in an enhanced photo collage.

2. The student alters the images using conventional materials: white-out, scissors, pencil, pen, crayon, marker, etc.).

3. The student pastes the images into an invented landscape that was established using primarily conventional materials.

4. The student scans the final work, producing a digital graphic as the final step in the process.

Alternately, the project can be completed entirely within technology applications that mimic and expand the capabilities of traditional art materials and processes.

DAY 1

1. **Research and preparation**

    a. Direct the students to do Web-based research on Surrealist artists, paying particular attention to landscape works. Dali and Magritte offer particularly good examples.

    Suggested focus questions:

    *   How would you describe the work of the Surrealists?

    *   What do you think they were trying to achieve?

    *   Are there aspects of these works that are realistic? What are they?

    *   How did the Surrealists' choices of what to include in their works and how to combine these elements help them achieve the special quality that we call Surreal?

    *   What do you think the initial viewing public's reaction was to their work?

    Discuss the answers to these questions as a group, listing discoveries that may help focus the students as they create an original work in this genre.

DAY 2

2. **Create a theme**

    b. Having now seen a number of Surrealist landscapes, the students should form a general idea about a theme for a Surrealist landscape of their own. It is useful for them to write brief descriptions and save them for reference.

The first step will be to collect images that they will include in their work. As they find possible images, students can save them in a folder on their computer desktops. Eventually, they will choose the ones that they feel are the most valuable for realizing their original ideas. These "keeper" images can be imported into an intermediary program, such as Word, through which they can be examined and manipulated.

   c. Direct the students to use a search engine to find photographic images of real subjects, objects that appear natural when found in an ordinary setting, such as automobiles, apples, pipes, hammers, and so on. Roughly half a dozen images should be collected at this stage of the project, although they may not all be used in the final piece.

   d. Print and/or save the found images in graphics file format.

Note: For the purposes of this project, simple images that are easy to read on their own will work best. In other words, the images should be ones that are easily identified by appearance and not by the context in which they are found. Assuming the students will produce a finished work for this project in an 8.5 x 11 inch format (or larger), the selected images should be of appreciable size in order to allow for the manipulation that will be part of subsequent steps.

DAYS 2–3

3. Move from the real to the surreal

   e. One surrealistic aspect of the picture is established as a result of the artist giving impossible characteristics to the subjects (e.g., Dali's melting clock, burning giraffes, madonnas with windows through their torsos, etc.) and/or impossible relationships between subjects (e.g., Magritte's flying trains, floating businessmen, etc.).

   f. Once the students have selected subject images for their project, the next step will be to transform the objects they've printed out by the application of lines, color, shading, and other techniques. This can be accomplished by applying traditional materials to the photos (hair may be drawn or painted on; flames may be drawn and painted to emanate from the subject; photos of handles, switches, hooks, and other hardware may be pasted on; images may be stretched by cutting them into strips and pasted at a distance from one another with a connecting line drawn to join them; the possibilities are limited only by the students' imaginations.

The challenge involves changing the real (or ordinary) into the surreal (or extraordinary). Students may want to refer to museum works in order to get ideas and inspiration. When finished, several of the students' subject images should be changed significantly by adding or removing features or by altering their visual characteristics.

Note: It may prove fruitful to have the group stop once or twice during this phase of the project to share ideas and successes and failures. The sharing of discoveries made during the process can be a very useful motivator and model for collaborative learning.

DAY 4

4. Composition

   g. The students can next scan the transformed images using a conventional flatbed scanner. Next, the files should be imported into an intermediate application and printed out again. This process yields a series of subject items ready to be placed within the final composition. This last step produces a smooth, processed image that already has aspects of the new dimension of reality that the final project will depict. This step will produce a graphics file that can be printed out repeatedly, offering the student artists great flexibility in working toward a finished piece (students may use various copies to make several attempts at an idea without ruining the original source image).

h. The next step involves freeing the transformed objects from their backgrounds so that they can be placed within the landscape. The students can accomplish this step by cutting the around the image contours with scissors. It will become apparent at this point whether the selected subject matter is too delicate or has too difficult an outline to navigate around with scissors. Students, however, can facilitate this process by using a pen to enhance or define the outline before attempting to cut away the background.

Because these images can be reprinted on demand, the artist may need to try several times to get this step right. By importing several copies of it, the image can be resized several times on the page, thus giving the artist the opportunity to cut out several identical images. This will be important for the landscape composition.

DAYS 5–6

5. **Refinement and completion**

i. Students establish the landscape aspect of the project by applying basic principles of this pictorial format (e.g., horizontal orientation of the picture, horizon line, and diminishing size of objects and higher placement within the picture plane, two representational devices that create the effect of filled space receding in the distance). Now that the subject images have been freed from their backgrounds, the next step involves creating a world in which to place them.

j. At this point students should have on hand a blank piece of paper that is heavy enough to support drawing, painting, or collage. Students will scan this finished work later on, so cutting it to conform to the dimensions of 8.5 x 11 or 8.5 x 14 inches ahead of time will move this project along nicely.

The subject images, freed from background material, can be laid on the blank paper that will hold the finished piece. (Alternately, students can keep them in an envelope until the process of developing the composition begins).

Students easily establish the empty space of the paper as a landscape by drawing a horizontal line across it, either freehand or with the aid of a straight-edge. They must make the important decision of how high or low on the page to place this horizon. Although one third of the way down from the top is a good starting point, establishing the horizon initially as a tentative light pencil line (which can be changed as other factors of composition are introduced) will allow students to make this decision in final form later on.

Students will discover a number of important concepts.

1. By placing several of their transformed subjects that are identical or nearly identical except in scale within the same composition, they can use the diminishing size to create the illusion of depth and space.

2. Students will then discover that subject elements appear to be further from the viewer the closer they are placed to the horizon.

3. And, if subject elements are placed so that they overlap, the suggestion of depth is created by the effect of closer elements obstructing the view of those behind them.

4. They will also notice that it is important to carefully plan the placement of each subject element in order to create an effective and pleasing arrangement that tells the story of the picture. Students can most easily understand this concept by laying the free elements out on the paper before committing any of them to final placement with the application of an adhesive.

k. After students decide on the placement of all elements, they carefully glue or paste them into their final place. The final phase of the process, adding details, shading, cast shadows, and color, is undertaken before the work is finished.

Alternately, the teacher can extend the project further with the following steps.

1. Direct the students to scan their work.

2. They next print the scan on a full sheet of paper the same size as the pre-scanned original.

3. If they use a black-and-white printer, the students may wish to add color to the work with water color, water-color marker, or other color-bearing materials (transparent media may provide the best results as they won't obscure lines they cover).

Project Sample

Figure 7.1. Project Sample—Surrealist Landscape

Process Used to Develop this Sample

Before the artist began work he mined the Web for a variety of raw reference images that relate to the medieval theme of the piece. He started the art-making process after he had located sufficient material, producing the work in the following four phases.

Phase I. The artist processed the selected images in a variety of ways to prepare them for insertion as elements of the finished piece.

    a. Graphic material and photos were cropped and adjusted for contrast.

    b. Portions of the images were eliminated or altered using the brush function of a paint program. Elements were also added by copying them, holding them on the clipboard, and then pasting, moving and manipulating size, as saving as part of image components (e.g., the eyes within the helmet, rose window in cowled monk statues, etc.). Some were drawn using the brush tool (e.g., unicorn's horn, monks' hands, etc.).

    c. Lines were accentuated by going over them with the brush tool, and muddy or fuzzy areas were cleaned and sharpened by covering grays and middle tones with white using the brush (e.g., knight's armor).

Phase II. The artist drew a landscape using the brush tool in a blank field of white to receive the prepared image elements mentioned above. Lines that form hills and a horizon leading back into space were created.

Phase III. He next inserted the various image elements into the landscape using the copy and paste function of the paint program. Once inserted he moved and sized them as appropriate and then saved them.

Phase IV. Using the airbrush tool, he added shading to make transitional areas within the piece more appealing to the eye (e.g., shadow under the unicorn and shading on the hills).

Sharing the Work

This project is likely best shared through variations of a traditional group exhibition of hard copy works of art. An interesting variation on this can be achieved by having the students take close-up digital photos of sections or details of their individual works. These can be imported into a slide show using PowerPoint or similar software. This enhancing digital presentation can be set up to run on a continuous loop at the entrance to the exhibit with the aid of an LCD projector and screen. This technique will set a special tone for the exhibit and will cue the visitors to what they are about to experience as they enter. The slide show can also be sent out (via e-mail attachments) as an invitation to the show, and they can be retained as a souvenir of the exhibit after it has been taken down.

Note: See unit 18, "Sharing Student Art Work" for an overview of possibilities in sharing technology-supported student art projects.

Assessment

This project involves toggling back and forth between work on paper in a somewhat traditional manner, and the use of new digital technology to extend what can be done by artists. One element of assessing the work is evaluating the students' understanding of this and their response to it. Have the technology-supported dimensions been incorporated without over-reliance on them as supports? Has the student used her personal hand-done drawing, collaging, coloring, and shading without missing aspects of what the technology can add? Are both aspects balanced in a well-thought out way?

Suggested General Assessment/Accountability Rubric for Unit 7

Project Components	Excellent	Proficient	Partially Proficient	Not Sufficiently Proficient or Incomplete
Completion of Project • Student crops and tunes graphic material to serve as collage elements • Student transforms images by altering and adding/deleting details with paint functions • Student sharpens and strengthens visual impact of collage elements • Student draws a setting into which to place the elements • Student inserts elements in optimum locations of collage • Student uses software to refine the appearance of the elements' insertion into the background	All portions of the project are completed successfully at a high level.	Most portions of the project are completed successfully at a high or satisfactory level.	Some important (and other) portions of the project are completed successfully at a satisfactory level.	Few of the project portions are completed successfully at a satisfactory level.
Research and Preparation • Student searches for and collects raw graphic material with which to develop collage	Conducted the needed research/preparation in a way that allows for a full level of participation in the project.	Conducted the needed research/preparation in a way that allows for a high level of participation in the project.	Conducted the needed research/preparation in a way that allows for a satisfactory level of participation in the project.	Conducted the needed research/preparation in a way that allows for a minimal level of participation in the project.

(Continued)

Suggested General Assessment/Accountability Rubric for Unit 7 *(Continued)*

Project Components	Excellent	Proficient	Partially Proficient	Not Sufficiently Proficient or Incomplete
Theme and Concept Learning • Student understands the concept of collage as a medium for artistic expression, its characteristics, and its advantages and shortcomings • Student understands the genre of surrealism and the freedom for artists it established	Fully understood the concepts and goals of the project. Understood the contextual background content. Understood how to apply the above in the creation of an original work.	Understood a good deal of the concepts and goals of the project. Understood the contextual background content to a high degree. Understood how to apply the above in the creation of an original work to a high degree.	Understood some of the concepts and goals of the project. Understood the contextual background content to a degree. Understood how to apply the above in the creation of an original work to a degree.	Did not adequately understand the concepts and goals of the project. Did not adequately understand the contextual background content. Did not adequately understand how to apply the above in the creation of an original work.
Technical Proficiency • Student develops images using drawing, painting, and collage approaches effectively • Images and elements sufficiently communicate the student's intended meaning • Finished piece is visually engaging and communicates ideas as required by the assignment	Demonstrated a very high degree of understanding and mastery of the concepts and skills involved in the techniques required of the project.	Demonstrated a good degree of understanding and mastery of the concepts and skills involved in the techniques required of the project.	Demonstrated a satisfactory degree of understanding and mastery of the concepts and skills involved in the techniques required of the project.	Did not demonstrate an adequate degree of understanding and mastery of the concepts and skills involved in the techniques required of the project.
Technology Use • Student performs image searches • Student imports images and uses drawing/paint functions appropriately • Student saves and manages files appropriately	Handled the technology portions of the project in a highly effective, insightful, and responsible fashion.	Handled the technology portions of the project very proficiently and in an effective, insightful, and responsible fashion.	Handled the technology portions of the project in a satisfactorily effective, insightful and responsible fashion	Did not handle the technology portions of the project in a satisfactorily effective, insightful, and responsible fashion.
Creativity-Expression • Student uses the assignment as an opportunity to create a personal and unique work	Conceived, developed, and executed a work of art that is highly original and that takes full advantage of the medium's possibilities	To a good degree, conceived, developed, and executed a work of art that is original and that takes full advantage of the medium's possibilities	To a satisfactory degree, conceived, developed, and executed a work of art that is somewhat original and that takes advantage of some of the medium's possibilities	Did not well conceive and execute a work that is original or takes good advantage of the medium's possibilities.

Art as Report

As one of the purposes of this project is to report what's been learned about a subject in a way that communicates this to an audience, assessing it can be enriched by treating it as a visual report. Accordingly, the following criteria might be applied to this project.

- Quality of information—Are there sufficient details given? Are they accurate?

- Is the information presented in a way that effectively communicates the content?

- Is the theme presented in a way that will effectively interest the viewer?

Suggested discussion question: Which part of this project is really best accomplished by the artist's own hand? Which part by the use of technology?

Note: See chapter 7, "Assessing Digital Art Projects" for an overview of assessing technology-supported student visual art projects.

Tech Tip. A large scanned image can be sized and converted to JPEG format by importing it into PowerPoint, adjusting the size by grabbing and pulling in the corners tabs, and then selecting JPEG format before using the Save As function. Be sure to label the file and select a save destination so that it can be easily located afterward.

Cross-Curricular Connection

Surreal Montage in Social Studies and Language Arts

This project is a good jumping off place for an activity that combines social studies and language arts. The approach is one of expressing in an art work content learned as a result of focused research.

From the point of view of a social studies activity, a research project that might ordinarily result in a written report or classroom-based oral presentation can culminate instead in a collage. The surrealist twist to this lends motivation and provides for personal expression in the project. Virtually any theme can be handled through this approach.

The research phase can be facilitated through the use of a chart that facilitates holding students accountable for accuracy and understanding. Here's a suggestion as to how this can be structured.

List each visual element that appears in your finished collage and give the source, rationale for inclusion, and message.

TOPIC OF YOUR COLLAGE:			
Visual Element	**Source**	**Rationale** *(How does this element* *relate to your topic?)*	**Message** *(What does this element* *communicate about your topic?)*

From the language arts perspective, based on the information listed in the above chart, assign the student to write a composition to accompany the finished work of visual art. This essay may take the form of a purely descriptive passage that explains what is presented visually and defends it from the point of view of historical accuracy. Or, alternatively, it may be a narrative story written about the visual piece.

UNIT **8**

Hard-Edge Color Study
Following in the Footsteps of Joseph Albers

We live in a beautiful and orderly world, not in a chaos without norms, even though this is how it sometimes appears.

— M. C. ESCHER

Please see the sections "Using this Book" and "Assessing Digital Art Projects" for more information about these standards, the interaction between them, and connecting these standards to the lessons in this book.

STANDARDS

NETS•S

Although all or most of the NETS•S are touched on in this unit, the connection is strongest and easiest to see and understand in the standards listed below:

1. a, b	4. b, c, d
2. a, b	5. a, b
3. a, b	6. a, b

Note: In this and other units, when students pursue the creation of a work of art as a focused solution to a defined design problem that is developed sequentially and systematically they are *planning and managing activities to develop a solution or complete a project* (NETS•S 4.b).

National Standards for Arts Education (Visual Arts)

CS–1, AS–b

CS–2, AS–a, b, c

CS–5, AS–a, c

UNIT OBJECTIVES

Students will be challenged to:

- Understand various aspects of color theory and its historical context in art.

- Understand how artists apply these theories in their work.

- Create an original work that demonstrates an understanding of hard-edge non-objective painting and the design elements that influence it.

- Engage in accountable talk to explain how dimensions of color interaction and theory affect works of art.

CENTRAL IDEAS

Of the many design elements that influence the outcome of a work of art, none is more powerful than the element of color. If color is to be part of a student's work, then an understanding of its underlying principles and rules of behavior will help tremendously. An effective step to take toward this is the production of work in which color exists on its own, without having to serve as part of a presentation or other dimensions of art.

One artist whose work can shed great light on this approach is Joseph Albers. Albers did a great deal of investigation into *The Interaction of Color* (the title of his book). But unlike other color theorists whose work precedes his, he produced finished works of art that were composed of just a few fields of color in varying relationships to each other, usually in the form of geometric shapes. His work influenced many artists and a style of painting based on it called "Hard-edge painting" evolved, which is essentially design built from color-bearing, interacting geometric shapes.

In addition to observing my students thoroughly enjoy making hard-edge designs and learning a good deal about how colors influence one another, I've seen many of them take these understandings away from this exercise and transfer the knowledge to the application of color in representational art. This understanding is infinitely more difficult if attempted directly within artistic realism.

TECHNOLOGY RATIONALE

The artists who established and developed the hard-edge approach to image creation were painters. They expended a great deal of effort in developing painting techniques that would result in very even surfaces and well-drafted shapes. In many instances they went to great pains to avoid even slight imperfections, such as brush strokes, light pencil lines used to plot shapes on canvases, and tape ridges left behind when masked shapes were filled in with paint. This attention to controlling and perfecting the paint as an object in its own right, was due in large part to the understanding that the desired effect of the painting is best achieved when there is little to distract the eye from it.

Today's students actually have a better chance of achieving this ideal through the use of computers than the Hard-edge painters of the 1960s and 1970s. Software that supports drawing allows for the precisely straight and consistent drafting of lines and shapes and perfectly smooth fields of tone with which to fill them.

On a practical basis, the execution of art works that must progress through the stages from roughing in a sketch, to carefully plotting and correcting shapes, and finally to filling them in with flat fields of color, is a time consuming process. I've found that in most classroom situations and for many students (who may have a limited amount of patience), using the computer to create these works offers many logistical advantages. Furthermore, the finished product they are likely to produce will be more pleasing if done using software. It is unlikely that any amount of care in student use of traditional drafting tools will produce lines in varying and uniform thickness and shapes so well-drawn as can be achieved with software.

Even classes determined to execute this type of work in traditional materials will find that doing it first on the computer offers a great advantage in planning the work before the final version is attempted.

Principal Technology Skills Addressed

- Web research

- Digital drawing/painting

Technology Resources Needed

- Drawing/painting program

WEB RESOURCES

Art Icons (overview of Albers work with examples)
http://articons.co.uk/albers.htm

Interaction with Web-Safe Colors (examples of Albers works)
www.sylloge.com/5k/entries/176/1.html

Kunstwissen (overview of Alber's life and work):
www.kunstwissen.de/fach/f-kuns/b_mod/albers.htm

Color Theory (comprehensive collection of information on color theory)
www.cs.brown.edu/courses/cs092/VA10/HTML/start.html

Wikipedia (overview of color theory)
http://en.wikipedia.org/wiki/Color_theory

Big Black Pig Studio (overview of color theory with examples)
www.bigblackpig.com/painting/colour.html

Guggenheim Museum—Hard-edge painting (annotated examples of art works and artists associated with this movement)
www.guggenheimcollection.org/site/movement_works_Hard_edge_painting_0.html

Tate (definition of Hard-edge painting with examples)
www.tate.org.uk/collections/glossary/definition.jsp?entryId=133

Princetonol (Hard-edge painting activity)
www.princetonol.com/groups/iad/lessons/middle/HardEdgeMS.html

About (Op Art painting activity)
http://painting.about.com/library/projects/blpaintingproject11.htm

MasterWorksOf FineArt (Vasarely and works)
www.masterworksfineart.com/inventory/vasarely.htm

Artfact (Vasarely and works)
www.artfact.com/features/viewArtist.cfm?aID=23131

Unit Conceptual and Pedagogical Overview

All artists must work with color. Even those who work in black-and-white do so knowing that they are making a statement about color, albeit its absence.

Students find color to be very attractive, but often have difficulty finding ways to apply it that involve making smart choices and informed decisions rather than simply reacting to it. During my career as an art teacher I've often observed students use every last color in their crayon box on a single piece of their work. Schooled artists, on the other hand, understand the natural laws in effect when working with color and that adhering to them is one approach to increasing the chances of success in their art. By engaging students in projects that encourage them to gain a degree of control over color, I've found they frequently gain much appreciated sophistication in this area, something that serves them well as they continue to grow as artists.

If we go back through the history of art we discover that art makers didn't always fully understand how colors behave. Color theory is a body of knowledge that's been added to in spurts, generally whenever new technologies to support mankind's art production have come into being.

One such advance was the work of M. E. Chevreul, which is documented in his classic book *The Principles of Harmony and Contrast of Colors.* This 19th-century work was motivated by the needs of industry, but it became a major source of inspiration and direction for the impressionists and later schools of French painting. In Chevreul's work, for the first time, a methodology by which colors could be mixed and understood was established and systematized.

Later on during the 20th century, Joseph Albers published *The Interaction of Color,* which advanced further understandings by which artists could comprehend and predict the powerful visual effects achieved through the interaction of colors.

More than mere exercises to facilitate the learning of a theory, some of the exploratory projects color theorists have conducted can be reproduced by students to create products that support learning and are wonderful finished works of art at the same time. The project presented in this unit is such an opportunity, an invitation to make a beautiful work of art while learning about color, one of the artist's greatest potential allies.

ACTIVITIES

DAY 1

1. **Background and preparation**

   a. Organize a group activity to provide background information for this unit. Assign groups to research the following subjects that impact the understanding of hard-edge color painting.

   Theory:

   - Color wheel

   - Primary and secondary colors

   - Complementary and analogous colors

   Artist practitioners:

   - Op Art painters

   - Hard-edge painters

   b. Lead a class discussion to digest and reflect on the information gathered.

   Some focus questions that may prove effective include the following.

   - Which artists associated with the development or application of color theory did you discover?

   - Whose work did you find to be particularly interesting or effective?

   - What theories or understandings about color can we come to from analyzing those works?

DAY 2

2. **Exploring the interaction of colors**

   c. Working individually, each student will create an original hard-edge digital design to explore the interaction of colors. For this project any software program that offers simple drawing/painting features (i.e., draw line, auto shapes, adjust line width, fill with color, etc.) can be used.

   - Students create a grid of squares that are equal in size. Any number of squares will work so long as all students produce a finished work that has the same number. A piece composed of 25 squares arranged five by five will be fine, as would 63 squares, with nine across and seven down (such as the project example). By keeping the class members to an agreed-on number, comparisons of the finished pieces will be made easier and more worthwhile.

- Each segment is to be filled with a shape within that square. This interior shape should be consistent, appearing in all squares the same way. This consistency will allow the students to concentrate solely on color, the focus of this project. In order to accomplish this other design elements must be kept to a minimum.

DAYS 3–4

3. **Exploring the interaction of colors, continued**

 - Each of the shapes, both square and interior shape, is to be filled with a solid color

 d. Students are directed to look for interactions between the colors that they feel are particularly effective. This is more challenging than it may appear at first, as the interactions between the square and its interior color, as well as the colors of adjacent squares and their interiors shapes all affect one another. Furthermore, the colors of neighboring and even distant squares influence one another and should be considered in producing a successful finished piece.

Note: Teachers may elect to permit more variation in shapes or an additional layer of a shape within the interior shape in subsequent implementations of this project. Furthermore, those who wish to teach formal color theory may set design parameters, such as "only complementary colors may touch," or "only colors that are analogous to the color of a square may be used to fill the shape within," and so on. The variations on this project are fascinating and endless in variety.

 e. Save the work in an appropriate file format.

Project Sample

Process Used to Develop this Sample

This piece was completed using the drawing functions of Microsoft Word.

Figure 8.1. Project Sample—Hard-edge Design

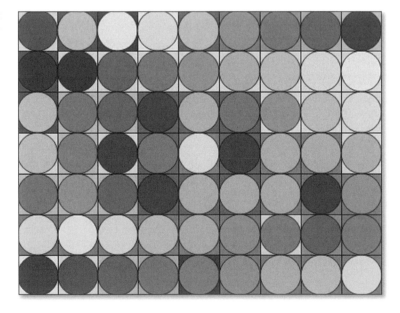

The project may be executed with a grid of fewer elements if time, grade level, and ability level indicate that would be advantageous. Furthermore, the project may be extended by the insertion of a third shape within the shape within each square.

After the artist drew a single, large square using the AutoShapes tool, he broke it up into a grid by using the Line tool. Next, he drew separate squares and sized them to fit into each grid space. These were maneuvered into place and colored using the Fill Color tool. Similarly, he drew the circles separately, maneuvered them into place, set each above a square, and then colored it with the Fill Color tool.

Note: Colors photographed in black-and-white will reveal their values (relative light and dark characteristics). Helping student artists understand color value and incorporating it into their work process is an important dimension of learning about color. A preliminary work finished in black-and-white can be a useful additional exercise to support students in understanding and mastering color value.

Sharing the Work

This work can be shared in a variety of ways. One approach that may produce a startling effect follows a modular approach. Because the work of each student in the class is built upon the principle of interlocking modules (squares of identical dimensions, in this case), by extension, each student's work may be viewed as a module, allowing the class to combine individual works to create a giant extended work. This wall of hard-edge paintings will both show off the individual taste and decisions of each student as well as further illustrate predictable or unpredictable effects when colored elements are placed near one another and interact.

Figure 8.2. Using an online photo sharing resource to share student art

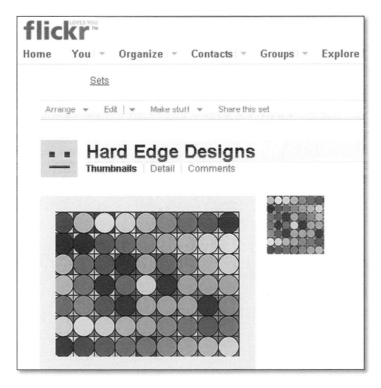

Disseminating the work can be simple and polished when it is uploaded to an online photo sharing resource such as Flickr. The link to this Web album then can be e-mailed individually or in a group of links. These can also be placed online in a blog or shared in other ways.

Note: See unit 18, "Sharing Student Art Work" for an overview of possibilities of sharing technology-supported student art work.

Assessment

This project involves research and discussion about established theories and principles of the behavior of colors. These touchstone art-making concepts have generated their own vocabulary over the years. Because this project is intended to be done with an awareness of these principles in mind, referring to them in evaluating and reviewing the work offers a valuable tool for assessment. Students may be asked to explain why certain combinations of colors give the effect they do in terms of color theory.

Suggested discussion questions:

- Name some artists in whose work there are similarities to the color effects created in your own.

- Can you explain why certain aspects and areas of your work are less or more effective, in terms of color theory?

Suggested General Assessment/Accountability Rubric for Unit 8

Project Components	Excellent	Proficient	Partially Proficient	Not Sufficiently Proficient or Incomplete
Completion of Project • Student opens and prepares a blank page to function as grid support for the design to come • Student fills the grid with a field of shapes • Shapes are varied using drawing software tools in order to create the design	All portions of the project are completed successfully at a high level.	Most portions of the project are completed successfully at a high or satisfactory level.	Some important (and other) portions of the project are completed successfully at a satisfactory level.	Few of the project portions are completed successfully at a satisfactory level.

(Continued)

Suggested General Assessment/Accountability Rubric for Unit 8 *(Continued)*

Project Components	Excellent	Proficient	Partially Proficient	Not Sufficiently Proficient or Incomplete
Theme and Concept Learning • Student understands the background of hard-edge abstract designs • Student understand that abstract design is the result of conscious choices made by the artist	Fully understood the concepts and goals of the project. Understood the contextual background content. Understood how to apply the above in the creation of an original work.	Understood a good deal of the concepts and goals of the project. Understood the contextual background content to a high degree. Understood how to apply the above in the creation of an original work to a high degree.	Understood some of the concepts and goals of the project. Understood the contextual background content to a degree. Understood how to apply the above in the creation of an original work to a degree.	Did not adequately understand the concepts and goals of the project. Did not adequately understand the contextual background content. Did not adequately understand how to apply the above in the creation of an original work.
Technical Proficiency • Student effectively generates a grid, shapes, and patterns to produce a finished design	Demonstrated a very high degree of understanding and mastery of the concepts and skills involved in the techniques required of the project.	Demonstrated a good degree of understanding and mastery of the concepts and skills involved in the techniques required of the project.	Demonstrated a satisfactory degree of understanding and mastery of the concepts and skills involved in the techniques required of the project.	Did not demonstrate an adequate degree of understanding and mastery of the concepts and skills involved in the techniques required of the project.
Technology Use • Student uses drawing software tools and functions effectively • Student saves and manages files appropriately	Handled the technology portions of the project in a highly effective, insightful, and responsible fashion.	Handled the technology portions of the project very proficiently and in an effective, insightful, and responsible fashion.	Handled the technology portions of the project in a satisfactorily effective, insightful, and responsible fashion.	Did not handle the technology portions of the project in a satisfactorily effective, insightful, and responsible fashion.
Creativity-Expression • Student develops a unique and personal work that reflects creativity and insight into how tools and resources can be used inventively	Conceived, developed, and executed a work of art that is highly original and that takes full advantage of the medium's possibilities.	To a good degree, conceived, developed, and executed a work of art that is original and that takes full advantage of the medium's possibilities.	To a satisfactory degree, conceived, developed, and executed a work of art that is somewhat original and that takes advantage of some of the medium's possibilities.	Did not well conceive and execute a work that is original or takes good advantage of the medium's possibilities.

Cross-Curricular Connection

Hard-edge Art and Mathematics

This project involves a good deal of simple mathematics. This aspect can become the basis for many math challenges and can offer an opportunity for math and art teachers to work together. Alternately, the math teacher may use this as an opportunity to give an art assignment in order to lay the groundwork for mathematical concepts.

As a series of identical spaces is required, a grid must first be created. The teachers can stipulate the dimensions of the rectangular grid spaces as well as the overall dimensions of the entire piece. The grid may be created by using the software application's ruler and line functions to draw equally spaced lines from top to bottom and then from left to right.

Once the project is completed the following strategies may form the basis for worthwhile activities:

- Compute the area of one of the squares in your design.

- Compute the perimeter of a square.

- Figure the entire area covered by the interior shapes.

- Compute the perimeter of all shapes from which your entire design is constructed. Explain the process by which you arrived at this figure.

UNIT **9**

Enviroscapes
Drafting the Built Environment

Architecture is inhabited sculpture.

— CONSTANTIN BRANCUSI

Please see the sections "Using this Book" and "Assessing Digital Art Projects" for more information about these standards, the interaction between them, and connecting these standards to the lessons in this book.

STANDARDS

NETS·S

Although all or most of the NETS•S are touched on in this unit, the connection is strongest and easiest to see and understand in the standards listed below:

1. a, b

2. a, b

3. a, b

4. b, c, d

5. a, b

6. a, b

Note: In this and other units, when students pursue the creation of a work of art as a focused solution to a defined design problem that is developed sequentially and systematically they are *planning and managing activities to develop a solution or complete a project* (NETS·S 4.b).

National Standards for Arts Education (Visual Arts)

CS–1, AS–b

CS–2, AS–a, b, c

CS–3, AS–a, b

CS–5, AS–a

CS–6, AS–b

UNIT OBJECTIVES

Students will be challenged to:

- Gain an understanding of the needs for and techniques involved in basic architectural drafting.

- Gain insights into the advantages and challenges involved in using computer assisted drafting (CAD).

- Consider the fine art aspects of functional drawings.

- Produce an original floor plan as a functional and art-oriented drawing.

CENTRAL IDEAS

The act of representation is central to art and educational activities with art at their core. Representing architectural space is a specialized aspect of this, one that poses unique challenges. It's also one that I found students relate to particularly well.

Perhaps the thought, "I could do better than that!" comes naturally to them, or so it seems to me whenever I've directed students to consider the physical reality of our classroom and have asked them to opine about the decisions that went into its design. For many, I suspect this project may have been the first time they'd considered occupied space from the perspective of design and designer.

Over the years a distinct set of approaches, techniques, and conventions have evolved within the art and craft of architectural drafting. This is a difficult art to practice. However, the new digital technologies offer many advantages and shortcuts that make this a practical and satisfying type of drawing to include in a program for student artists.

TECHNOLOGY RATIONALE

Like other projects presented in these pages, this one relies on the drawing/drafting capabilities of commonly used software. In addition to the ease of drawing perfectly and consistently formed lines and shapes, something that is an absolute standard for architectural plans, software also offers the element of measurement.

By establishing a grid that aligns with the ruler function of the software, the size (relative to scale) of all elements of a drawing is tracked continually as the student develops it. Changes in size of shapes, as well as distances from one spot to another, are done relative to the grid that underlies everything. This allows the student artist to maintain a consistent ratio of all elements to the whole. Although some aspects of this could be done with conventional drawing tools, the software outstrips them in capability, making labor-intensive and skill-dependent dimensions of technical drawing doable for students. It even allows the grid to be hidden or shown at will.

As the depicted space is filled with copies of identical symbols for the furniture and room features, it is easy to grasp whether or not the size calculations will support the finished plan and make adjustments if need be. I've observed many students (who without the support of the software would be highly frustrated by the level of accuracy required for this sort of project), rise to the occasion and produce very satisfying drawings.

Principal Technology Skills Addressed

- Digital drawing (CAD—Computer Assisted Drafting/Drawing)

Technology Resources Needed

- Software with technical drawing/drafting capabilities

Note: This unit involves students in the art of drafting, a specialized variety of drawing.

Drafting, also referred to sometimes as *technical drawing* or *mechanical drawing*, is used to represent spaces in precise terms so that architects, construction personnel, and future occupants can visualize the space aided only by the reading of a drafted plan (drawing). The craft of drafting involves straight or other geometrical lines in precisely measured increments. In many respects, drafting embraces aesthetic qualities that are the opposite of the vast bulk of artists' handmade drawings. For instance, they generally exhibit no variations in line quality and do not reveal personality through the unique and imperfect *handwriting* of the artists.

Since the advent of computers, drafting has become a technology-supported art, taking the acronym CAD (computer assisted drafting) as its generic name. Numerous varieties of this type of software have been developed to support drafting; however, these programs are generally dedicated exclusively to drafting and do not offer other uses to purchasers. They also require a fair degree of training, and are expensive. Furthermore, apart from those attending technical and career schools, few teachers and students have access to CAD applications. Fortunately, some software applications that schools commonly possess already offer functions that can be tapped for use in activities that involve drafting. Word and PowerPoint are two that are nearly ubiquitous. Their Draw and AutoShapes functions provide all that is needed for the level of drafting required in this unit, with the added bonus that they are relatively easy to use and understand. Although a Web search may well turn up downloadable freeware and shareware titles that offer CAD capability, these programs often require a good deal of time to absorb and understand.

WEB RESOURCES

Math-Kitecture (real-life math, architecture, and computers):
www.math-kitecture.com

DesignWorkshop Lite (Free downloadable 3-D software):
www.artifice.com/free/dw_lite.html

ArtEdventures (Drawing Floor Plans):
www.alifetimeofcolor.com/main.taf?p=2,2,1,1

CUBE Center for the Understanding the Built Environment:
www.cubekc.org

ArchiTech Gallery (examples of architectural plans as works of art):
www.architechgallery.com/arch_info/exhibit_docs/exhibitions_2000/master_plans.html

Classroom Architect (floor planning activity guide):
http://floorplan.altec.org

eMints Classroom Design (comprehensive listing of classroom floor plan related resource links)
www.emints.org/ethemes/resources/S00001368.shtml
www.more.net/technical/netserv/diagrams/classroom.html

Unit Conceptual and Pedagogical Overview

Art and Architecture go hand in hand. The principles of fine art often make their way into the design considerations of those who plan buildings. The reverse is also true. Buildings are sculptural in the way they express forms in three dimensions, although their multitude of flat surfaces (both interior and exterior) can function in the same ways that two-dimensional paintings do.

Furthermore, the fourth dimension, the temporal experience of movement around a sculpture, a design element in and of itself, is never more apparent or important than in buildings; designed constructions in which the experience of moving within, through, and around forms is of prime importance.

Buildings begin with drawings. This is so for a myriad of practical reasons, but the drawings also free architects to dream and imagine without being restricted by the possible. Drawing allows them to engage in pure design first and then make something that works in the real world once their ideas are on paper.

Drawings, even those that are primarily functional in their intent and use, can't escape being aesthetic objects as well. As soon as marks are put down on paper, the drawing's existence as an art object has begun. Interestingly, architects, designers, and draftsmen often take great pleasure in the functional drawings they produce. It is part of a continuum of pride and creativity that they bring to a project, to produce beautiful drawings even though they act simply as plans for those who will build the object in the real world or illustrations to help clients envision how the structure will look after it is built.

In fact, it is this interesting relationship between the functional requirements of a technical drawing and its inevitable aesthetic existence that can be exploited to produce a worthwhile project for student artists. How can a drawing bring to life the idea of a physical object such as a building or a room and simultaneously be a beautiful two-dimensional work when viewed on its own? I've observed many students consider this possibility for the first time. It is a great eye-opener for them, a new understanding about the world they are preparing themselves to enter, and a revelation of unimagined possibilities of what they might accomplish in it.

ACTIVITIES

One easy project to get students started on this path is to have them create a floorplan of their idea of an improved classroom. The classroom, a space they are familiar with that is right there to be observed, measured, and evaluated, offers the perfect subject.

DAY 1

1. **Research and preparation**

   a. Conduct a class discussion to establish the context for drafting a floorplan for the classroom. One approach is to brainstorm with the students on improvements they would like to see made in the classroom (new furniture, additional sinks, built-in storage shelving and cabinets, skylights, etc.). Explain that the starting point for making these changes would be to define the classroom as they find it now. Explain that any additions or alterations would have to be made to fit the existing space and that some sort of map of the classroom must be sent to all those involved in the project.

   Focus questions may include the following.

   - How can we accurately show others the precise dimensions and features of our classroom? (Typical responses might include photos, videos, written descriptions, maps, etc.)

   - What information should be included to assist all who will help in the renovation? (measurements, materials, features such as doors and windows, etc.)

   - Is there an angle or point of view from which the classroom should be represented? One that is especially useful for those looking at it and trying to interpret it?

   b. Present the class with examples of professionally prepared floorplans (these can be found on the Internet).

   Focus questions for this section may include the following.

   - What tools and supplies will we need to create a floorplan for our classroom?

   - Where should we begin? What steps come first?

   - How can we make our floorplan also be an attractive work of art? What aspects of beautiful drawings and painting can we bring to it?

   c. As a group, record and analyze all responses.

DAY 2

2. Measuring up

d. Assign each student to create an original floorplan of the class. Even though each student will produce his own finished piece, it may be useful to have them work as small collaborative groups. This will also support classroom management in having them share measuring devices or any traditional art materials used.

Students should take measurements of everything that will be included in the floor plan.

Note: The logical first step of this project is measuring the classroom dimensions and the dimensions of the furniture and architectural features within it. It may be best to implement this portion of the project in mixed groups and with collaborative group exercises. A good way to begin might be to have a brainstorming session in which the class lists all of the objects that must be measured (walls, windows, doors, desks, etc.) and then to divide measuring assignments among pairs or threesomes of students.

If several groups work on the assignment, a further discussion (in which measurements are compared and those agreed upon are accepted, and those for which there isn't agreement repeated after re-targeting approaches), may enrich the experience.

It may be fruitful to review the use of measuring tools before this step is undertaken or to collaborate with a math teacher on this.

DAY 3

3. Making an original floorplan

e. Once the students have a solid, standard set of measurements the creation of the drawings can begin. On any sheet of paper, ask the students to render a rough sketch of the floorplan. This dry run is important because it will be the first attempt at translating a set of ideas into a real artifact, and it will give them an indication of the technical difficulties they will be challenged with as they move toward the finished piece.

It is essential that this step be done with marks that are erasable, changeable, and moveable. This project will involve many tentative attempts and course corrections. During this rough stage students may change their mind about what they will include or leave out in the finished piece.

DAYS 4–7

4. Creating the floor plan

f. To complete the finished floorplan, a grid is a perfect support for the initial work. A useful approach would be to set up a ratio that will help when translating the measurements taken into the drawn elements (each ¼ inch, for instance, might equal a foot of the real-world classroom). Although it is useful to draw the quick-sketch map of the classroom in traditional paper and pencil, it is far more practical to do the finished floorplan digitally.

Computer Assisted Drafting (CAD)

It takes professional draftsmen a great deal of practice to produce a clean and attractive technical drawing that is accurate and functional. The materials involved in this type of work are challenging to manipulate, especially for newcomers. I found that using a computer-assisted drafting (CAD) approach is perfect for student artists, as the technical aspects of creating the drawing are greatly facilitated, leaving the artist to concentrate on what is being represented rather than the mechanics of the process. Furthermore, the difference between both sets of materials and their advantages and drawbacks are important understandings for the students to come to.

Many software programs can be employed for a project such as this one. However, several ubiquitous programs, such as Microsoft PowerPoint and Word, have drawing features that can be tapped to produce good results in this project.

The features of these two programs (or any other considered for this project) should include: ruler, grid, adjustable line drawing tools, auto shapes, arrows, text box (insertion), font and type adjustments, and so on. The ability to import graphics (clip art, photos, etc.) will also help produce a functional, highly attractive drawing.

Essentially, the procedure is the same in rendering the drawing digitally as it would be with traditional materials: lines are drawn to represent walls; gaps are left to indicate openings for doors or windows; basic shapes are used to indicate a bird's-eye view of furniture (square for desk, circle for stool, rectangle for table, etc.); lines terminating with arrows; text and numerical annotation that indicate dimensions; and captions within text boxes. All of these functions can be overlaid on a grid that aids in calculating and measuring the depiction of dimensions. When finished, the grid can be kept or removed, depending on the aesthetic considerations of the artist.

Numerous, detailed, step-by-step guides to this type of basic CAD-generated floorplan are also available on the Internet.

DAY 8

5. **Finishing and assessing**

   g. As a final step in the project, have the students compare their plans up to this point and facilitate a short discussion about how the now-functional floorplans can be made to assume more of the identity of an aesthetic art object. After brainstorming possible approaches (vary line width, import graphics, add color, create or add texture to various portions, etc.) allow the students to apply as many of these techniques as they choose in order to finish the project.

Project Sample

Figure 9.1. Project Sample—Floorplan for an imaginary classroom.

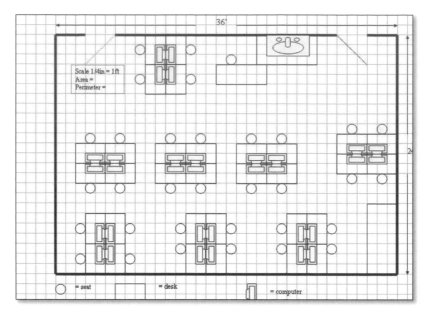

Process Used to Develop this Sample

Using PowerPoint, the artist turned on the "display grid" setting of the Grids and Guides function and selected a grid setting of .25 inches.

Next, using the line tool and the displayed grid, the artist drew a virtual graph paper as a base for the drawing to come.

The draftsman of this piece next used the Draw function's "line" and "arrow" tools to define the walls, door openings, and other physical characteristics of the space.

Using the Auto Shapes function, simple-shaped drawings were selected to serve as symbols of the furniture. He then filled them with color, grouped them, and copied and pasted them as needed to produce the quantity of furniture needed to fill the room.

Sharing the Work

This project lends itself well to either a gallery exhibit of the printed out works hung on a wall or a virtual exhibit accomplished through the use of a thumbnail gallery software. Although PowerPoint may be a practical program within which to render the drawing, floorplans are complex, have much detail to absorb, and require greater time to inspect than a public slide show would ordinarily provide. Whatever the application selected, slide show, photo gallery, or other, it is advisable for it to be offered to the viewer in a way that will allow him or her to direct the navigational flow and the pace through which the work is be investigated and appreciated.

Figure 9.2. This thumbnail gallery was created using JAlbum, a free downloadable software available for most platforms. JAlbum is easy to use and offers many different styles of gallery.

Note: PowerPoint permits files to be saved as JPEG graphics files, a format which may facilitate the use of a variety of applications for digital sharing.

Note: See unit 18, "Sharing Student Art with an Audience" for an overview of other possibilities.

Assessment

This project calls for the student to produce a work that is equally functional and beautiful. Assessment should reflect both aspects, as well as the interplay between the two. It is relatively easy to ascertain the functionality of the student's computations and measurements. However, the functionality of the planned space, in terms of how it will create an environment worthy of the people who will use it, will require some probing and analysis.

Suggested discussion questions:

- What will people be doing in the environment you've designed?

- How does the layout of furniture, passages for the movement of people, and placement of windows and doors support that activity?

- What special features does your environment offer that will make living and working within it especially worthwhile?

- In creating the drawing to represent the environment, what decisions did you make to influence the final look of your work?

Suggested General Assessment/Accountability Rubric for Unit 9

Project Components	Excellent	Proficient	Partially Proficient	Not Sufficiently Proficient or Incomplete
Completion of Project • Student prepares a digital environment (page) on which the floorplan will be drawn • Student uses drawing/drafting functions of software to create a drawn floorplan • Student uses software functions to create appropriate symbols for furniture and features of depicted space • Student uses the on-screen rulers and other tools to plot the floorplan to an appropriate scale, ratio, etc.	All portions of the project are completed successfully at a high level.	Most portions of the project are completed successfully at a high or satisfactory level.	Some important (and other) portions of the project are completed successfully at a satisfactory level.	Few of the project portions are completed successfully at a satisfactory level.
Research and Preparation • Student reviews existing floorplans and architectural drawings to gather background information on the project • Student takes measurements, calculations, and estimations, on which to base the project drawing	Conducted the needed research/preparation in a way that allows for a full level of participation in the project.	Conducted the needed research/preparation in a way that allows for a high level of participation in the project.	Conducted the needed research/preparation in a way that allows for a satisfactory level of participation in the project.	Conducted the needed research/preparation in a way that allows for a minimal level of participation in the project.
Theme and Concept Learning • Student understands the concept of technical drawings and floorplans as tools to functionally depict living/working spaces	Fully understood the concepts and goals of the project. Understood the contextual background content. Understood how to apply the above in the creation of an original work.	Understood a good deal of the concepts and goals of the project. Understood the contextual background content to a high degree. Understood how to apply the above in the creation of an original work to a high degree.	Understood some of the concepts and goals of the project. Understood the contextual background content to a degree. Understood how to apply the above in the creation of an original work to a degree.	Did not adequately understand the concepts and goals of the project. Did not adequately understand the contextual background content. Did not adequately understand how to apply the above in the creation of an original work.

(Continued)

Suggested General Assessment/Accountability Rubric for Unit 9 *(Continued)*

Project Components	Excellent	Proficient	Partially Proficient	Not Sufficiently Proficient or Incomplete
Technical Proficiency • Student executes lines, shapes, symbols, and other technical design elements appropriately to create a functional drawing of a space	Demonstrated a very high degree of understanding and mastery of the concepts and skills involved in the techniques required of the project.	Demonstrated a good degree of understanding and mastery of the concepts and skills involved in the techniques required of the project.	Demonstrated a satisfactory degree of understanding and mastery of the concepts and skills involved in the techniques required of the project.	Did not demonstrate an adequate degree of understanding and mastery of the concepts and skills involved in the techniques required of the project.
Technology Use • Student uses drawing functions of software appropriately to create the design elements required of the project • Student saves and manages files appropriately	Handled the technology portions of the project in a highly effective, insightful, and responsible fashion.	Handled the technology portions of the project very proficiently and in an effective, insightful, and responsible fashion.	Handled the technology portions of the project in a satisfactorily effective, insightful, and responsible fashion.	Did not handle the technology portions of the project in a satisfactorily effective, insightful, and responsible fashion.
Creativity-Expression • Student creates an attractive and functional technical drawing that is easy to read and interpret and that conveys an original conception of a living/working space	Conceived, developed, and executed a work of art that is highly original and that takes full advantage of the medium's possibilities.	To a good degree, conceived, developed, and executed a work of art that is original and that takes full advantage of the medium's possibilities.	To a satisfactory degree, conceived, developed, and executed a work of art that is somewhat original and that takes advantage of some of the medium's possibilities.	Did not well conceive and execute a work that is original or takes good advantage of the medium's possibilities.

Note: Refer to chapter 7, "Assessing Digital Art Projects" for an overview of assessing technology-supported student visual art projects.

Cross-Curricular Connection

Floorplans and Mathematics

The project described in this unit is a convenient hands-on project through which a great many core curriculum mathematics skills and understandings can be learned and practiced, and through which competence may be demonstrated. As examples, a variety of learning standards published by the New York State and New York City departments of education are listed below.

New York City Department of Education Performance Standards Addressed (Middle School):

M2a: Is familiar with assorted two- and three-dimensional objects (to recognize different shapes within the basic structures of architecture).

M2c: Identifies three-dimensional shapes from two-dimensional perspectives, can draw two-dimensional sketches of three-dimensional objects (to recognize different shapes within the basic structures of architecture).

M2d: Determines and understands length, area, and volume (to measure length, area, and volume of classrooms and/or bedrooms, as well as floor plans/elevations of famous buildings).

M2f: Analyzes and generalizes geometric patterns, such as tessellations (to recognize tessellations in architecture, as well as learn to create their own).

M2j: Reasons proportionally with measurements to interpret maps and makes smaller and larger scale drawing (to convert the measurements from bedroom at home into a scale drawing).

M6c: Estimates numerically and spatially (to estimate the length and area of classrooms and/or bedrooms).

M6d: Measures length and area correctly (to draw a floor plan of classrooms).

M6h: Uses pencil and paper, measuring devices, and computers to achieve solutions (to draft floor plans to scale).

New York State Education Department Core Curriculum (Grades 7–8)

Key Idea 4: Modeling/Multiple Representation

    4A. Visualize represent, and transform two- and three-dimensional shapes

    4B. Use maps and scale drawings to represent real objects or places

    4I. Use appropriate tools to construct and verify geometric relationships

    4J. Develop procedures for basic geometric constructions

Key Idea 5: Measurement

    5A. Estimate make and use measurement in real world situations

    5B. Select appropriate standard and non-standard measurement units and tools to measure to a desired degree of accuracy

Key Idea 7: Patterns/Functions

    7A. Recognize, describe, and generalize a wide variety of patterns

    7G. Use properties of polygons to classify them.

    7H. Explore relationships involving points, lines, angles, and planes

UNIT **10**

Marisol-Style Box Sculpture
Ideas That Stand on Their Own

The job of the artist is always to deepen the mystery.

— FRANCIS BACON

Please see the sections "Using this Book" and "Assessing Digital Art Projects" for more information about these standards, the interaction between them, and connecting these standards to the lessons in this book.

STANDARDS

NETS•S

Although all or most of the NETS•S are touched on in this unit, the connection is strongest and easiest to see and understand in the standards listed below:

1. a, b   4. a, b, c, d

2. a, b   5. a, c

3. a, b, c, d   6. a

Note: In this and other units, students use *multiple processes and diverse perspectives to explore alternative solutions* (NETS•S 4.d) when they develop art works through a series of stages involving a variety of software applications and their uses, as well as approaches to making and presenting images.

National Standards for Arts Education (Visual Arts)

CS–1, AS–b

CS–2, AS–a, b, c

CS–3, AS–a

CS–4, AS–a

CS–5, AS–a, c

UNIT OBJECTIVES

Students will be challenged to:

- Understand basic design aspects of sculpture in the round.

- Understand how sculpture in the round can be seen as a composition of multiple planes, and understand the relationship between individual planes to the whole sculpture.

- Understand that some sculpture, such as the work of Marisol, is frontal with applied motifs, and recreates this historical approach (as seen in the sculpture of ancient Egypt).

- Apply these understandings to the creation of an original work of art.

CENTRAL IDEAS

What is sculpture? On examining its history, one sees that for much of it, sculpture has been the creation of complex representational forms that occupy three-dimensional space. Classically, these forms are a sophisticated melding of many subsidiary shapes into a single, seamless biomorphic entity. In presenting these ideas to students I've found that although they can appreciate the beauty and emotional power of classic sculpture, they don't easily comprehend how to create their own work in this idiom.

Furthermore, learning to model realistic sculpture in the round requires far more time, physical resources, and prerequisite skills than have been available to my own classes. It is often the case that only purely abstract sculpture projects can be undertaken practically in school settings. Although many 3-D design concepts can be learned through abstract creations, keeping the representational dimension of sculpture is important for preserving the communicative, expressive, and cross-curricular dimensions of sculpture-based learning projects. The project presented in this unit is one that I developed with students that takes advantage of both approaches and that is made practical by the availability of technology.

In classically realistic sculptures (e.g., Michelangelo's Pieta) individual planes are not prominent features or easy to discern. More recently though, modernists have developed an alternative approach, and they often construct sculptures out of basic geometric shapes that present a series of flat surfaces to the viewer. Numerous sculptors, Marisol for example, have exploited this approach to beautiful effect. Her "box sculptures" are works that are easy for young artists to comprehend and draw on as they conduct their own first experiments in making sculpture in the round.

Sculpture that is intended to be experienced as a series of two-dimensional planes may be enriched by incorporating two-dimensional graphic elements. Technology is of particular value in acquiring or generating graphic elements for this purpose.

TECHNOLOGY RATIONALE

In this project a traditionally created sculpture functions as a support for graphic material gathered by a student as a result of online research. Together, the sculpture and the graphics combine to make a unique and highly meaningful work of art. The use of a search engine to locate images associated with the project theme is but the first reason why technology makes this project a good example of a 21st-century literacy-driven learning activity.

The graphic material in this project is not simply affixed to the surface of an existing sculpture; but rather it should be searched for and selected based on how well it works with the sculptural surface it will be affixed to. The student artist may wisely elect to complete the shape of the sculpture as the images are selected and suggest the ideal shape with which they will ultimately work.

As is true when working on two-dimensional collage projects, the advantage of using digital images is that as many copies of the image as desired can be produced and saved in a wide variety of sizes. This would not be true if traditional hard copy materials were used. Collage elements gathered from magazines, for instance, are available generally in just the single copy and size in which they are found.

Digital graphics are particularly helpful in producing the type of sculpture in the round indicated in this project, as extra copies and versions of images can follow the flow of planes around the sculpture, conforming to sculptural elements that themselves are of varying sizes and shapes. The repetition of images is something that, when traveling around a solid form, makes for an especially interesting visual experience.

Principal Technology Skills Addressed

- Digital photography
- Use of scanners

Technology Resources Needed

- Digital cameras
- Scanners
- Printers

WEB RESOURCES

Art Museum of the Americas (Marisol Escobar work: Magritte III in heaven):
www.museum.oas.org/exhibitions/museum_exhibitions/marisol/sculptures_01.html

Basic Principles of Egyptian Sculpture:
www.cartage.org.lb/en/themes/Arts/scultpurePlastic/SculptureHistory/ArtofEgypt/
BasicEgyptianSculpture/BasicEgyptiansculpture.htm

Neurberger Museum of Art (exhibit and background information and examples
of Marisol Escobar art works):
www.tfaoi.com/aa/2aa/2aa661.htm

Princeton Online—Incredible@rtDepartment (related activity guide):
www.princetonol.com/groups/iad/lessons/middle/Dawn-marisol.htm

the-artists.org (background information and examples of Marisol Escobar art works):
www.the-artists.org/ArtistView.cfm?id=8A01F3F6-BBCF-11D4-A93500D0B7069B40

Unit Conceptual and Pedagogical Overview

Marisol Escobar is an artist who has created uniquely expressive and personal works of sculpture. Her work is generally considered "assemblage," a kind of modern sculpture that is composed of found or ready-made objects that are adapted, adjusted, and assembled to produce an original work that reveals the artist's vision.

Marisol's work combines block-like basic shapes from which figures are constructed as well as highly graphic painted images, usually somewhat realistic faces. These are affixed to the surface of other elements that retain the same identity as the materials of their construction, often unpainted wood. The addition of found elements, such as shoes and cloth, are also affixed strategically, giving personality and identity to the work.

Marisol's figures generally assume a rigid, static, and frontal posture, breaking with the realism and naturalism of the smoothly flowing forms in motion seen in the work of traditional masters of sculpture such as Michelangelo or Rodin. In this sense, her work bears some resemblance to the figurative sculpture of antiquity: the sculpture of ancient Egypt or early Greek sculptures such as the Kouros. Part of the visual effect of Marisol's work is the sense of how her figures remain partly embedded in the blocks of materials that define their shape and from which they seem to emerge.

Although her work has a decidedly frontal sensibility to it, it also exhibits the qualities of sculpture in the round, with different visual information and impact delivered when viewed from the back or sides.

The ready availability of mass-produced, small cardboard boxes that hold everything from tubes of toothpaste to food items to hardware, as well as the plethora of graphic images that represent literally every aspect of our world, make adapting this type of sculpture as a student project highly practical.

I've found this style of sculpture to be a valuable first experience with sculpture in the round for students. It allows them to transition from conceiving and producing art exclusively in two dimensions to finding a level of comfort in working with three dimensions. It's been my experience that creating sculpture can be conceptually challenging for them, and this project can represent an important step in overcoming that challenge.

This project makes good use of technology to develop the graphic elements that afford visual emphasis and punch to the sculpture. Technology is also particularly useful in sharing student work of this type, as will be seen toward the end of the unit.

ACTIVITIES

Produce a sculpture in the round, the creation of which is accomplished by combining the basic shapes of common, found objects with graphic material that communicates information.

DAY 1

1. **Research and preparation**

    a. Review the work of Marisol Escobar with the students (see links in the Web Resources section for possible sources). Present the concept that a three-dimensional form, like a box, is composed of numerous two-dimensional flat planes that occupy space simultaneously. Show them examples of sculpture by Marisol (and other sculptors) that illustrate this idea.

    Suggested focus questions include the following:

    *   Give examples of how three-dimensional shapes have two-dimensional components (rectangle as one side of a box, triangle as a side of a pyramid, circle as a manner of representing a sphere, etc.).

    *   Can flat graphic elements be incorporated into sculpture?

    *   What information about their subjects can sculptures that are portraits give to the viewer?

DAYS 2–3

2. **Gather source materials**

    b. The students should gather a body of digital images (approximately 8 to 15) that can be incorporated into a "portrait sculpture" that gives information about the art work's subject. The images should reveal information about the personality, circumstances, culture, history, or any other facet of the subject.

    The teacher may choose to allow students to set their own challenge with this project in terms of what types of information will be communicated, or he or she may choose to use the production of this sculpture as a focus for study and research into a specific, agreed-upon theme. In the second case the completed sculpture would serve as a visual report.

    Images may be acquired in two ways: 1) mined from the Web using a search engine, or 2) as scans of material gathered from magazines, newspapers, or other printed matter. Teachers may choose to limit the implementation of this project to one of these methods.

    If students mine images from the Web, they may do so directly at their desks, saving the images to the hard drives on their laptops, or in the computer lab, saving files to portable storage devices, whichever is most practical and available. If students are scanning images from hard copy, setting up several scanners at stations around the classroom may be most practical.

If both methods are employed for the project, it may be more practical from a classroom management standpoint to limit the class to one method per designated session, depending on the time available, maturity level of the students, and familiarity with technology on the part of the teacher and students. It may also be advantageous to assign students to bring in digital images for use in their project as homework, saving class time.

It may be helpful for students to keep a running list or other record of the images they acquire, with an eye toward the work of art they are developing. When they have collected all the visual elements they need, the next step will be to assemble the sculpture. In preparation, the image files they have selected should be placed in a folder and saved.

DAYS 4–5

3. Creating box sculptures

c. The student images are printed on a laser or other printer and given to the students. For more flexibility, they may be given two or three copies of each in varied sizes. Students may be permitted to print images on their own, depending on practicality.

d. The students next affix the photos to a collection of cardboard boxes that they have brought in for this purpose.

By connecting boxes of varying sizes and shapes to one another at varying angles, an interesting arrangement can be achieved. This arrangement of shapes, in connection with the graphic elements that will be affixed to its multiple surfaces, is the visual material from which the sculpture will take its form.

A good method for affixing the boxes to one another is to glue them with white glue, scoring their surface first with the rough end of a straightened paper clip (or similar item) to aid adhesion. Holding the boxes in place with masking tape while the glue dries will also help. Students may wish to cover the surfaces of the boxes with blank paper before gluing their graphic images to them.

Note: Correlation of the size of the photos to the size of the boxes should be discussed ahead of time with students.

e. Finally, students may opt to add color with paints or markers or add other decorative elements to finish their sculpture.

Project Sample

Process Used to Develop this Sample

After identifying a theme for the sculpture, the artist gathered a body of raw photographic material from the Web using a search engine (Google images, in this example).

Figure 10.1. Project Sample—Box Sculpture. This piece was created based on the theme of personal adornment in African cultures.

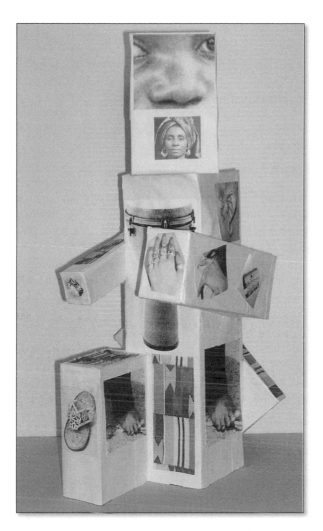

Using photo-editing software (Picasa, in this example) he cropped the photos; adjusted them for brightness, shadows, and contrast; and transformed them using a variety of effects offered in the software.

Next he imported the processed photos (in JPEG file format) into a word processing program (Word, in this example) so that they could be adjusted in size, printed them in a variety of sizes, and made multiple copies for application to the surface of the sculpture.

Finally, he cut the images from the paper and glued them onto the surface of the sculpture in a traditional manner.

Note: The artist constructed the base sculpture from small cardboard boxes that originally held food. These were glued together and covered in white paper.

Sharing the Work

This project calls for the creation of larger works of sculpture than are practical for public schools to store for very long. The use of technology to archive and present these works will enable teachers and students, however, to overcome storage issues that might ordinarily discourage them from even undertaking a project of this scale. Therefore, it may be more practical to see the lifespan of the physical presence of the original work in school as a short one, with the use of technology to capture the experience of the sculptures as a way to extend that presence and lifespan.

One interesting and relatively easy way to capture the essence of the sculpture produced in this project is through a digital video. This video can be made by first taking a series of digital photos while moving around the piece, and then stringing them together. The individual frames are imported into a simple movie editing software (Windows Movie Maker, for example), and then saved as a video presentation. This can next be uploaded to a free video resource on the Web, such as YouTube or TeacherTube, with the link embedded in a simple e-mail announcement.

Alternately, an actual video can be taken instead of a series of stills. If care is taken to keep the camera steady and at a consistent angle, a satisfactory video piece can be produced.

The stills approach is somewhat more manageable, as each individual view can be selected, and the eye will accept the somewhat jerky transition from view to view because it will be clear that the video is made of individual frames, without the benefit of a perfect transition from one to the next. Furthermore, the artist may wish to enhance each individual view in photo-editing software before putting them together as a single presentation.

Figure 10.2. In Windows Movie Maker still photos of the sculpture are imported in series and transformed into an uploadable video.

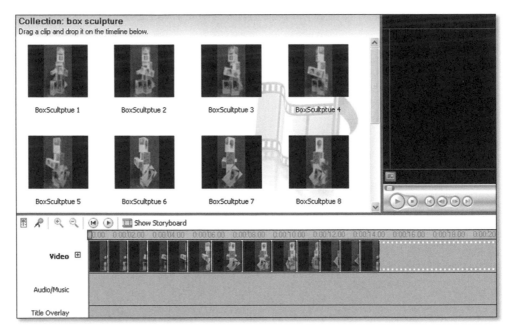

Figure 10.3. View of the finished uploaded video's presence on the Internet.

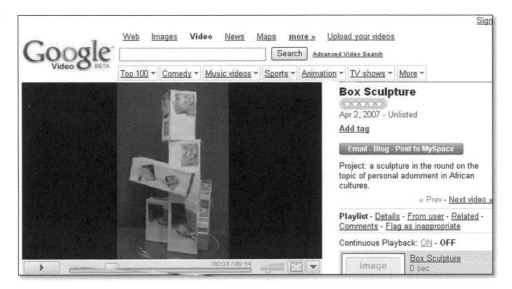

Note: See "A Virtual Sculpture Gallery Tour" in unit 20 for more information on virtual sculpture exhibits.

Note: See unit 18, "Sharing Student Art with an Audience" and "Sharing Student Art Work" for an overview of sharing technology-supported student art projects.

Assessment

This project involves a fairly simple set of directions and procedural steps. Assessment therefore may be most effective if it reflects more than the student's diligence in following the steps. As a work of art, this sculpture's value lies not in its inclusion of the required elements, but in how it can communicate something beyond the total of the parts. How does it relate mood, personality, or humor, for instance?

Suggested General Assessment/Accountability Rubric for Unit 10

Project Components	Excellent	Proficient	Partially Proficient	Not Sufficiently Proficient or Incomplete
Completion of Project • Student searches and acquires raw graphic material • Student adjusts and processes selected graphics • Student sizes and prints the graphic elements • Student affixes graphic elements to a conventional sculpture	All portions of the project are completed successfully at a high level.	Most portions of the project are completed successfully at a high or satisfactory level.	Some important (and other) portions of the project are completed successfully at a satisfactory level.	Few of the project portions are completed successfully at a satisfactory level.
Research and Preparation • Student researches and mines the Web for reference images • A body of images that gives information about the art work's subject is selected	Conducted the needed research/preparation in a way that allows for a full level of participation in the project.	Conducted the needed research/preparation in a way that allows for a high level of participation in the project.	Conducted the needed research/preparation in a way that allows for a satisfactory level of participation in the project.	Conducted the needed research/preparation in a way that allows for a minimal level of participation in the project.
Theme and Concept Learning • Student understands the concept of sculpture in the round and its history as a major vehicle for artistic expression • Student understands the function and possibilities of applying graphics to surfaces as a manner of conceiving and enhancing sculpture	Fully understood the concepts and goals of the project. Understood the contextual background content. Understood how to apply the above in the creation of an original work.	Understood a good deal of the concepts and goals of the project. Understood the contextual background content to a high degree. Understood how to apply the above in the creation of an original work to a high degree.	Understood some of the concepts and goals of the project. Understood the contextual background content to a degree. Understood how to apply the above in the creation of an original work to a degree.	Did not adequately understand the concepts and goals of the project. Did not adequately understand the contextual background content. Did not adequately understand how to apply the above in the creation of an original work.

(Continued)

Suggested General Assessment/Accountability Rubric for Unit 10 *(Continued)*

Project Components	Excellent	Proficient	Partially Proficient	Not Sufficiently Proficient or Incomplete
Technical Proficiency • Student creates and affixes graphic elements using graphic editing software that effectively communicate ideas and are visually effective	Demonstrated a high degree of understanding and mastery of the concepts and skills involved in the techniques required of the project.	Demonstrated a good degree of understanding and mastery of the concepts and skills involved in the techniques required of the project.	Demonstrated a satisfactory degree of understanding and mastery of the concepts and skills involved in the techniques required of the project.	Did not demonstrate an adequate degree of understanding and mastery of the concepts and skills involved in the techniques required of the project.
Technology Use • Student effectively conducts image searches and downloads images appropriately • Student uses editing software effectively to improve and transform raw material • Student imports, sizes, and prints graphics appropriately to support project creation • (If done by student) photographs, edits, and imports pictures of finished sculpture into medium for sharing work	Handled the technology portions of the project in a highly effective, insightful, and responsible fashion.	Handled the technology portions of the project very proficiently and in an effective, insightful, and responsible fashion.	Handled the technology portions of the project in a satisfactorily effective, insightful, and responsible fashion.	Did not handle the technology portions of the project in a satisfactorily effective, insightful, and responsible fashion.
Creativity-Expression • Student exercises personal interests, taste, and sensibilities in working on project • Student creates a unique and original work that communicates ideas and information effectively	Conceived, developed, and executed a work of art that is highly original and that takes full advantage of the medium's possibilities.	To a good degree, conceived, developed, and executed a work of art that is original and that takes full advantage of the medium's possibilities.	To a satisfactory degree, conceived, developed, and executed a work of art that is somewhat original and that takes advantage of some of the medium's possibilities.	Did not well conceive and execute a work that is original or takes good advantage of the medium's possibilities.

Suggested discussion questions:

- Which view of the model do you feel is most effective? Why?

- Do you feel you've provided a proper support (box) for it to be presented on? Have you affixed it at the best angle and in the best proportion? How might this be improved if revised?

Note: See chapter 7, "Assessing Digital Art Projects" for an overview of assessing technology-supported student visual art projects.

Cross-Curricular Connection

Box Sculpture and Cultural Studies

Personal adornment is a window into a culture. Because the box conforms to the human figure, it becomes a perfect platform to convey information learned through research about a culture as expressed through body adornment (clothing, hairstyle, jewelry, tattooing, and other body modification), as well as the natural physical characteristics of an ethnic group associated with a given culture.

Because the box stands in for the body, the details that carry the cultural identity can be isolated and concentrated on, both from the point of view of study and from that of pure aesthetics in the creation of the sculpture.

UNIT 11

Mythical Creatures— Mask Making

The function of Art is to disturb. Science reassures.

— GEORGE BRAQUE

Please see the sections "Using this Book" and "Assessing Digital Art Projects" for more information about these standards, the interaction between them, and connecting these standards to the lessons in this book.

STANDARDS

NETS•S

Although all or most of the NETS•S are touched on in this unit, the connection is strongest and easiest to see and understand in the standards listed below.

1. a, b	4. a, b
2. b	5. a, c
3. a, b, c	6. a, b

Note: In this and other units, when students are engaged in the implementation of focused searches for raw graphic material and approaches to use it as part of the creation of an original art work produced to satisfy a design problem or project challenge, they are *planning strategies to guide inquiry* (NETS•S 3.a).

National Standards for Arts Education (Visual Arts)

CS–1, AS–b

CS–2, AS–c

CS–3, AS–a, b

CS–4, AS–a

CS–5, AS–a, b, c

CS–6, AS–a, b

UNIT OBJECTIVES

Students will be challenged to:

- Research and share discoveries about the history of, societal uses for, and techniques associated with traditional mask making.

- Create an original mask employing a variety of traditional and technology-supported techniques in three-dimensional design.

- Balance approaches to mask making derived through the study of traditional art with the artistic possibilities posed by contemporary media and technology.

CENTRAL IDEAS

Mask making is one of the most basic and well-established approaches to making art known to man. It is an art that combines imagination and creativity with information about the observed world, blending all elements into something quite magical. Throughout history, humankind has used this ancient form of visual expression in attempts to derive meaning from the surrounding world and to gain a measure of control over it.

By searching the World Wide Web students can recreate early man's exploration of a world of images, picking and choosing those that strike a chord and help tell an important story. An array of software is available with which they can process these raw visual materials into powerful and thought-provoking masks. The project outlined here will support them in fluidly combining traditional art-making approaches with the use of technology.

Over the years I've guided students through a variety of units of study that feature the creation of masks. These mask-making activities serve as models for the special role art projects can play in the focus of extended, multidisciplinary learning experiences. As an integral part of these units my students have enthusiastically studied foreign and ancient cultures and their literature in order to acquire background information for the creation of masks. And the masks, in turn, have served as supporting documents for the oral and print delivery of original plays, poems, and prose—student writing that flowed surprisingly freely from a source of inspiration and motivation found in the art-making process. The power of masks and the process of their creation is indeed unique and powerful.

TECHNOLOGY RATIONALE

Athough students often make masks by traditional means that feature the application of their own drawing to the mask, the project presented in this unit pushes the envelope, creating an end-to-end continuum of elements, all of which are enhanced by the use of technology.

I assigned mask-making projects to students for years before the introduction of computers into the classroom. The methods and materials available then generally only allowed students to produce pieces that were somewhat crude. Traditional materials such as papier-mâché and tempera paint applied with school-grade brushes afforded them little control, and realistic imagery or fine detail were the exception not the rule in what was created. By using current technology, the results students can expect to produce are far more compelling, motivational, and useful for cross-curricular purposes.

The practice of doing studies or drawings to plan a major piece before actually executing it is a useful aspect for teaching art. Interestingly, this process echoes the use of outlines and drafts in the process of writing, an important core curriculum connection with which students are likely to be familiar.

As is the case with the craft of writing, technology makes the process easier and more effective, as drafts can be created directly over outlines (which have been previously saved as distinct versions), and various versions of the draft can be saved as it is developed into the finished piece. The advantages are obvious as time and effort are saved by eliminating the need to laboriously copy everything in multiple states. False starts are no longer the disasters they were before the availability of digital files, as students can go back to a previous version and continue exploration from there with no loss. In fact, formative assessment is facilitated, as a record of the process, not just the final product, is available.

In the mask project, by rendering a sketch in a simple drawing/painting program, tentative studies can be developed into a finished two-dimensional version of the mask. This can be kept as the culminating product (see the following project sample) or it can become the raw material for producing a three-dimensional version.

The process of producing the graphic dimension of the mask is similar to the creation of a digital collage. The Web can be searched for useful reference images, or images found in hard copy can be scanned into digital form. In either case, painting and image processing programs will allow this material to be transformed so that it conforms to the specific needs of the mask maker. These processes may include altering contrast, accentuating or minimizing characteristics, or adding elements from the student's imagination.

Equally important, many versions of a useful image can be created by virtue of the copy and paste functions, and the image can be sized or flopped as needed, as well. This gives the artist terrific flexibility.

Principal Technology Skills Addressed

- Internet research/image mining
- Digital photography

Technology Resources Needed

- Internet access/browser/search engine(s)
- Digital camera

WEB RESOURCES

Chenowith School District (Mask Making and Use in Different Cultures):
www.chenowith.k12.or.us/TECH/subject/art/masks.html

Dick Blick (catalog of materials, techniques, and sources):
www.dickblick.com/categories/maskmaking/

Leisure Cambodia (The craft of mask making—informational overview):
www.leisurecambodia.com/Leisure_Cambodia/No.16/Mask_making.html

Masks from Around the World (the tribal mask):
www.masksoftheworld.com

Teachnet (Art of Mask Making):
www.teachnet-lab.org/miami/2002/mgil2/art_of_mask_making.htm

Unit Conceptual and Pedagogical Overview

Mask making is one of the human family's oldest art-making traditions. Like the representation of animals on cave walls, its roots can be traced to primitive man's deep-seated need for magic (or at least magical thinking), a way to gain a measure of control over the world.

Traditional mask making is often associated with human societies that developed in close relationship with the natural world. There, the observation of animals, the ascribing of supernatural powers to them, and the anthropomorphization of their behavior led to a pantheon of animals as totems, deities, and spirits; characters that appeared prominently in important folklore.

Extending this process, mankind eventually created mythical creatures—characters based on observed animals, but with fantastic physical characteristics and imbued with greater powers than their real-world relatives. These creatures were the product of a creative process that not only combined real features from disparate animals in impossible ways, but one that combined animal features with those of men, as well. The phoenix, chimera, unicorn, minotaur, and centaur are but a few examples.

The preoccupation with these creatures is reflected in the mask-making arts of numerous cultures. In the culture of Native Americans of the Pacific Northwest, for instance, we see large-scale masks used in transformation ceremonies that combine the attributes of several creatures. This combining is seen consistently in the highly imaginative masks of traditional African peoples, as well. Similar concepts are seen in the art of the Caribbean, Oceanic Pacific, Southeast Asia, and other areas. It truly is a universal theme.

Closely associated with a belief in these creatures is the production of masks for the use in ceremonies. In these rites, mankind fostered a relationship with the creature the mask represents, acquired or borrowed some of its powers, and honored and celebrated it.

Although in many societies the core beliefs behind mask making have faded, the artistic tradition of mask making and the themes and techniques associated continue as important aspects of their art and culture.

Consequently, in addition to being an ideal platform for their creative expression, mask making can engage student artists in learning various important areas of social studies. I've found it to be one of the most enjoyed and fruitful of all art-making activities completed in school and quite possibly the most perfect one from the point of view of cross-curricular connections.

ACTIVITIES

DAY 1

1. Research and preparation

a. Direct students to do Web-based research on traditional or folk art masks as well as on mythical creatures. Ask the students to select and print out a picture of a mask they find particularly interesting or inspiring.

b. Follow-up group discussion: Have the students present to the group photos of the mask they selected and relate their understanding of its function (within the social context of its creation), what ideas and feelings it conveys to them, and so on.

DAY 2

2. Create the shell of an original mask

Note: In this project students will use technology to harvest raw graphic material from which they will produce finished art. The base of the mask, the shell, will serve as a support for this technology-generated material.

c. The mask shell can be produced or acquired in one of three different ways. Teachers can acquire blank masks in many craft stores; depending on the art capacity of the school or classroom, students can produce the shell by covering half of an inflated balloon with papier-mâché or Paris Craft (gauze impregnated with plaster of Paris available from craft stores or surgical supply houses); or by directly applying Paris Craft to the student's face, which has been covered with Vaseline. For those unfamiliar with these last two classic art-class approaches, a great deal of information is available on the Web or in the library that describes these non-technology-dependent aspects of student mask making. Alternately, a paper bag (stuffed with newspaper) will work well as a mask shell.

As a pre-art-making exercise, the students list the features to be incorporated into their mask (i.e., snake eyes, goat nose, tiger mouth, etc.)

Using an image search engine (Google images, for instance) reference material relating to the listed features are mined from the Web. In the process of gathering the images, full pictures of creatures may be located from which, either by use of a photo processing software or using scissors, the needed features are acquired and freed from their background. The digital approach offers the advantages of allowing the student to create multiple copies of an element.

DAYS 3–4

3. Create the exterior of the mask

d. The printed elements are next permanently affixed onto the mask shell with glue. Because the printed element will be paper-based, using a non–water-based adhesive, such as vinyl wallpaper paste will create the cleanest effect. This type of adhesive can be simply brushed on with student-grade paintbrushes that are easily cleaned.

In a slightly more advanced version of the project, cardboard (or other light material) scraps, papier-mâché, or Paris Craft can be used to build up the relief of features (the nose, for instance), and the graphic material can be scored, folded, or stretched to fit over it.

Any conventional wet or dry art material (paint, crayon, marker, etc.) can be used to enhance and finish the piece. This finish may involve sharpening, darkening, and widening the lines that define the features, adding color, erasing or covering aspects of the features, adding texture, and so on.

Project Samples

Process Used to Develop this Sample

Students can create this project in either a flat, two-dimensional version or in a more traditional three-dimensional version. Both versions offer the full value of the process of creating the mask. A sample of each version is shown here.

Figure 11.1. Project Sample—Graphic Mask, two-dimensional version.

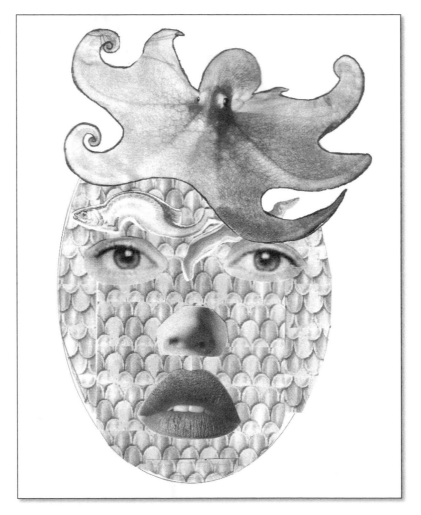

Figure 11.2. Project Sample—Graphic Mask, three-dimensional version.

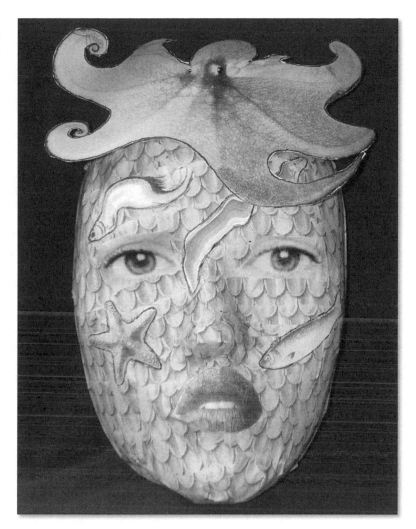

From a body of raw reference material mined from a variety of sources on the Web, the artist selected a group of elements to use in the mask. One of these was a segment of fish-style chain mail armor, an artifact based on fish scales that truly resembles the scales. This segment was imported into a painting program (in this example, Paint), further cropped using the crop tool, and then copied. He pasted multiple copies of this into a new document in the painting program and positioned them so that they formed a continuous pattern. Where segments met he used the brush and airbrush tools of the program to touch up the areas and to enhance the effect of one continuous expanse of fish scales.

Flat version

1. Using the auto shapes function of a word processing or painting program (in this case, Paint) the artist used the oval tool to create a large oval roughly the same shape and orientation as a human head. He then adjusted the size and orientation on the page until satisfactory and then printed it on 8.5 x 11 inch white paper.

2. The rest of the mask was finished by printing images of facial elements (animal and human) and pasting them onto the oval in traditional collage manner.

3. Using the oval tool again, the artist applied an oval identical in size to the oval in step 1 over the page of the fish scale pattern. Next, using a scissors, he cut out the form and pasted it on top of the oval in step 1.

4. The eyes, nose, mouth, fish (eyebrows) and octopus (hat) were all found as individual images on the Web. He adjusted some (e.g., the fish eyebrows) for contrast to accentuate the lights and darks in a photo-editing software (Picasa, in this case), imported them into a word processing program (Word), and adjusted them to be a size that would fit the oval. He then printed, cut out, and pasted the images onto the oval created in step 3.

5. He then scanned the completed mask collage on a digital scanner and saved it as a JPEG file.

6. The artist then imported the JPEG file back into Paint and processed it (e.g., drawing a black line around the features using the brush tool, applying tone under the mouth using the airbrush tool, etc.). The flat version of the mask was now finished.

3-D Version

Using the same elements as above, the artist freed printouts of the features from background material with scissors and glued them onto a mask form. In order to make the flat-printed features conform to the three-dimensional contours of the mask, he cut slits allowing the wet elements to better fit around them. In numerous cases, multiple versions of the features were printed out and cut to provide the extra material required.

Sharing the Work

The finished masks make an excellent exhibition within the school. Because they are lightweight and made of a soft material, they can be hung on the wall in a variety of ways (e.g., a string looped through holes punched at the edges of the mask and hooked over a nail or hook taped to the wall).

An important extension of making the masks is documenting the process. To do this, assign a student to photograph each step of the mask-making process by circulating throughout the classroom as the masks are being created. These photographs will make a wonderful addition to the exhibition of the masks themselves. These process photos will mean more with the addition of captions, which in turn lays the groundwork for a narrative procedure writing assignment.

Alternately, an exhibit composed entirely of photographs will produce a good result. This provides the opportunity to photograph the masks on their own as sculptural art objects, as well as the chance to photograph them while being worn or posed with their student creators. These photos, along with the captions, can also become the content for a class book: a catalog of the exhibit.

Note: See unit 18, "Sharing Student Art Work" for an overview of sharing technology-supported student art projects.

Assessment

Assessment of this project might effectively cover a number of its dimensions: diligence in following directions and procedures, how the finished piece reveals an understanding of the cultural role of masks in traditional societies, and creativity in adapting the raw material found on the Web to the purpose and context of this project.

Suggested discussion question: If your mask were to be used in a ceremony in a traditional culture, what would it identify and what qualities would it communicate?

Suggested General Assessment/Accountability Rubric for Unit 11

Project Components	Excellent	Proficient	Partially Proficient	Not Sufficiently Proficient or Incomplete
Completion of Project • Student prepares framing shape on which to develop the mask • Student adapts found images to paste onto the framing shape for clarity, scale, design quality • Uses applicable software (photo-editing, painting, drawing, etc.) • The adapted images are pasted onto the framing shape and positioned as facial features and details as a traditional (non digital) collage 1. The 2 D mask collage is scanned, reworked with software (as applicable), and saved as a graphics file *or* 2. The 3-D mask collage is digitally photographed and saved as a graphics file	All portions of the project are completed successfully at a high level.	Most portions of the project are completed successfully at a high or satisfactory level.	Some important (and other) portions of the project are completed successfully at a satisfactory level.	Few of the project portions are completed successfully at a satisfactory level.
Research and Preparation • Student mines the Web for reference graphics with potential to be mask elements	Conducted the needed research/ preparation in a way that allows for a full level of participation in the project.	Conducted the needed research/ preparation in a way that allows for a high level of participation in the project.	Conducted the needed research/ preparation in a way that allows for a satisfactory level of participation in the project.	Conducted the needed research/ preparation in a way that allows for a minimal level of participation in the project.

(Continued)

Suggested General Assessment/Accountability Rubric for Unit 11 *(Continued)*

Project Components	Excellent	Proficient	Partially Proficient	Not Sufficiently Proficient or Incomplete
Theme and Concept Learning • Student understands the history and significance of the art of mask making • Student understands the ritual mask is a specialized form of sculpture	Fully understood the concepts and goals of the project. Understood the contextual background content. Understood how to apply the above in the creation of an original work.	Understood a good deal of the concepts and goals of the project. Understood the contextual background content to a high degree. Understood how to apply the above in the creation of an original work to a high degree.	Understood some of the concepts and goals of the project. Understood the contextual background content to a degree. Understood how to apply the above in the creation of an original work to a degree.	Did not adequately understand the concepts and goals of the project. Did not adequately understand the contextual background content. Did not adequately understand how to apply the above in the creation of an original work.
Technical Proficiency • Student uses drawing, painting, and collage techniques effectively to produce an attractive mask that succeeds in communicating story and idea	Demonstrated a very high degree of understanding and mastery of the concepts and skills involved in the techniques required of the project.	Demonstrated a good degree of understanding and mastery of the concepts and skills involved in the techniques required of the project.	Demonstrated a satisfactory degree of understanding and mastery of the concepts and skills involved in the techniques required of the project.	Did not demonstrate an adequate degree of understanding and mastery of the concepts and skills involved in the techniques required of the project.
Technology Use • Student uses software functions effectively to scan, draw, paint, and so on, as needed to develop the project • Student saves and manages files appropriately	Handled the technology portions of the project in a highly effective, insightful, and responsible fashion.	Handled the technology portions of the project very proficiently and in an effective, insightful, and responsible fashion.	Handled the technology portions of the project in a satisfactorily effective, insightful, and responsible fashion.	Did not handle the technology portions of the project in a satisfactorily effective, insightful, and responsible fashion.
Creativity-Expression • Student creates a visually compelling mask that communicates ideas and information as required by the project • Student uses available resources, materials, and tools inventively to maximize artistic effect and expression	Conceived, developed, and executed a work of art that is highly original and that takes full advantage of the medium's possibilities.	To a good degree, conceived, developed, and executed a work of art that is original and that takes full advantage of the medium's possibilities.	To a satisfactory degree, conceived, developed, and executed a work of art that is somewhat original and that takes advantage of some of the medium's possibilities.	Did not well conceive and execute a work that is original or takes good advantage of the medium's possibilities.

Note: See chapter 7, "Assessing Digital Art Projects" for an overview of assessing technology-supported student visual art projects.

Cross-Curricular Connection

Mask Making and Language Arts

Mythology is a content area frequently drawn on in a variety of K–12 curricula. It comprises an appreciable portion of materials used in the teaching of reading. The *Mythology in the Classroom* section of the Internet School Library Media Center is but one example of the rich resources for teaching and learning mythology that can be found on the Web.

It is common practice for language arts teachers to assign books on general themes rather than individual titles. Assigning a book on mythology, or in a more focused manner, Greek mythology, for instance, would make an appropriate and effective curricular alignment to accompany the mask-making project. Because each student can elect to read about a different myth, each would produce a different mask as part of the class exhibit. Greek mythology figures strongly in Greek history and culture, which are almost universally included in the standard social studies curriculum.

As opposed to writing a book report or making an oral presentation based on the reading assignment, the creation of a mask establishes a context and focus for a highly motivating and effective project.

Some focus items to direct the assignment might include the following:

- Identify the character your mask is based on, as well as the myth associated with it.

- What is the domain or power of the character for whom you are creating the mask? (God of the sea? God of war? Denizen of the underworld? Resident of a heavenly realm? etc.)

- Describe your character's powers, special abilities, and weaknesses.

- Describe your character's personality, behavior, quirks, and so on.

- Give a short synopsis of the portion of the myth your character appears in.

In order to accomplish the above, the student will have to read a book or other text of a classic myth and do so in a focused, purposeful manner. The information obtained through the reading will guide the creation of the mask.

As a culminating activity, the student could present the mask to the class in a theater piece. In a darkened setting, holding or wearing the mask so that it alone appears in a pencil spotlight, the student could present a short narrative written to introduce and explain the character brought to life through the creation and presentation of the mask.

UNIT **12**

A New Dimension
for **Origami**

In whatever one does there must be a relationship
between the eye and the heart.

— HENRI CARTIER-BRESSON

*Please see the
sections "Using
this Book" and
"Assessing Digital
Art Projects" for
more information
about these
standards, the
interaction
between them,
and connecting
these standards to
the lessons in this
book.*

STANDARDS

NETS·S

Although all or most of the NETS·S are touched on in this unit, the connection is strongest
and easiest to see and understand in the standards listed below:

1. a, b, d	4. a, b, d
2. a, b, c, d	5. a, c
3. a, b	6. a, b

Note: In this and other units students *develop cultural understanding of global awareness by engaging with
learners of other cultures* (NETS·S 2.c) when they use technology to immerse themselves in content
produced by other cultures, publish content intended to further the understanding and appreciation
of cultures for a worldwide audience, and/or collaborate directly with peers in other cultures.

National Standards for Arts Education (Visual Arts)

CS–1, AS–a, b

CS–2, AS–a, c

CS–3, AS–a, b

CS–4, AS–a, b

CS–5, AS–a, b, c

CS–6, AS–a, b

UNIT OBJECTIVES

Students will be challenged to:

- Learn about the traditional Japanese art of Origami and its derivation and function within the context of Japanese culture and society.

- Use a traditional art form as inspiration for a contemporary work based in that tradition.

CENTRAL IDEAS

Origami, the traditional Japanese art of paper folding, embodies many of the characteristics of traditional decorative crafts at the same time that it expresses the design qualities of fine art sculpture in the round. This dual nature makes it an especially handy focus for teaching three-dimensional art to students.

I have had many successful experiences using Origami as an entry point to making sculpture. From a practical standpoint, its small scale and relatively low demand on materials, space, and other resources, make it an activity that can be easily completed practically anywhere.

Many of Origami's classic themes affirm it as a form of stylized, but representational, sculpture in the round. Even though it is typically not displayed as such, but held in the hand or suspended from a string, we can easily see that it has the same form as many free-standing sculptures.

The stylization of Origami's subjects, which involves breaking the forms represented into many flat planes, stems from the technique of constructing these three-dimensional sculptures from two-dimensional sheets of paper.

That Origami is made from paper offers a potential for design that is usually not taken advantage of. Using digital technologies, the paper from which the Origami are constructed can be made to carry images that relate to the theme of the Origami's form. This provides an unusual opportunity for student artists to focus on the differing approaches to representation between two- and three-dimensional works and to explore the relationship between them.

I've found that students naturally enjoy making Origami. However, they especially appreciate this project's added dimension of creating personalized and expressive Origami, as opposed to simply making traditional designs that a great many others have done previously in nearly identical manner. This is the type of challenge that today's students find engaging and through which both art and technology skills and understandings are well learned.

TECHNOLOGY RATIONALE

The purpose of this project is to inform and involve students in the traditional Japanese art form of Origami and at the same time have them reflect on how its boundaries can be pushed and explored. Technology is essential to this later part and is highly useful in making the first part successful.

Web-based research can make any study of traditional Origami easier, as it turns up photos of examples of completed projects, historical and practical information about how it evolved, its place in society, and illustrated instructions on how to do it oneself.

The approach to expanding the form taken here is to custom-produce graphically enhanced paper from which to fold Origami projects. This is a technique that cannot be accomplished in any way other than through the use of computers and ancillary technology resources.

For this project students acquire, either by searching and downloading or by hand-collecting hard copy material that is scanned, the raw material on which to base the themed pattern of their custom Origami folding paper. The student artists then size and process this, generally to simplify and strengthen the design quality. The pattern is created by repeatedly copying and pasting the image into software that lays the design out in a controlled order. Finally, the printer provides as many copies of draft and finished copies as needed to complete the process.

Principal Technology Skills Addressed

- Web-based research/image mining

- Image processing

- Digital photography

Technology Resources Needed

- Internet access/browser/search engine(s)

- Image processing software

- Digital cameras

WEB RESOURCES

Opane.com (comprehensive listing of Origami resource links):
www.opane.com/origami.html

Tammy Yee's Origami Page (variety of Origami resources for students):
www.tammyyee.com/origami.html

WannaLearn.com (comprehensive listing of resource links for Origami):
www.wannalearn.com/Crafts_and_Hobbies/Origami/

Web Japan (Origami Trivia):
http://Web-jpn.org/kidsWeb/virtual/origami2/trivia.html

Unit Conceptual and Pedagogical Overview

Although Origami is sometimes made as a school-based activity, it is seldom done as a serious art project. In reality Origami is a highly respected art form in Asian cultures. In addition to offering much of the same art content learning associated with the study of any vibrant form of sculpture, Origami offers many other benefits.

Understanding the Japanese mindset, culture, and artistic tradition is greatly facilitated by exposure to, and involvement with, Origami. Making Origami requires planning, problem solving, discipline, and an appreciation of aesthetic subtleties. Origami reflects the traditional Japanese preoccupation with nature, fine craftsmanship, and the miracle of paper, a material that is not often given the respect it deserves and which is an important element for student artists to consider. It's been my observation that through projects such as this one, in which students must produce the paper they'll use for their project, their understanding of the function of paper and an appreciation of its qualities is greatly enhanced.

Origami projects generally expose students to process, procedure, and technique, as well as traditional form. What is often lacking, though, is a fostering of understanding of how Origami literally transforms a material from having a two-dimensional existence to a three-dimensional one. Reflecting further, we can see that although finished Origami are three-dimensional, they are composed entirely of two-dimensional planes that can retain the qualities and artistic properties of two-dimensional work. The tension between 2-D and 3-D inherent in Origami can be exploited by artists and art students to produce visually and conceptually compelling work.

In U.S. schools Origami projects are often made with packaged Origami papers (usually of Japanese manufacture) that provide little more than the convenience of being cut to the traditional size and aspect ratio, along with having pretty pastel colors. In the great Origami tradition, as practiced by masters in Japan and other parts of Asia, the weight, texture, and patterns of the paper used to create these sculptures are also valued for what they can add to the art form.

This unit leverages convenient technology in order to explore the graphic dimension of the creation of Origami as fine art. Students will reflect on the theme and form of a traditional Origami motif and mine the Web for raw graphic material with which they will produce a unique paper to enhance the realization of that motif.

ACTIVITIES

DAY 1

1. Research and preparation

a. Have students research via the Internet the history and dimensions of Origami as an art form. Engage them in a discussion and brainstorming session about what was learned.

Focus questions that may prove especially useful include the following:

- Who makes Origami in Japan and where might one find exceptional examples of it?

- Is Origami intended to be permanent, or is it a collection of works that are recorded and intended to be produced again and again on an ongoing basis?

- What is the relationship between the paper Origami is made of and the ideas and feelings that finished Origami convey?

b. Based on their online research, have students select an Origami project to produce on their own. The project should be selected from those for which step-by-step directions (especially illustrated ones) are available from informational sources on the Web or in the library. (The Web abounds in such materials—see suggested sites in the Web Resources section).

DAY 2

2. Hands-on practice

Note: Traditional Origami can be difficult to make, especially the first time around, even though step-by-step directions and illustrations are often available. The following are prudent steps to take in order to ensure success.

c. Walk the class through a single, simple exploratory and background project. By doing this, an understanding of what the experience of producing Origami is like will put all members of the class on informed footing. Those individuals with a particular aptitude for paper folding will be identified, who may then prove to be invaluable resources for the success of the entire class.

d. As a concluding activity for this step, have the class brainstorm what they feel they've discovered about Origami, what the problems and pitfalls in producing it are, and how they may better prepare themselves for success as they continue making the paper sculptures.

e. After the walkthrough, students should search for images of two-dimensional graphics (drawings, photos, etc.) that they feel accompany and complement their particular Origami subject. For instance, if the subject is a frog, then graphics of frogs, pond plants, flies, and so on, would work well.

Note: As an alternative to steps b. through d., structure the selection of an Origami theme (Day 1) and the folding and presenting aspects of the project (Day 2) as collaborative group work in which groups of roughly four students work together to support one another. If the hands-on exercise identified students to whom paper folding comes particularly easy, these students may be placed strategically within groups to aid others who have difficulty with it.

DAYS 3–4

3. **Making an original Origami**

    f. The Origami sculpture (of the previously-selected motif) is executed in the traditional way using plain white paper. The sculpture is unfolded and flattened to reveal a series of small, two-dimensional planes (most often triangular in shape).

    g. Using the images collected in the previous session, a digital photo collage is designed by placing the images within the picture plane to correspond to the sections that the unfolded, flattened finished Origami sculpture revealed in step **f.**

    h. The collage is printed (either scan, save, and print this collage using a computer, scanner, and printer or use a photocopier) and then the paper is trimmed to size. This is the material from which an identical Origami is folded. When finished, the two-dimensional graphics become an integral part of the sculpture and its visual statement.

Note: This project involves students becoming aware of and facile with a process of pre-visualization, trial-and-error experimentation, and making course corrections as a visual idea is refined and worked toward realization. For students to get the full benefit of this experience, they should be given the opportunity to repeat the above steps several times until they are satisfied.

Project Sample

Figure 12.1. Project Sample—Origami Cranes

Process Used to Develop this Sample

After deciding on the subject of "The Crane" as the theme on which to base his pattern, the artist found and downloaded images relating to cranes using a search engine (Google images, in this case).

After analysis, he selected several elements as the best raw material for the pattern. He then simplified and processed the images using photo-editing software (Picasa) to increase the images' contrast, and then used a painting program (Paint) to isolate segments for use in the pattern. In the case of the crane head, he placed this segment within an oval using the program's auto shapes function.

Once imported into a word processing program (Word), the artist used the size, rotate, copy, and paste functions to create the pattern.

The pattern was applied to both sides of the paper by simply printing it once and then flipping the paper in the paper tray and printing it again.

Finally, the artist cut the printed paper to size (8.5 x 8.5) and folded it into the desired Origami shape.

Figure 12.2a. A full 8.5 x 11 inch sheet of Origami paper created for this sample.

Figure 12.2b. Close-up of a segment of the paper.

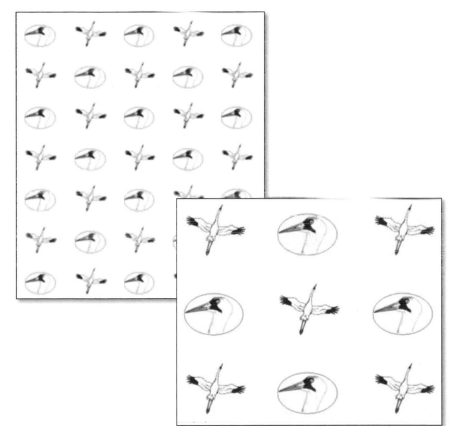

Sharing the Work

Origami figures can be exhibited easily and effectively by suspending them from the ceiling on nylon monofilament fishing line (which can often be attached to classroom lighting fixtures).

Additionally, a digital photo of Origami is easy to take. The photos can be displayed in a classic gallery exhibit on the wall or incorporated into a book or catalog of the class's work on Origami. This can be finished as an e-book, a format that is easy to prepare by composing the book in a word processing software and then saving the file in PDF format. PDF files are stable, can't be altered, and can be attached to e-mail or uploaded to a Web site. By producing a class exhibit catalog in which each student's work represents just one page of a single file, distribution of the classes work is manageable.

Figure 12.3. A page from a class catalog of Origami projects.

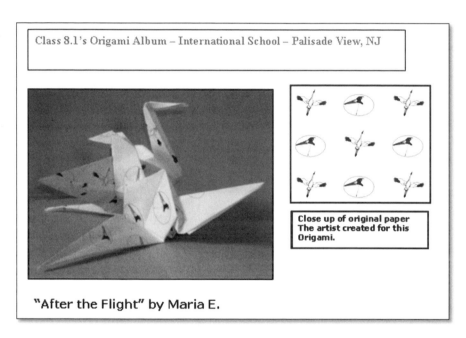

One classic approach to picture making is the diptych, a compound picture made up of two equally-sized images. A natural outcome of this unit's project would be a diptych composed of the finished Origami and the patterned paper that the student created.

Figure 12.4. A diptych of an Origami piece and the artist-made paper from which it is constructed.

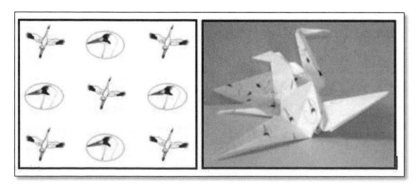

A worthwhile extension of this project would involve directing the students to create an illustrated narrative procedure that shows, through captioned digital photos, all of the steps taken in the creation of their Origami.

Another more advanced use of digital photography would involve virtual reality software. Because Origami is sculpture in the round, a series of photos taken from all possible angles can be converted into a virtual reality view of the finished art work.

Note: See unit 18, "Sharing Student Art Work" for an overview of possibilities in sharing technology-supported student art projects.

Assessment

The value of this project comes from imparting an understanding of how digital technology can preserve a traditional art form. It also empowers young artists to pick up where tradition leaves off, taking what they find useful and inspirational and expanding upon its possibilities. Accordingly, what we are looking for in student performance are indicators that both aspects are understood, explored, and honored. Can the finished work stand on its own as a quality example of traditional Origami? Furthermore, will closer examination show that the motif revealed through sculptural shape is echoed in the graphic elements, and that the two blend to create a third, more powerful dimension in their union?

Suggested discussion question: Does the combination of the two representational states of your sculpture, 2-D and 3-D, give the viewer something that neither could provide on its own?

Suggested General Assessment/Accountability Rubric for Unit 12

Project Components	Excellent	Proficient	Partially Proficient	Not Sufficiently Proficient or Incomplete
Completion of Project • Student selects and downloads appropriate range of reference images • Student processes the images appropriately for inclusion in patterned paper for Origami piece • Student produces an effective patterned paper • Student successfully folds the final Origami sculpture	All portions of the project are completed successfully at a high level.	Most portions of the project are completed successfully at a high or satisfactory level.	Some important (and other) portions of the project are completed successfully at a satisfactory level.	Few of the project portions are completed successfully at a satisfactory level.
Research and Preparation • Student researches and acquires background information about the chosen subject and the possible traditional Origami connection	Conducted the needed research/preparation in a way that allows for a full level of participation in the project.	Conducted the needed research/preparation in a way that allows for a high level of participation in the project.	Conducted the needed research/preparation in a way that allows for a satisfactory level of participation in the project.	Conducted the needed research/preparation in a way that allows for a minimal level of participation in the project.
Theme and Concept Learning • Student understands the historical and cultural background of the art of Origami • Student understands the relationship between the paper material and finished Origami • Student understands the play between the 2-D-graphics of the patterned paper and the subject represented by the 3-D sculpture	Fully understood the concepts and goals of the project. Understood the contextual background content. Understood how to apply the above in the creation of an original work.	Understood a good deal of the concepts and goals of the project. Understood the contextual background content to a high degree. Understood how to apply the above in the creation of an original work to a high degree.	Understood some of the concepts and goals of the project. Understood the contextual background content to a degree. Understood how to apply the above in the creation of an original work to a degree.	Did not adequately understand the concepts and goals of the project. Did not adequately understand the contextual background content. Did not adequately understand how to apply the above in the creation of an original work.

(Continued)

Suggested General Assessment/Accountability Rubric for Unit 12 *(Continued)*

Project Components	Excellent	Proficient	Partially Proficient	Not Sufficiently Proficient or Incomplete
Technical Proficiency • Student transforms raw 2-D-material to support the graphic requirements of envisioned finished 3-D art work • Student creates an effective, scale-appropriate pattern from processed images • Student successfully folds finished Origami piece	Demonstrated a high degree of under-standing and mastery of the concepts and skills involved in the techniques required of the project.	Demonstrated a good degree of under-standing and mastery of the concepts and skills involved in the techniques required of the project.	Demonstrated a satisfactory degree of understanding and mastery of the concepts and skills involved in the techniques required of the project.	Did not demonstrate an adequate degree of understanding and mastery of the concepts and skills involved in the techniques required of the project.
Technology Use • Student searches and downloads needed materials • Student imports and processes images in paint/drawing application and/or word processing program • Student prints materials as appropriate for completion of project	Handled the techno-logy portions of the project in a highly effective, insightful, and responsible fashion.	Handled the technology portions of the project very proficiently and in an effective, insightful, and responsible fashion.	Handled the technology portions of the project in a satisfactorily effective, insightful, and respon-sible fashion.	Did not handle the technology portions of the project in a satisfactorily effective, insightful, and respon-sible fashion.
Creativity-Expression • Student chose an appro-priate subject to satisfy unique needs of project • Student participated in a way that resulted in the creation of a unique piece based on a traditional theme • Student's personal interests, concerns, and sensibilities are evident in finished piece	Conceived, developed, and executed a work of art that is highly original and that takes full advantage of the medium's possibilities.	To a good degree, conceived, developed, and executed a work of art that is original and that takes full advantage of the medium's possibilities.	To a satisfactory degree, conceived, developed, and executed a work of art that is somewhat original and that takes advantage of some of the medium's possibilities.	Did not well conceive and execute a work that is original or takes good advantage of the medium's possibilities.

Note: See chapter 7, "Assessing Digital Art Projects" for an overview of assessing technology-supported student visual art projects.

Cross-Curricular Connection

Origami and Math

A variety of mathematics skills are used in this project. The first part of the work involves the students in creating a unique patterned paper from which each will construct an Origami sculpture. The raw material they will be working with is 8.5 x 11 or 8.5 x 14 inch printer paper. However, most Origami constructions require square paper for folding. The conversion of the rectangular printer paper to the square folding paper involves measurement and calculation.

How much paper must be removed from the long side in order to have all sides be equal? Once this has been determined, a ruler is needed to plot where the cut should be made. And afterward, the ruler should be used again to check that a square has indeed been produced successfully.

The second part of this project involves the creation of a pattern on the paper from which the Origami will be folded. This may be seen as an application of tᵒessellation, a common subject in mathematics courses.

The pattern will be produced using word processing functions that allow for easy copying and pasting of as many versions of an image as desired, as well as the easy adjustment of their size. The pattern involves numbers of repetitions of images laid out in rows. An interesting challenge can be created by assigning the students mathematical parameters within which they must produce the pattern (e.g., no more than ten and no fewer than five per line). Alternately, the student might be tasked to try several different versions of a pattern and report on the density of the images on each of the versions.

If time permits, an effective version of the project would involve the creation of an Origami, and then an adjustment of the size and character of the paper's pattern based on the artist's reaction to the results achieved the first time. Measurement, estimation, and recalibration of the pattern may produce a more effective interplay of pattern and sculpture the second or third time the Origami is folded. Increasing the size of the pattern elements (consequently reducing the number of repetitions of the elements it holds) may produce a better fit between the 2-D pattern and 3-D figure. Or, conversely, decreasing their size and increasing their number may be more effective artistically.

Some valuable resources for establishing further connections between Origami and math learning include the following:

Math and Origami: www.utc.edu/Faculty/Deborah-McAllister/camta04origami. html

Origami Cube: www.mathematische-basteleien.de/oricube.htm

Origami and Math: www.paperfolding.com/math/

Sadako and the Paper Cranes

The tale of Sadako, a young Japanese girl, and how she used Origami to get the world to focus on peace is a famous story. It is perhaps most well known through the popular book for young people by Eleanor Coerr titled *Sadako and the Thousand Paper Cranes.*

Reading and discussing this book in class as part of this unit on Origami will establish a natural and meaningful connection to language arts and social studies as well as touch on a number of inspiring dimensions of character education.

Born in 1943, a native of Hiroshima, Sadako was very young when the atom bomb was dropped on her city. At age 11 she became sick with leukemia, which was also known then as "atom bomb disease." She began a personal project to make 1,000 paper cranes (the crane is the Japanese symbol of peace) as a way to keep herself positive and muster the will to survive her severe illness. She continued making cranes until she died at the age of 12.

Sadako's schoolmates were so inspired by her courage and strength that they put together a book of her letters and published it. Since then many millions have become familiar with her inspiring story and have made paper cranes that they've sent to join others at the International Peace Memorial in Hiroshima Japan.

The Web abounds with versions of this story, additional information about Sadako and the popular movement for young people to make cranes for peace.

The Sadako story and related Origami-based activities are an interesting introductory or extension activity for this project. Students can find a great deal of "how to" information on making Origami cranes.

A few of the many Web sites that can be used as resources include:

Cranes for Peace—A project to learn about creating World Peace:
www.networkearth.org/world/peace.html

The Sadako Story:
www.sadako.org/sadakostory.htm
http://japan.lisd.k12.mi.us/resources/jumppages/sadako.html

Sadako and the Thousand Paper Cranes—A Web Quest for Grades 3–5:
http://asterix.ednet.lsu.edu/~edtech/Webquest/sadako.htm

Wikipedia— Sadako Sasaki:
http://en.wikipedia.org/wiki/Sadako_Sasaki

UNIT **13**

Beyond the Third Dimension
Graphic Mobiles

I begin with an idea and then it becomes something else.

— PABLO PICASSO

Please see the sections "Using this Book" and "Assessing Digital Art Projects" for more information about these standards, the interaction between them, and connecting these standards to the lessons in this book.

STANDARDS

NETS•S

Although all or most of the NETS•S are touched on in this unit, the connection is strongest and easiest to see and understand in the standards listed below:

1. a, b, d   4. a, b, c, d

2. b   5. a, b, c

3. a, b, c, d   6. a, b, d

Note: In this unit and others, students produce works that involve multiple processes (e.q., digital photography, image processing, printing and affixing images to surfaces), blend two dimensional and three-dimensional aspects of images, and share their work through traditional exhibits as well as by publishing them, which *communicate information and ideas effectively to multiple audiences using a variety of media and formats* (NETS•S 2.b).

National Standards for Arts Education (Visual Arts)

CS–1, AS–b

CS–2, AS–a, b, c

CS–3, AS–a, b

UNIT OBJECTIVES

Students will be challenged to:

- Understand the form and function of mobiles as a development in modern sculpture.

- Understand how both graphic elements and three-dimensional elements can be combined to give the viewer a powerful visual experience.

- Create an original mobile embracing these ideas and incorporating traditional and new possibilities presented by technology.

CENTRAL IDEAS

One of the artist Alexander Calder's greatest accomplishments was the invention of a new sculptural form, one that broke with the long-standing convention of sculpture as a stationary object. He named it the *mobile*, a moving sculpture. No longer did the viewer have to move in order to see the sculpture completely. Employing simple engineering, mobiles present themselves as continually shifting collections of shapes suspended in space. They are generally playful, whimsical works of art that students find very appealing.

Traditionally, mobiles have been primarily abstract works of art made up of collections of simple shapes. An additional dimension, however, can be added to them by bringing in the element of representation. This technique is accomplished by affixing representational images to the surfaces of the shapes. These graphically enhanced mobiles are an art form that I've successfully made with students, exploring the unique possibilities of shapes that carry images as they move in space. When the right image is selected for a specific shape, and then is carefully prepared to conform to the contours, scale, and overall character of the shape, the result is an exciting and effective mobile element.

Doing all this, however, is a tall order for even an accomplished artist and would be a difficult challenge for students if not for the advent of imaging technologies, which aid students in researching and acquiring images, as well as in processing, tailoring, and transferring them to the sculpture.

TECHNOLOGY RATIONALE

This project guides the student in an exploration of the differences between two-dimensional and three-dimensional design and how the characteristics of both can be brought together to produce an especially interesting approach toward creating art.

The mobile, a sculptural form that's been around for roughly three-quarters of a century, has traditionally been conceived of and understood as composed of unadorned flat planes that move in space. Wonderful student work has been created following this simple tradition. However, other possibilities may be explored with students that will yield valuable learning experiences, as well.

By enhancing the planes from which a mobile is composed with realistic images, new dimensions of design and meaning can be explored. Technology makes this possible and relatively easy, empowering the student to concentrate on the message aspect of the project, rather than struggling to master the techniques required to produce it.

Because mobiles are devoted to the element of movement, movement becomes a subject upon which their themes may be derived and developed. What things in our world move, particularly through the air? How can we depict them? How can we do so in a way that is aligned with the production of a mobile?

In addition to mining the Web for ideas and for graphic materials that answer those questions, other applications of technology can be used for this project. By using the painting/drawing aspects of software, the raw visual material can be processed for size and visual characteristics. In the sample described, the visual material has been subjected to special software effects that alter the nature of the subject depicted in accordance with the theme and taste of the student artist.

Additionally, the graphics are imported into computer-drawn shapes that evoke the theme and heighten the visual message. This project is very much a product of what contemporary, technology-using students can do in the creation and expansion of a traditional art product.

Principal Technology Skills Addressed

- Web research/image mining

- Digital photography

Technology Resources Needed

- Digital cameras

WEB RESOURCES

Calder Foundation (information and collections of Alexander Calder's works): www.calder.org/SETS/work/work.html

Google Video (video of large Calder mobile at National Gallery): hrrp://video.google.com/videoplay?docid=-5552815781795311388

Math Cats (Virtual Mobiles—mobile mechanics simulations): www.mathcats.com/explore/virtual/mobile.html

Mathew Brand (information on mobile movement and mechanics): http://alumni.media.mit.edu/~brand/about-mobiles.html

Virtual Calder (mobile mechanics simulations and related information): www.mine-control.com/zack/balance/balance.html

Unit Conceptual and Pedagogical Overview

Mobiles, moving sculptures, are generally considered to have been invented by Alexander Calder, although the Russian artist Naum Gabo began experimenting with similar constructions a few years earlier. Mobiles represent a fascinating step forward in the field of art in which sculpture had always been conceived of as static. During the era of Pop Art, mobiles were explored again with renewed interest. The result was mass-produced mobiles with graphic elements, as opposed to the highly simplified abstract shapes they had been made up of traditionally.

In the project presented in this unit, technology will be used to produce the hanging design elements that are suspended from the structural elements. The hanging, graphic elements can add great visual interest and punch to the overall effect of a mobile and will be the thrust of this unit. Unlike the Pop-Art era mobiles, which were largely about having random two-dimensional images move (the mobile is primarily seen as a vehicle on which the images would ride), this project will explore a further dimension in which (for a combined effect) the shapes of the hanging elements will be designed to work with the images they carry.

ACTIVITIES

DAY 1

1. **Research and preparation**

   a. Display a hanging mobile for the class to observe (preferably with blank hanging elements); alternately, numerous photo and video examples can be found on the Web. Discuss with the students their impressions of how the mobile is constructed, how it moves, and the relationship between the two. Ask them to associate the movement of the mobile with what they believe such movements remind them of (birds, planes, kites, swaying palms, drifting clouds, etc., are likely responses).

DAY 2

2. **Associating design subjects**

   b. In this project the students will design a mobile that incorporates the subject of their association. In other words, they'll create a mobile in which graphic depictions of clouds, birds, comets, and so on, are part of the overall design, cueing the viewer to make the same association of shape and movement as the artist.

   c. Have the students use an image search engine to mine the Web for a variety of graphics to use in the visual realization of their idea. Students should first develop a list to use as the basis for their mobile (e.g., glider, orbit, balloon). Three to six images should be sufficient reference material.

   Note: If the students are not already adept at performing Web-based searches, some background in this methodology is worthwhile; conversely, this project offers a good rationale for teaching this necessary 21st-Century skill.

DAYS 3 4

3. **Creation of graphic hanging elements**

   d. Direct the students to print out the various graphics that they will use in the creation of the hanging elements of their mobiles.

   Note: In addition to locating raw graphics, it is effective to have the students process them. This may involve the elimination of gray tone within the Image, adding a line drawing effect, or using a photo-editing application that employs a continuum of visual effects. It is essential that the finished hanging element display a simple and strong visual that is easy to read and recognize from a distance and in motion.

   Furthermore, it is good design to repeat the elements but vary their size and other visual characteristics (e.g., three otherwise identical drawings of an airplane but in varied size, value (lightness and darkness, color, etc.)

   e. The printed graphics are pasted smoothly to light cardboard and, using scissors, the shape is freed from its background.

DAYS 5–6

4. Creating a finished mobile

    f. The hanging elements are affixed to the structural arms of the mobile to finish the sculpture.

Note: The arms of the mobile can be fashioned from a variety of inexpensive and easy-to-find materials. Mobiles made of wire coat hangers, thin dowels, rolled construction paper, plastic drinking straws, and so on are classic activities in art classrooms. The hanging elements can be suspended from the arms by varying lengths of nylon monofilament fishing line and attached with staples, paper fasteners, bent paper clips, or glue. A little creativity, imagination, and scrounging will make this an easy to accomplish project.

Project Sample

Figure 13.1. Project Sample—Graphic Mobile

Figure 13.2. Project Sample—Graphic Mobile (closer view)

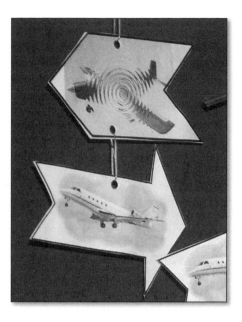

Process Used to Develop this Sample

The hanging elements of this classic mobile exert a great deal of impact on the overall design of the piece. Their creator produced them in the following manner.

1. Using a search engine, raw photos were mined that conform to the previously selected theme of the piece—airplanes.

2. He then processed these raw elements using a variety of software applications and techniques.

   a. The images are imported into a painting or other image processing application (Paint, in this example). He used the cropping tool to select and save just the area of the raw reference material to be used.

   b. Using a photo processing application (Picasa, in this case) he adjusted the photos for contrast, ensuring the airplane subject would be easy to read in relation to any background or other elements present.

   c. In some cases the photo was next processed using an effects tool (in this example, the application Pixie, a Tech4learning product, was used). The finished photo was then exported in JPEG file format.

3. Next he imported the file into a word processing program (Word, in this example) and adjusted it to a size that would be appropriate for the hanging element of the finished collage. Then, using the auto shapes function, an arrow shape was selected and inserted onto the same page as the photo.

4. In order to have the shape function as a border for the photo, the Format AutoShapes function menu was opened and "no fill" was selected in the Fill Color area. Using the nudge function and the arrow keys, the artist positioned the arrow shape to frame the photo appropriately.

5. Selecting both the photo and the arrow shape simultaneously, they were copied and pasted onto another area of the page. Next, using the "Rotate or Flip" direction in the draw tool, they were flipped horizontally to produce a mirror image of the original photo and arrow frame. After adjusting the two images to make certain the position of both (not adjusting the size) was visually appropriate, the artist printed them out on a laser printer.

6. Using scissors he cut both figures from the blank background. One figure was glued onto a light cardstock (or tag board) and then cut out again with the scissors to free the background and extra cardstock. The other image (the mirror image of the first) was glued to the opposite side. The result was a free shape with an identical (but reversed) image on each side.

7. These digitally produced, hanging elements were then incorporated into the finished mobile using a traditional approach.

Sharing the Work

Mobiles can be exhibited easily and effectively by suspending them from the ceiling on nylon monofilament fishing line (they can often be attached to lighting fixtures or from heavier lines run between them).

A worthwhile extension of this project would involve directing the students to create an illustrated narrative procedure showing, through captioned digital photos, all of the steps taken in the creation of this mobile.

Another approach would be short digital videos. An MPG file (digital video) can capture the gist of a student mobile in a few seconds and can be played on a computer with digital-media software. These videos might be uploaded to media-sharing Web sites or blogs.

Figure 13.3.
Animated GIF showing three views of the mobile.

Additionally, a digital photo of the mobile is easy to make, but an interesting variation on it would be to take a small series of time-lapse photos. By moving the air next to the mobile, it can be gently encouraged to move and reveal the varieties of its potential configurations.

By placing a camera on a tripod or other stable support and taking many photos from an identical angle, an approximation of the mobile's special qualities, as well as how the student artist has taken advantage of them, can be captured.

A particularly appropriate way to use these time-lapse photos is with a GIF animator—a piece of software that creates an animated effect by showing a series of images, one after another, at a set interval. GIF animators are widely available as downloads, usually at very modest cost and often free (or free for short-term trials), and they are available for Windows, Mac, and other operating systems. Generally, the programs allow the user to select the number of images to include and the time interval between them. Most often they are set to repeat on an endless loop.

Once completed, the GIF animations can be uploaded to a Web site or viewed directly from a disk (or other storage device) or played from the hard drive of a computer. They can also be e-mailed and imported into other applications such as PowerPoint and thumbnail galleries, where they will retain their functionality.

More traditionally, the images can also be incorporated into a book or catalog of the class's work.

Assessment

Successful mobiles created in this project will convey the dimension of movement and the power of graphics to enhance its appearance through the selection, refinement, and placement of appropriate images. Has the student located two-dimensional images that can perform this function as design elements in a mobile? Has the student's adjustment and manipulation of these images maximized their potential effect in this regard? Has the student adjusted the shapes of the elements to take advantage of the contribution that the graphics can offer?

Suggested discussion question: How do the sculptural and two-dimensional elements of your mobile work together?

Suggested General Assessment/Accountability Rubric for Unit 13

Project Components	Excellent	Proficient	Partially Proficient	Not Sufficiently Proficient or Incomplete
Completion of Project • Student uses painting editing software to refine, transform, and strengthen the raw graphics • Student draws outline shapes to receive images that are imported into them • Student sizes and prints finished graphic elements • Student cuts printed graphics from background, affixes them to support material, and cuts to final shape • Student arranges finished hanging elements and arranges them on arms	All portions of the project are completed successfully at a high level.	Most portions of the project are completed successfully at a high or satisfactory level.	Some important (and other) portions of the project are completed successfully at a satisfactory level.	Few of the project portions are completed successfully at a satisfactory level.
Research and Preparation • Student searches and acquires raw reference graphics and selects a small group to use as basis for project	Conducted the needed research/ preparation in a way that allows for a full level of participation in the project.	Conducted the needed research/ preparation in a way that allows for a high level of participation in the project.	Conducted the needed research/ preparation in a way that allows for a satisfactory level of participation in the project.	Conducted the needed research/ preparation in a way that allows for a minimal level of participation in the project.
Theme and Concept Learning • Student understands the principles of mobiles as sculpture • Student understands the idea of communication by graphic means	Fully understood the concepts and goals of the project. Understood the contextual background content. Understood how to apply the above in the creation of an original work.	Understood a good deal of the concepts and goals of the project. Understood the contextual background content to a high degree. Understood how to apply the above in the creation of an original work to a high degree.	Understood some of the concepts and goals of the project. Understood the contextual background content to a degree. Understood how to apply the above in the creation of an original work to a degree.	Did not adequately understand the concepts and goals of the project. Did not adequately understand the contextual background content. Did not adequately understand how to apply the above in the creation of an original work.

(Continued)

Suggested General Assessment/Accountability Rubric for Unit 13 *(Continued)*

Project Components	Excellent	Proficient	Partially Proficient	Not Sufficiently Proficient or Incomplete
Technical Proficiency • Student manipulates and transforms raw graphics effectively • Student selects and draws shapes of hanging elements • Student imports and positions graphics into shaped hanging elements • Student crafts finished hanging elements from graphics • Student constructs finished mobile	Demonstrated a very high degree of under-standing and mastery of the concepts and skills involved in the techniques required of the project.	Demonstrated a good degree of under-standing and mastery of the concepts and skills involved in the techniques required of the project.	Demonstrated a satisfactory degree of understanding and mastery of the concepts and skills involved in the techniques required of the project.	Did not demonstrate an adequate degree of understanding and mastery of the concepts and skills involved in the techniques required of the project.
Technology Use • Student uses search engine, drawing, and image editing software effectively • Student sizes and prints graphics effectively	Handled the tech-nology portions of the project in a highly effective, insightful, and responsible fashion.	Handled the technology portions of the project very proficiently and in an effective, insightful, and responsible fashion.	Handled the technology portions of the project in a satisfactorily effective, insightful, and respon-sible fashion.	Did not handle the technology portions of the project in a satisfactorily effective, insightful, and respon-sible fashion.
Creativity-Expression • Student develops a cohesive design that effectively communicates a motif • Student uses materials and resources to realize a visually effective finished piece that satisfies project requirements	Conceived, developed, and executed a work of art that is highly original and that takes full advantage of the medium's possibilities.	To a good degree, conceived, developed, and executed a work of art that is original and that takes full advantage of the medium's possibilities.	To a satisfactory degree, conceived, developed, and executed a work of art that is somewhat original and that takes advantage of some of the medium's possibilities.	Did not well conceive and execute a work that is original or takes good advantage of the medium's possibilities.

Note: Refer to chapter 7 "Assessing Digital Art Projects" for an overview of assessing technology-supported student visual art projects.

Cross-Curricular Connection

Research Report for Social Studies, Science, or Other Subject Area

The crux of a mobile is that it is composed of related elements that continually combine in different ways as they make a whole. Although the elements don't change, the view is ever changing, always presenting a new facet of the complete mobile. This movement makes the mobile a unique way to present information, a kind of randomized presentation of views and understandings.

These characteristics of a mobile lend themselves to a project in which students create a visual report of information they've gathered. Students will need to reflect on the information and make decisions on which elements to include and how they can best be displayed. An investigation into a topic will produce many possible images that are emblematic of the topic and that give information about it. For instance, as part of an elementary-level historical unit on the American Colonial period, a student might find a body of images composed of items such as the Old Glory flag, a flintlock pistol, a tri-cornered hat, a Red Coat soldier, coins from the colonial period, and a portrait of George Washington. Many of these would make easy-to-read, visually interesting elements for a mobile. Likewise, in a middle school science unit on simple machines, a student might turn up a group of pictures that include gears, levers, pulleys, screws, cogs, and wedges.

To enhance the content learning of a project that calls for a report in mobile format, a simple chart will keep the student accountable for choices made and focus his or her thinking.

Sample Focusing Chart for a Report in Mobile Form

Mobile Element	Source	Connection to Topic

UNIT 14

Drawn Sculptures

Inspired by Keith Haring

A sculpture is just a painting cut out and stood up somewhere.

— FRANK STELLA

Please see the sections "Using this Book" and "Assessing Digital Art Projects" for more information about these standards, the interaction between them, and connecting these standards to the lessons in this book.

STANDARDS

NETS•S

Although all or most of the NETS•S are touched on in this unit, the connection is strongest and easiest to see and understand in the standards listed below:

1. a, b, c, d	4. a, b, d
2. b	5. a, c
3. b, c	6. a, b, d

Note: By producing a virtual reality product (the sculpture produced in this unit) and sharing it with broader audiences than those that might attend a real-world exhibition, students *transfer current knowledge to learning of new technologies* (NETS•S 6.d).

National Standards for Arts Education (Visual Arts)

CS–1, AS–a, b

CS–2, AS–a, c

CS–3, AS–a, b

UNIT OBJECTIVES

Students will be challenged to:

- Understand how digital images can be manipulated and transformed with image-processing software.

- Understand the relationship of free-standing two-dimensional planes to sculpture in the round.

CENTRAL IDEAS

Over the years, I've guided many students through their first experiences with sculpture. Although they intuitively understand the difference between two-dimensional and three-dimensional objects, translating those understandings into the planning and focused development of a work of art does not follow so easily.

Young artists are challenged to understand how sculptors use two-dimensional preparatory sketches to inform and guide their work on three-dimensional sculptures. This is indicative of their perception of the two types of work as being entirely of either one variety or the other. In reality, art works lie somewhere on a continuum between the two extremes, and the understanding that a 3-D work may be seen as embracing many 2-D faces is an eye-opening, "ah-ha" moment for them. It's a profound understanding though, either when directly applied to making art or when extended into parallels in life.

Consequently, the intersection of the workings of flat, two-dimensional art and those of three-dimensional sculpture is an interesting area to explore with students, and this project is one I've found to be the most effective in opening their eyes.

Keith Haring was a daring young artist who invented his own methods of drawing and picture making. He carried this relationship to making art into his later forays into sculpture, as well. Many of his cutout sculptures can be understood as drawings that have been freed of their background and made to stand on their own. This is a fresh approach, and one that is remarkable in its inventiveness as well as in the finished work.

This manner of freeing a drawing from its background and having it stand in space provides a thought-provoking focus for student artists, one that I've seen them find highly engaging and satisfying. As will be seen in this project, technology aids immensely in the production of these works.

TECHNOLOGY RATIONALE

Through the use of classroom computing technology, an art project that ordinarily would be of heroic scale in both its physical presence in the world and in the amount of work and acquired skills needed to implement it, has been pared down to a student-friendly, classroom-friendly activity.

Rendering a convincing representation of a human figure, particularly one that is fully involved in the action of a sport, is difficult by any means. Executing it with a heavy, single-line contour is particularly challenging. This would be beyond the ability of most students to complete satisfactorily.

However, by mining images on the Web or scanning harvested hard copy pictures and then processing them in a painting software application, such images can be acquired as needed by students. Transforming them into line drawings through a series of technology processes defines the next major step.

Fine tuning the size of each image so that it maintains a convincing and pleasing proportional scale to the others in its group is another portion of the process that can only be achieved by most students through the use of computers and printers.

Above all, this project gives students good insight into how artists beginning in the latter half of the 20th century have continually appropriated "business" technologies for their own purposes in making fine art. In doing so they have expanded their own vocabulary and repertoire, making art a living, growing field of human effort.

Principal Technology Skills Addressed

- Web research/image mining

- Digital image processing

Technology Resources Needed

- Printer(s)

- Image processing software

WEB RESOURCES

Emporis.com (related sculpture by Dubuffet):
www.emporis.com/en/il/im/?id=263130

Keith Haring Foundation (follow Art link to view sculptures 1985–1989):
www.haring.com

Keith Haring Foundation—Two Dancing Figures:
www.haring.com/cgi-bin/art_lrg.cgi?date=1989&genre=Sculpture&start=0&id=00235
www.haring.com/cgi-bin/art_lrg.cgi?date=1989&genre=Sculpture&id=00269
www.haring.com/cgi-bin/art_lrg.cgi?date=1989&genre=Sculpture&id=00112

Unit Conceptual and Pedagogical Overview

In the latter half of the 20th-century, artists explored the interesting territory formed by the overlap of two-dimensional and three-dimensional representation. Just as painters (namely post-impressionist through abstract expressionist) worked their way from the restrictions of realistic representation to explorations of flatness and the liberation of pure design, sculptors found that the flattening and simplifying of subjects yielded exciting possibilities in the area of sculpture, as well.

Keith Haring was one of these inventive souls, an artist who continually invented his own language and the rules by which it could be spoken. Haring originally emerged as an artist who was concerned with two-dimensional work. His initial involvement with quickly-rendered graffiti relied on recognizable, although intentionally hyper-simplified, cartoon-like figures. As he gained success in this direction, his work expanded in scale, migrating to full-scale, color murals. As success propelled him, his work moved to more traditional fine art formats on the walls of galleries and museums. Eventually, he explored placing his subjects in three-dimensional space as sculpture, retaining the heavy, personal outlines that defined his figures, a design characteristic that was his trademark.

Recreating many of the interests, decisions, and experiments taken by Haring as he progressed from painting to sculpture is a focus that offers students numerous opportunities to reflect on the process of making art, as well as the role of imagery and the relationship of technique to it. Haring's work is particularly relevant for students because of its accessible imagery. It also celebrates the personal touch in artistic expression, particularly the development of line drawing as a personal "handwriting" of the artist. The whimsical images that Haring created are derived from subjects that students will enjoy: youthful figures, animals, and fantasy creatures.

ACTIVITIES

This project guides students through the process of stretching their understanding about making art to be able to conceive of the transformation of line drawings into free-standing sculptures. Consequently, an appropriate mindset can be achieved either by showing students examples of work of this type (i.e., Keith Haring or Jean Dubuffet) or by engaging them in a discussion in which they are encouraged to imagine how such a process might work and the type of object it would produce.

Each student will create a sculpture comprised of three free-standing drawing cutouts. These should be different versions of the same figure involved in the same activity. Either of two approaches may be taken depending on the ability level of the students and their experience in making two- and three-dimensional art.

Variation A: A single drawing is reproduced three times as the basis for the sculpture.
Variation B: Three different drawings of the same figure in the same activity are used (e.g., a basketball player at three different points in the process of a jump shot).

DAY 1

Part I: Producing the drawings

a. Direct the students to obtain reference image(s) of a figure (person or animal) involved in an action (sports figures are particularly effective for this). The images will be used as the basis for the creation of a drawing. They can be acquired by shooting photos of peers, scanning hard copy pictures (perhaps taken at school sporting events), or by mining the Web for images.

DAYS 2–3

b. Based on the reference image(s), the students produce a line drawing of the figure. The finished drawing should consist of heavy outline only. This may be accomplished either by processing and enhancing a photo (creating an outline and eliminating the tonal material within) or by using a drawing program (selecting a heavy line setting) and copying the observed figure.

Note: The effect of transforming a tonal photograph to an outlined black-and-white drawing can be achieved in a variety of ways. One particularly effective approach is to import a saved photo into a paint program (e.g., Microsoft Paint). Within the paint program the outline of the figure can be traced with the mouse cursor (after selecting a heavy line setting for the brush function). Next, by selecting white as the line color, the background and tonal material within the photo can be erased. It is usually necessary to switch back and forth between the black line color (which draws the line) and the white line color (which erases unwanted lines and background) until a satisfactory outline effect is achieved. As with all other aspects of producing images, a degree of trial-and-error is required before final results can be achieved. This experimentation phase should be included as part of the learning activity.

DAYS 4–7

Part II: Making the sculpture

    c. After a satisfactory outline drawing has been produced, print out three copies using any type of black-and-white printer *or*, if attempting Variation B, make one copy of each of three drawings. They should be a different pose or stage of the action, but all of the same subject and rendered in line to look similar.

    d. The images should then be pasted onto a support material (tag board, cardboard, foam core board, etc.).

    e. The background (and any negative spaces within the figure) should be cut away with scissors, an X-Acto knife, or other tool.

    f. Arrange the figures at different angles so that they appear to intersect (pass through one another). One or two of the figures must be cut into two sections and glued to butt against one that is designated as the prime support for the other two. By having two or more figures connected and occupying different angles (like a house of cards) a freestanding sculpture is created.

Project Sample

Figure 14.1. Project Sample—Drawn Sculpture

Process Used to Develop this Sample

The artist scanned several photographs found in old school yearbooks using a digital scanner. He saved the scans in JPEG file format.

Next, the artist adjusted the scanned photos for the greatest possible contrast using photo-editing software (Photoshop Elements, in this case). The resulting images had the darks and lights accentuated and as few middle tones left as possible. They were converted to black-and-white format in the software, as well.

The artist imported the edited photos into a painting program (Paint, in this example) in which:

A. the contour lines of the figures were enhanced by going over and accentuating them with a black line (using the brush tool of appropriate thickness); and

B. all visual information other than these lines (both within and outside the figure) was covered with white using a variety of brush settings.

The artist imported the finished files into a word processing program, adjusted them for size, and printed them out.

Using scissors, the black line figures were cut from the paper and pasted on tag board (light cardboard). After the adhesive dried the tag board was cut to leave free-standing figures. These sculptures were arranged to work (visually) as a group and glued to one another on a cardboard base.

Figures 14.2. These drawings are actually processed photos. Once reduced to black-and-white lines only, they became the raw material for the 3-D-sculpture that resulted.

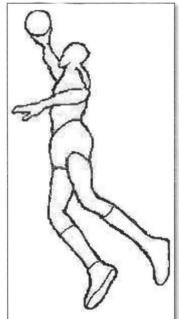

Sharing the Work

These free-standing sculptures can be displayed easily on tabletop surfaces, and it is not necessary to create a base for them. Covering the surface with a material that provides contrast to the tonal value of the sculpture will make it easier to view and photograph the work. In the scale that these sculptures will be produced in a school setting, they will gain in visual presence as part of a class grouping when exhibited.

An interesting variation can be achieved if these projects are displayed virtually. Begin by photographing the works to prepare for a virtual reality presentation (details given in unit 20). This involves taking photographs from every important angle that the work may be viewed. However, these photos can be extended by disassembling the sculptures, making the minor repairs necessary to begin afresh with whole figures, and then reassembling them in different configurations to be photographed as an entirely new sculpture. By combining the photos of two or three versions of the same sculpture, the virtual reality presentation will offer the viewer a presentation that is greater than any individual version of the work.

Note: See unit 18, "Sharing Student Art Work" for an overview of opportunities in sharing technology-supported student art projects.

Assessment

Assessment should reflect the many decisions and manipulations involved in the process of evolving the sculpture from start to finish. How has it progressed from exploratory image searches, through translation to simplified figures, and the arrangement of the transformed images, to final, free-standing, three-dimensional arrangements of shapes. It should also evaluate the impact of the completed work.

If the virtual reality option for sharing (mentioned previously) is chosen, then a unique opportunity for assessment may be had. The students will each have several completed versions of the same sculpture to compare (in photographic form).

Suggested discussion questions: Which version of the sculpture do you feel is most effective? Why?

Suggested General Assessment/Accountability Rubric for Unit 14

Project Components	Excellent	Proficient	Partially Proficient	Not Sufficiently Proficient or Incomplete
Completion of Project • Student scans raw graphic material and saves it in graphic format • Student reworks them to support the project by transforming them to black-and-white, heavy outline drawings • Student adjusts the size of graphics and prints them out to be affixed to their final support	All portions of the project are completed successfully at a high level.	Most portions of the project are completed successfully at a high or satisfactory level.	Some important (and other) portions of the project are completed successfully at a satisfactory level.	Few of the project portions are completed successfully at a satisfactory level.
Research and Preparation • Student acquires appropriate reference graphics	Conducted the needed research/ preparation in a way that allows for a full level of participation in the project.	Conducted the needed research/ preparation in a way that allows for a high level of participation in the project.	Conducted the needed research/ preparation in a way that allows for a satisfactory level of participation in the project.	Conducted the needed research/ preparation in a way that allows for a minimal level of participation in the project.
Theme and Concept Learning • Student understands the qualities of sculpture in the round • Student understands the dimensions of portraying action figures in three-dimensional work	Fully understood the concepts and goals of the project. Understood the contextual background content. Understood how to apply the above in the creation of an original work.	Understood a good deal of the concepts and goals of the project. Understood the contextual background content to a high degree. Understood how to apply the above in the creation of an original work to a high degree.	Understood some of the concepts and goals of the project. Understood the contextual background content to a degree. Understood how to apply the above in the creation of an original work to a degree.	Did not adequately understand the concepts and goals of the project. Did not adequately understand the contextual background content. Did not adequately understand how to apply the above in the creation of an original work.
Technical Proficiency • Student produces graphics that are defined by an attractive functional outline • Student affixes printouts of graphics to supports neatly and effectively • Student arranges individual figures into an effective, attractive finished sculpture	Demonstrated a high degree of understanding and mastery of the concepts and skills involved in the techniques required of the project.	Demonstrated a good degree of understanding and mastery of the concepts and skills involved in the techniques required of the project.	Demonstrated a satisfactory degree of understanding and mastery of the concepts and skills involved in the techniques required of the project.	Did not demonstrate an adequate degree of understanding and mastery of the concepts and skills involved in the techniques required of the project.

(Continued)

Suggested General Assessment/Accountability Rubric for Unit 14 *(Continued)*

Project Components	Excellent	Proficient	Partially Proficient	Not Sufficiently Proficient or Incomplete
Technology Use • Student scans photos effectively • Student uses photo processing software to maximize line contour of figure • Student uses paint/drawing software to restate lines as contour outlines, eliminating background and other extraneous middle tones	Handled the technology portions of the project in a highly effective, insightful, and responsible fashion.	Handled the technology portions of the project proficiently and in an effective, insightful, and responsible fashion.	Handled the technology portions of the project in a satisfactorily effective, insightful, and responsible fashion.	Did not handle the technology portions of the project in a satisfactorily effective, insightful, and responsible fashion.
Creativity-Expression • Student selects raw material that reflects personal interests and sensibilities • Student develops an interesting, expressive arrangement of figures • Student develops a finished piece that is personal and unique, taking advantage of design possibilities presented by materials and reference materials	Conceived, developed, and executed a work of art that is highly original and that takes full advantage of the medium's possibilities.	To a good degree, conceived, developed, and executed a work of art that is original and that takes full advantage of the medium's possibilities.	To a satisfactory degree, conceived, developed, and executed a work of art that is somewhat original and that takes advantage of some of the medium's possibilities.	Did not well conceive and execute a work that is original or takes good advantage of the medium's possibilities.

Note: Refer to chapter 7, "Assessing Digital Art Projects" for an overview of assessing technology-supported student visual art projects.

Cross-Curricular Connection

Sculpture and Language Arts

Writing fiction is a classic part of the language arts curriculum. The project presented in this unit makes an excellent focus, prompt, and organizing topic for a short exercise in fiction writing.

Inform students at the beginning of the sculpture project that they will be writing a story about the finished sculpture and that they should keep this in mind as they create the sculpture.

After the piece is completed, direct the students to write a short story using the sculpture as the subject. Inform the students that this story will be read out loud and that they should script it for the spoken voice. A story that can be read in roughly a minute would be a good length for this project.

Have the student take several digital photos of the sculpture, both full-figure and close-up shots. The photos can be cropped and improved by using photo-editing software.

Have the student select three to ten photos and import each onto its own slide in a PowerPoint presentation.

Using the sound recording feature of PowerPoint, have the student read the story into a microphone so that the finished presentation is the student reading his story as an accompaniment to the slides.

UNIT 15

Stained Glass in the Round

What I expect from any work of art is that it surprises me, that it violates
my customary valuations of things and offers me other, unexpected ones.

JEAN DUBUFFET

*Please see the
sections "Using
this Book" and
"Assessing Digital
Art Projects" for
more information
about these
standards, the
interaction
between them,
and connecting
these standards to
the lessons in this
book.*

STANDARDS

NETS•S

Although all or most of the NETS•S are touched on in this unit, the connection is strongest
and easiest to see and understand in the standards listed below:

1. a, b   4. b, d

2. a, b   5. a, c

3. a, b, c   6. a, b, d

Note: In this unit and others, a wide spectrum of digital tool functions (e.g., copy, adjust size, line quality,
flop, etc.) are available to students for processing the raw material they generate to express
their ideas. In choosing and employing the images to produce a work of art, they *select and use
applications effectively and productively* (NETS•S 6.b).

National Standards for Arts Education (Visual Arts)

CS–1, AS–b,

CS–2, AS–a, b, c

CS–3, AS–a, b

UNIT OBJECTIVES

Students will be challenged to:

- Design an original sculpture in the round that employs the element of transparency.

- Understand how the application of graphic elements can enrich the experience of three-dimensional art.

- Develop graphic images for use in a three-dimensional work.

CENTRAL IDEAS

Although they are appealing, it's been my experience that design-on-glass activities are difficult to implement in schools. The practical and logistical considerations involved are overwhelmingly difficult. Furthermore, the skills required are beyond what most students can bring to the activity.

Technology, though, can make this type of activity more doable for the student and infinitely easier for the teacher to implement than through traditional means. Through the use of digital technologies, classic approaches to the creation of stained glass images can be reconceived to produce visually effective, thought-provoking, and new types of student art projects.

Computer-assisted approaches to drawing and image making can be directly applied to producing a stained-glass-like product, eliminating laborious and difficult methods of drawing on glass that generally produce poor results. This is a great advantage for today's students. Student artists I've worked with clearly found working on a transparent surface to be a fascinating change of pace and an eye-opening experience.

The project presented in this unit combines a variety of traditional and new approaches to design on glass. It is highly relevant in our 21st-Century world as it involves the recycling of used, throw-away materials as well as Internet-powered "recycling" of images appropriated from previous contexts and processed for new ones. The result is a new approach to sculpture that is produced by combining traditional stained glass designs with a twist on traditional sculpture in the round.

TECHNOLOGY RATIONALE

Although the drawn elements of this project could be created through freehand drawing, certain aspects of the drawings make far more sense when created through technology. Drawings rendered for stained glass designs must be kept simple, often relying on simplified or abstracted shapes. Additionally, they must be finished in heavy outline, with a line that is consistent in width and weight. These qualities are easy to achieve through drawing software.

Furthermore, the key portion of the process that makes this piece come alive is printing the designs from the computer onto transparent paper that is affixed to glass. Again, although it is possible to draw directly on glass with specialized paints or dyes, affixing a preprinted design on transparent stock allows for images to be repeated, possibly in a variety of sizes, and positioned creatively and inventively, allowing for changes and experiments before committing to a final design decision.

Principal Technology Skills Addressed

- Internet research/image mining
- Computer drawing or image processing

Technology Resources Needed

- Internet access/browser/search engine(s)
- Drawing software
- Printer and specialized output (transfer) media

Note: This project will make use of decal paper, which can be acquired from specialty craft and art supply stores or on the Web from several suppliers. They are available for either laser or inkjet printers. The paper can be found by searching for "digital transfer decals, printer decals, or water slide decals" (these decal papers are most often sold for use on ceramics or other hobby items).

WEB RESOURCES

Metropolitan Museum of Art:
www.metmuseum.org/explore/tiffany/listsgw.htm

The Stained Glass Museum:
www.stainedglassmuseum.com/briefhis.html

Wikipedia:
http://en.wikipedia.org/wiki/Stained_glass

Unit Conceptual and Pedagogical Overview

The history of humans as a makers of art has produced vast amounts of material which teachers can draw upon to inform and direct projects for students. For a few projects, however, the truth in this is minimal. Stained glass simply hasn't been practical to explore with students. Fortunately, the new technology of digitally produced decals that can be applied to a wide variety of surfaces, including glass, opens up exciting and unprecedented possibilities in the production of student art.

Applying design to glass, whatever technique we use, recalls humankind's long-term fascination with stained glass. This technique was developed many centuries ago and represented a major step forward in image making. Activating color by allowing sunlight to pass through colored glass was a technological advance so inspiring that its principal application was the introduction of light and color into cathedrals, the most important works of their time.

Students seem to understand the project presented in this unit better if it is contextualized for them by reviewing the history of stained glass. Thus informed, they get more from being challenged to make a related work on their own. They also quickly come to appreciate the juxtaposition of using today's technology as an entry point in approaching such a historical medium of expression. The understanding of the art that man can create is contingent on the state of his technology is an important one. Furthermore, it's an idea I've observed students carry beyond art class into their understanding of the world in which they live.

The production of works in traditional stained glass is time consuming, somewhat dangerous, expensive, and inconvenient—qualities that make its implementation in most classrooms absolutely impractical. The attainment of similar visual properties by digital means, however, overcomes those limiting factors, freeing up the imagination by establishing new techniques through which its visions can be realized.

Beyond practical limitations, stained glass has had another important limitation in the realm of design. Traditionally, it has exclusively been produced as a flat, two-dimensional work. This challenge is now easily overcome with the use of computer-printed decals, which can be used to create a new art form—stained glass in the round. This unprecedented methodology offers a further advantage to school art activities by making the work produced with it far more durable, portable, and exhibitable than the original, flat approach ever could.

ACTIVITIES

DAY 1

1. Presenting the project to students

a. Establish the context for this project by showing students examples of classic stained glass and by presenting them with photos of such works and the settings into which their creators placed them.

I've found it to be particularly important to have a class discussion about the need for the stained glass artist to greatly simplify subjects as he uses the medium to represent them. Close-up photos that show the thick line created by the lead used to hold together the glass parts of the design are eye-opening for young artists who likely have never tackled the challenge of representation quite this way before. An interesting "ah-ha" moment that I've watched many students have is the realization that the very thick line the lead makes, a design element that might be seen as crude and clumsy in other media, is a beautiful asset in this one.

DAY 2

2. Selecting a subject

b. Students are to select several related images (photos) as the subject for their stained glass in the round sculpture (e.g, fish/wave/boat; tree/leaf/apple; hammer/saw/nail). Direct the students to choose the three that they feel work together best. The images can be mined from the Web or selected from hard copy of any source. Students will use them as references, but they will not directly become part of the project.

DAYS 3–4

3. Creating basic shapes

c. Direct the students to analyze the photos so that they can create a facsimile composed of a small number of basic shapes they'll draw with a very thick and heavy outline.

Students can use any drawing or painting program to produce the finished images. A program that offers an auto shapes function will give an excellent result, as the basic shapes and lines needed to portray the subject will acquire the consistent, flat, and highly geometric characteristics that are easily identifiable as those seen in stained glass.

After they've made a satisfactory initial attempt at reproducing the subjects as simplified images, encourage the students to experiment further by selecting different line thicknesses and types of lines and then filling them in with flat fields of color using the program's fill function. By saving several versions of each image, a choice will be available when they affix the images to the three-dimensional support (a glass jar).

DAY 5

4. Creating transfer decals

d. When satisfied with the final version of their designs, the student will create transfer decals. They should determine the size of each decal by considering how much of the surface of a clear glass jar or bottle they will cover. The students should be instructed ahead of time to bring in a bottle that will provide the base for their sculpture.

Students may produce one to three copies of each decal. These may be of various sizes, as well as flopped or reversed images.

Note: The teacher may choose to take the finished student graphics and import them into grouping pages on which as many of the images as can fit are placed. This will save time and money in the process of printing out the decals.

DAY 6

5. Completing the project

e. After carefully considering their placement, the students will affix the decals to the bottles.

The decals are two-dimensional design elements. However, by placing them around the bottle, they become part of a three-dimensional design. Furthermore, by incorporating the experiential factor of the images traveling around the bottle, as well as accounting for the fact that from certain angles, the decals may be placed to create an overlapped or combined image (when one is seen on the surface and one seen through the clear bottle affixed to the opposite side), an additional dimension is achieved.

Note: Once the decals are affixed permanently, the design cannot be changed at all. Therefore, positioning the decals tentatively in place with a lightly sticky tape before committing to their position will give the students the experience of planning a three-dimensional design with a great many variables.

Project Sample (2 views)

Process Used to Develop this Sample

The artist created most of the images used in this example in Word, using the auto shapes drawing function. They are each a conglomerate of shapes. In various spots the order function was used to have one element overlap and hide another. This can be seen in the tailfin of the sardine-like fish and in the upper wing of the flying fish that overlaps the fish's body (Fig. 15.2).

In some portions the artist used the fill function to fill the shape with tone, as can be seen in the body of the fish and turtle.

The sea grass image was produced using a freehand drawing tool.

Figures 15.1. Project Sample—Stained Glass in the Round

The finished images were then printed out on a conventional computer printer. However, they were printed using special transparency stock and then affixed to the glass bottle that serves as the base support of the three-dimensional glass design piece.

Figure 15.2. Graphics created using the auto shapes function

Figure 15.3. Graphics "ganged up" on a single page ready to be printed as a transfer decal

Sharing the Work

These works would lend themselves to both a traditional onsite exhibition or a virtual exhibition through the use of virtual reality software. In either case, the viewers' ability to travel around the work, seeing it from a variety of angles, is essential. Additionally, in the case of these transparent sculptures the value and color of surfaces behind the work become all essential, as seeing through them is one of the great parts of their visual impact.

Similarly, because they are transparent, the lighting is crucial, allowing the viewer to "get it" about the combined visual message of the surface being faced and the one that can be perceived on the opposite side of the work. As a more controlled environment will produce better results for sharing, a virtual exhibition may prove best, with the class working to establish the ideal setting and then photographing each work in that, in turn. Furthermore, because these works are produced by applying graphics to the surface of found objects (glass bottles) a startling effect may be achieved by running the virtual reality presentation through an LCD projector and onto a large surface, the result being that bottles of improbable scale are presented.

Note: See unit 18, "Sharing Student Art Work" for more suggestions about sharing technology-supported student art projects.

Assessment

The success of the student art produced through this project is highly dependent on understanding and working through the processes involved. An important element in assessing it, therefore, is the student's accountability for following the processes and the decisions made in doing so. Student statements to explain this will shed insight onto their levels of learning and achievement.

Suggested Prompt for Oral Response: Please describe the evolution of the motif you used in this piece and explain why it looks the way it does in its finished form.

- Where did you get the idea?

- How did you refine your initial attempt and why?

- How is the final version more effective for a piece done in this medium?

Suggested General Assessment/Accountability Rubric for Unit 15

Project Components	Excellent	Proficient	Partially Proficient	Not Sufficiently Proficient or Incomplete
Completion of Project • Preliminary drawings • Variety of finished versions of drawings • Arrangement of decals on support • Application of decals to glass support	All portions of the project are completed successfully at a high level.	Most portions of the project are completed successfully at a high or satisfactory level.	Some important (and other) portions of the project are completed successfully at a satisfactory level.	Few of the project portions are completed successfully at a satisfactory level.
Research and Preparation • Acquired a satisfactory number of reference images • Reference images were appropriate to the chosen theme and requirements for execution of project	Conducted the needed research/ preparation in a way that allows for a full level of participation in the project.	Conducted the needed research/ preparation in a way that allows for a high level of participation in the project.	Conducted the needed research/ preparation in a way that allows for a satisfactory level of participation in the project.	Conducted the needed research/ preparation in a way that allows for a minimal level of participation in the project.

(Continued)

Suggested General Assessment/Accountability Rubric for Unit 15 *(Continued)*

Project Components	Excellent	Proficient	Partially Proficient	Not Sufficiently Proficient or Incomplete
Theme and Concept Learning • Chose a personal theme that reflects an understanding of the stained glass medium's history and characteristics	Fully understood the concepts and goals of the project. Understood the contextual background content. Understood how to apply the above in the creation of an original work.	Understood a good deal of the concepts and goals of the project. Understood the contextual background content to a high degree. Understood how to apply the above in the creation of an original work to a high degree.	Understood some of the concepts and goals of the project. Understood the contextual background content to a degree. Understood how to apply the above in the creation of an original work to a degree.	Did not adequately understand the concepts and goals of the project. Did not adequately understand the contextual background content. Did not adequately understand how to apply the above in the creation of an original work.
Technical Proficiency • Line quality, shapes, and fills selected were appropriate to the project and were applied carefully in a way that supported the drawings	Demonstrated a high degree of understanding and mastery of the concepts and skills involved in the techniques required of the project.	Demonstrated a good degree of understanding and mastery of the concepts and skills involved in the techniques required of the project.	Demonstrated a satisfactory degree of understanding and mastery of the concepts and skills involved in the techniques required of the project.	Did not demonstrate an adequate degree of understanding and mastery of the concepts and skills involved in the techniques required of the project.
Technology Use • Understood the drawing functions and used and manipulated them properly • Used copy, paste, and size functions to good advantage • Properly saved and managed versions and files	Handled the technology portions of the project in a highly effective, insightful, and responsible fashion.	Handled the technology portions of the project very proficiently and in an effective, insightful, and responsible fashion.	Handled the technology portions of the project in a satisfactorily effective, insightful, and responsible fashion.	Did not handle the technology portions of the project in a satisfactorily effective, insightful, and responsible fashion.
Creativity-Expression • Used the project as an opportunity to make a personal statement • Execution of project shows a degree of originality	Conceived, developed, and executed a work of art that is highly original and that takes full advantage of the medium's possibilities.	To a good degree, conceived, developed, and executed a work of art that is original and that takes full advantage of the medium's possibilities.	To a satisfactory degree, conceived, developed, and executed a work of art that is somewhat original and that takes advantage of some of the medium's possibilities.	Did not well conceive and execute a work that is original or takes good advantage of the medium's possibilities.

Note: Refer to "Assessing Digital Art Projects" for an overview of assessing technology-supported student visual art projects.

Cross-Curricular Connection

Stained Glass Sculpture and Language Arts

One classic writing exercise is the writing of a story that is presented as a series of descriptions of characters and events from a variety of points of view. That this has become a much favored theme in writing for students can be observed in the publication and popular consumption of such books as *The True Story of the Three Little Pigs* and *The Wolf's Story: What Really Happened to Little Red Riding Hood*. In both of these works, the reader is treated to an alternate version of reality, one in which the wolf is not the bad guy.

Based on these two books and others like them, teachers often ask students to write an alternate version of a well-known fairy tale.

A variation on this can be observed in a popular assignment given in conjunction with reading the perennial favorite *Charlie and the Chocolate Factory*, Roald Dahl's tale about Willy Wonka. This assignment requests students to think of rooms in the chocolate factory that they know must be there, but that Dahl didn't describe in the book. After listing these, they are instructed to write descriptions about them.

In view of the above, an interesting writing assignment can be created in conjunction with the stained glass in the round project by asking the students to describe their sculpture from the point of view of each of the subjects (the graphic elements) that populate its surface. In order to do this, the student must be objective in what can be seen from the angle at which each element is most prominently depicted, while at the same time anthropomorphizing these subjects to bring them to life.

Instruct the students that they will present their writing to the class and that they should prepare themselves to defend their statements based on what others can clearly observe in the art work.

UNIT 16

Digital Zoetrope
Animated Drawings

Art does not reproduce the visible; rather, it makes visible.

— PAUL KLEE

Please see the sections "Using this Book" and "Assessing Digital Art Projects" for more information about these standards, the interaction between them, and connecting these standards to the lessons in this book.

STANDARDS

NETS·S

Although all or most of the NETS·S are touched on in this unit, the connection is strongest and easiest to see and understand in the standards listed below:

1. a, b, c, d	4. b, d
2. a, b	5. c
3. c	6. a, b, c, d

Note: In this and other units, students often must work in an experimental fashion with applications that produce and process images. To fully satisfy a design problem students must *troubleshoot systems and applications* (NETS·S 6.c) by analyzing the results an application produces, and adjusting its function and output according to individual sensibilities, apart from the standard ideas of results and performance.

National Standards for Arts Education (Visual Arts)

CS–1, AS–b

CS–2, AS–a, b, c

CS–3, AS–a, b

CS–5, AS–c

UNIT OBJECTIVES

Students will be challenged to:

- Understand the history of drawn animation and its role as a visual art form.

- Learn and apply the principles of animation.

- Understand how digital technology can be adapted to produce animation.

- Create an original work of art that applies the concepts and skills learned in this unit.

CENTRAL IDEAS

An important development in the field of media and entertainment was the emergence of animated films based on drawings. This art form relies on a two-part process. The first part involves the creation of a series of drawings that illustrate a change or movement of the subject. This change happens gradually, with little difference between any two drawings. However, a significant cumulative change happens over the course of a large body of drawings. In the second part, the drawings are presented to the viewer, one after the other, in the same sequence they were created and at a rapid pace. The resulting effect is the illusion that the subjects in the drawings are actually moving.

This technique, one the film industry tapped and used successfully in its early days, can form the basis of highly valuable student art projects. Few activities generate more excitement from students.

I've created drawn animation projects with students both with and without technology, and although the initial excitement exists for both varieties, the difficulties of execution (as well as resulting products that look meager to members of today's wired generation), make animation by mechanical means (i.e., flip books) too dull. The case for using technology for this project is a naturally strong one.

With simple digital technology, student artists can produce reasonably sophisticated works of drawn animation relatively easily. Projects that result in this type of animation offer a unique set of art-making challenges that can be so enlightening to media-preoccupied students that they ought to be part of the body of activities all students participate in during the course of their education.

TECHNOLOGY RATIONALE

Every aspect of this project is tied to the use of technology.

The starting point and basis of the project is the execution of a series of drawings. From the beginning, therefore, students take advantage of technology's power tools—the drawings in this project are rendered directly in software. Most importantly, while working on a drawing the student artist may save his work at any point of completion, enabling him or her to conduct subsequent experiments and progress in a risk-free manner. The student can always revert back to the last saved version if it becomes apparent that the work is going in the wrong direction.

Furthermore, as the point of the series is animation, each drawing must bear a resemblance to the one executed before it. The most proven method of achieving this is to save each finished drawing as two versions, one that stands as finished and one from which to form the basis of the next in the series.

By creating sequential slides of the drawings, the artist may import them into PowerPoint (or other software) and size and position them using the tools and functions specifically designed for that purpose. In doing so, the student is using copies of the drawings that may be imported again into subsequent slides and re-sized or positioned. The effect of this approach is the elimination of the labor of attempting to create identical or similar drawings for each frame. The work is recycled—a great advantage for the student artist.

Finally, the artist creates the presentation of the finished, animated piece, by using the slide show software's ability to quickly present a series of slides in rapid-fire fashion.

Principal Technology Skills Addressed

- Digital drawing

- Creation of sequential presentation

Technology Resources Needed

- Drawing program

- Animation program

WEB RESOURCES

A Rather Incomplete but Still Fascinating History of Animation (comprehensive information organized as a timeline):
http://animation.filmtv.ucla.edu/NewSite/WebPages/Histories.html

Bennetonplay! Flipbook (related tool and posted examples of student work):
www.benettonplay.com/toys/flipbookdeluxe/

Drawings That Move (related info and activities):
http://home.att.net/~RTRUSCIO/DRAWMOVE.htm

Origins of American Animation (comprehensive collection of information and examples from the Library of Congress):
http://memory.loc.gov/ammem/oahtml/oahome.html
http://memory.loc.gov/mbrs/animp/4064.mpg

Microsoft GIF animator (free download):
www.mrfreefree.com/free_software/free_gif_animator_tools.html

Private Lessons–2D Animation (roots and fundamentals of animation):
www.privatelessons.net/2d/sample/welcome.html

ReadWriteThink (simple online tool related to basics):
www.readwritethink.org/materials/flipbook/

Unit Conceptual and Pedagogical Overview

Invented in the 1830s, the zoetrope is a mechanical device that produces the illusion of action by presenting a rapid succession of static pictures. It anticipated the development of conventional film-based movies, achieving much the same effect by different means.

The film industry has since set a standard of 24 or more frames (separate images) per second as the speed at which images are shown in order to create the seamless illusion of motion. Early films and devices like the zoetrope produced this effect by showing fewer images at a slower speed. The result, which is considered choppy, actually offers a wonderful opportunity for students to learn about the concept of animation and evaluate the means by which it is achieved.

ACTIVITIES

In this project students will create a short animated series of drawings that tell a visual story. In addition to understandings about animation, several aspects of drawing can be learned here. The intersection of learning about both makes for a rich experience for students.

In this project, student artists will produce short animations in much the same way that the pioneers of animation did in their early, experimental work. Technology, however, will facilitate this traditional process for the students, making many of the subsidiary chores easier and quicker. This point will quickly become apparent to the students who will appreciate the power and functionality of technology.

DAY 1

1. **Research and preparation**

   a. Show the students examples of early films and pre-film devices that present animated drawings as a medium for entertainment and communication (many are available free on the web—see Web Resources for this unit).

   b. Engage the class in a discussion about drawn animation.

   Suggested focus questions include the following.

   - How does the effect of drawn animation work?

   - How do you think people learned about animating drawings?

   - How much time and effort might be expended to produce a five-minute movie based on animated drawings?

   - How can digital technology be used by animators to make their work easier? More effective?

   c. After discussing these questions have the class brainstorm on a common theme from which they will each produce a very short, simple animation.

A Note About Making the Drawings

In this portion of the project students will create a series of drawings that change very slightly from drawing to drawing, but when presented in a linear sequence represent a noticeable or even extreme change. The number of drawings they must produce is somewhat arbitrary and can be determined by weighing the implementation factors of time, student attention span, level of access to computers, and so on. However, to understand the point of this unit, a minimum of ten drawings, and preferably more, should be produced. Again, the use of technology will make this far easier to do than if it were attempted with traditional art materials alone.

Consequently, students will need many blank "pages" (digital or traditional) to work on—one for each drawing.

Because one of the principal points of this project is to understand how drawings can be animated or made to appear to move, selecting a theme that expresses the visual phenomenon of movement is essential. Students will discover that subjects can move in space, change direction, grow or shrink, change their shape by expanding or compressing, get lighter or darker, change color, and cast shadows of different dimensions in differing directions, among other actions or characteristics that tell the story.

DAY 2

2. Creating the home-base drawing

d. Direct the students to establish the first drawing as the start or home-base drawing, one that establishes the subject or character's identity and personality and that accommodates the action to follow (e.g., a man on a bicycle, two or three basic shapes, a stick figure or balloon). Label and save this first drawing.

Note: At this point it would be advisable to stop the class's work and discuss the duplication process that will follow.

A Note About Duplicating the Drawings

Once the base drawing is created (as well as the drawings that follow it), students must duplicate each image. Students will quickly come to realize that attempting to duplicate it by hand is very difficult. Not only does the subject need to be duplicated in terms of its appearance, but also in its size, placement, and orientation on the page.

Duplicating the first drawing, (either by traditional tracing, by photocopying, by scanning and printing, or by copying an already digital file), makes what would otherwise be very difficult quite easy and doable.

The difference in the subject between the first and the second drawing should be small but noticeable. Therefore, the man on the bicycle may change body position, arm and leg angles, facial expression, and his bicycle should move forward slightly.

Accomplishing this via traditional means is difficult, even with the technological advantage of keeping the original while copying it to produce a starting point for the second drawing. If, for instance, a photocopy machine were used, the copy would print out in toner, which is more difficult to alter than if the artist had taken the more traditional approach of tracing and then transferring pencil lines from one sheet to another. The use of white-out, however, allows portions of the copy to be "erased," and then fresh lines defining the change can be drawn by hand (any overlap of lines can be whited out, as well). Still, this is a challenging process.

Producing the drawings with a computer will be much easier. If a drawing or painting program is used to create the images, a much more fluid process can be had. If the program permits the creation of auto shapes that are established as separate objects, these may be used, allowing for their manipulation in terms of size, placement, and orientation. Additionally, only the portion that must change can be selected, the rest of the image remains identical. Or, if a freehand drawing of a man on a bicycle is attempted, the eraser function will make the elimination of lines easy and convenient.

DAYS 3–4

3. Duplicating the home-base drawing

e. Using an exact digital copy of the first drawing as the starting point, direct the students to create drawing number two, which is a slightly altered version of the first.

f. After drawing number two is completed, the process is repeated again to produce drawing number three, and so forth until all drawings required for the series are finished. Clearly, rendering the drawings in this set, linear order makes good sense, and attempting any drawings out of sequence is very problematic. You may wish to discuss this point with the students who will gain insight from it, as well.

DAYS 5–6

4. Making the drawings move

g. This portion of the project is easier. Students can employ a variety of technologies. One variation involves the use of PowerPoint (or other slide show software with similar functions). The procedure is simple: the students each create a slide show. They import each drawing into a separate slide in the order in which they were created and are to be shown. In the Set Up Show window, preferences should be selected for the show to be viewed at a kiosk and not as a presentation through a projector; the slides should run in a repeating loop; and they should change automatically (not manually by mouse click). In the transition dialog on the same pull-down menu, "00.01" should be selected as the interval between slides (Fig 16.3).

When the slide show is launched the individual slides are shown one after another in quick succession, giving a convincing zoetrope-like effect of movement and animation.

An alternate approach is to use GIF animator software. This type of program is included within some photo software (Photoshop Elements), or specialty art software (Tech4Learning's application Frames, which can be found online either at reasonable cost or as a free trial download).

Project Sample

Figure 16.1. Project Sample—Digital Zoetrope. A complete animated sequence composed of 16 drawings shown in PowerPoint's Slide Sorter view.

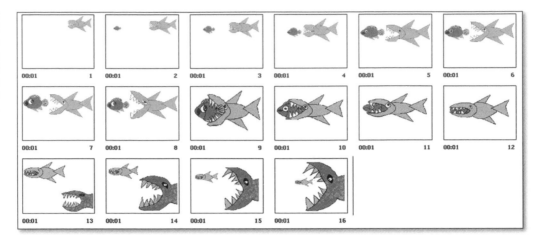

Process Used to Develop this Sample

I. Rendering the Drawings

In the first segment of the implementation phase of this project the artist created a series of drawings using a painting program (Paint, in this example). The functions used were the brush tool (to draw curved lines), auto shapes tool (to construct major segments of the figures' bodies from basic shapes), fill with color tool (to add color to the figures in the picture), and the airbrush tool (to shade and tone portions of the figures).

In order to show a lifelike change in the actions of the figures, the artist drew the drawings sequentially. He saved the initial drawing of a figure as version #1, which he copied and saved as version #2, and then altered it slightly. Over the course of creating many drawings, each of the versions is similar, but changed slightly in one or a few respects. Changing the position (within the frame) and size of the figures was left for Phase 2.

II. Creating the Slides

In the second phase of implementation, the artist created a series of slides using the drawings rendered in Phase I. These images were imported into a slide show software (PowerPoint, in this example).

Using the nudge function, he moved the drawings within the picture slides to support the story being told. Likewise, he adjusted the size of the figures using the size function in order to accentuate the action within the story. These two software functions are easy to use, which encouraged experimentation. The artist didn't undertake subsequent slides in the series until the preceding ones seemed right.

As was true in the creation of the drawings, the artist imported drawings and adjusted their size and location within the slides sequentially. This step was accomplished by saving slide A (for example), copying it to produce slide B, and then altering slide B slightly. He achieved a good sense of continuity by not working out of sequence.

By importing figure B into slide B (which was an exact copy of slide A), and then deleting figure A, a swap was accomplished, putting the next drawing in the series into the next slide in the series. Using figure A as a reference for size and position, a convincing continuity was easily achieved.

The Set Up Show menu was accessed, and "all" was selected under the Show slides setting, and "Using timings, if present" under Advance slides. Also, by selecting "loop continuously until 'Esc'" under Show options, the brief animation shows itself repeatedly (until manually turned off), heightening the effect of an individually crafted work of art.

Figure 16.2.
Individual drawings in PowerPoint's Normal view, which gives a measuring grid in the background and a full range of tools and functions.

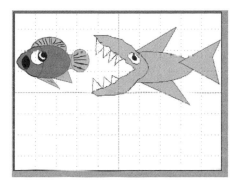
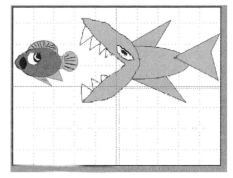
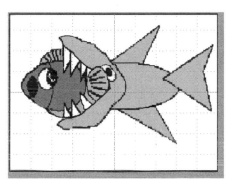

III. Setting up the Animated Show

For the final phase of implementation, the series of slides is set as a slide show. By selecting the No Transition effect, Modify transition speed: fast, and Advance slide: Automatically after 00:01 (seconds) are applied to all slides, a true animation effect is created that is similar in appearance to the zoetrope of the early days of animation experimentation (Fig. 16.3).

Figure 16.3.
PowerPoint menus used to set up the slide show as a continuous loop in which a very quick transition from frame to frame is selected, giving the effect of animation.

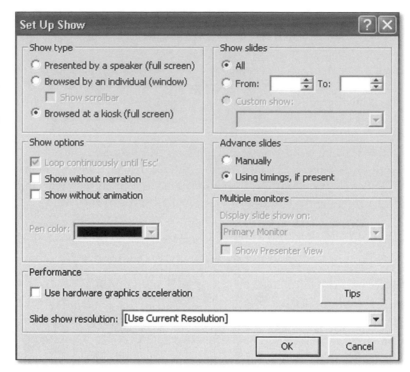

Sharing the Work

Student projects can be shown in a formal theater setting with an LCD projector (as a class or school animation festival) or on a dedicated desktop computer set up as a kiosk (presentation is set on a continuous loop or set up for the viewer to start). An interesting variation on this can be achieved by running each student's animation as a continuous loop on one of the computers in a lab. The class, or an invited group, can circulate throughout the lab to see the projects one after the other.

Additionally, the work can be published by burning it on disks in bulk.

Note: See unit 18, "Sharing Student Art with an Audience" for an overview of other possibilities.

Assessment

The goal of this project is to achieve the effect of movement through the creation of a series of drawings that is presented by software. The degree to which the student achieves this should be a prime point of assessment. Completion of the steps leading to the final product is another, subsidiary consideration.

Before a summative assessment is performed, it may be best to formalize some aspects of formative evaluations in which the students present (either to the teacher alone or to the class as a whole) the work with an eye toward gaining valuable feedback for improvement. This process is authentic and mirrors that of commercial producers of animated films.

Suggested discussion questions:

- How might you change the process of producing your animation to produce a better product?

- Would you change the number of drawings?

- Would you make alterations to individual drawings? Would you make other changes?

Suggested General Assessment/Accountability Rubric for Unit 16

Project Components	Excellent	Proficient	Partially Proficient	Not Sufficiently Proficient or Incomplete
Completion of Project • Student creates a series of sequentially altered drawings that show action or transformation • Student uses the drawings in a series of slides designed to illustrate the changes or transformation begun in the drawings • Student (if applicable) sets the slide show to effectively give the effect of animation	All portions of the project are completed successfully at a high level.	Most portions of the project are completed successfully at a high or satisfactory level.	Some important (and other) portions of the project are completed successfully at a satisfactory level.	Few of the project portions are completed successfully at a satisfactory level.
Research and Preparation *(if applicable)* • Student researches reference material on which to base drawings of subjects	Conducted the needed research/preparation in a way that allows for a full level of participation in the project.	Conducted the needed research/preparation in a way that allows for a high level of participation in the project.	Conducted the needed research/preparation in a way that allows for a satisfactory level of participation in the project.	Conducted the needed research/preparation in a way that allows for a minimal level of participation in the project.
Theme and Concept Learning • Student understands the concept of animation • Student is familiar with the history and varieties of animated film/art sufficiently to draw on in participating in this project • Student understands what makes an appropriate theme for the animation project	Fully understood the concepts and goals of the project. Understood the contextual background content. Understood how to apply the above in the creation of an original work.	Understood a good deal of the concepts and goals of the project. Understood the contextual background content to a high degree. Understood how to apply the above in the creation of an original work to a high degree.	Understood some of the concepts and goals of the project. Understood the contextual background content to a degree. Understood how to apply the above in the creation of an original work to a degree.	Did not adequately understand the concepts and goals of the project. Did not adequately understand the contextual background content. Did not adequately understand how to apply the above in the creation of an original work.
Technical Proficiency • Student uses lines, shapes, tones, and other design elements to create effective drawings that communicate ideas well • Student crafts and orders slides to establish a cohesive, effective animated presentation	Demonstrated a high degree of understanding and mastery of the concepts and skills involved in the techniques required of the project.	Demonstrated a good degree of understanding and mastery of the concepts and skills involved in the techniques required of the project.	Demonstrated a satisfactory degree of understanding and mastery of the concepts and skills involved in the techniques required of the project.	Did not demonstrate an adequate degree of understanding and mastery of the concepts and skills involved in the techniques required of the project.

(Continued)

Suggested General Assessment/Accountability Rubric for Unit 16 *(Continued)*

Project Components	Excellent	Proficient	Partially Proficient	Not Sufficiently Proficient or Incomplete
Technology Use • Student uses painting/drawing software functions effectively to create and refine drawings needed • Student uses slide show software effectively as a medium with which to create animation	Handled the technology portions of the project in a highly effective, insightful, and responsible fashion.	Handled the technology portions of the project very proficiently and in an effective, insightful, and responsible fashion.	Handled the technology portions of the project in a satisfactorily effective, insightful, and responsible fashion.	Did not handle the technology portions of the project in a satisfactorily effective, insightful, and responsible fashion.
Creativity-Expression • Student uses project as an opportunity to communicate a unique idea or set of artistic sensibilities	Conceived, developed, and executed a work of art that is highly original and that takes full advantage of the medium's possibilities.	To a good degree, conceived, developed, and executed a work of art that is original and that takes full advantage of the medium's possibilities.	To a satisfactory degree, conceived, developed, and executed a work of art that is somewhat original and that takes advantage of some of the medium's possibilities.	Did not well conceive and execute a work that is original or takes good advantage of the medium's possibilities.

Note: Refer to chapter 7, "Assessing Digital Art Projects" for an overview of assessing technology-supported student visual art projects.

Cross-Curricular Connection

Animated Drawings in Science

This project lends itself strongly to many hands-on science activities. A ubiquitous facet of science education involves conducting experiments in which students observe phenomena, take notes, and later report on their findings. These experiments frequently involve changes noted over a period of time.

One common family of such activities involves plant and animal growth. Seed germination and the culturing of mold are two common varieties. Students are often encouraged to make sketches of their observations and later to present them in a report on the data they collected and the conclusions they draw.

Drawings of plants going through the growth cycle would make a worthwhile adaptation of the project outlined in this unit. Drawings in this case might easily make far better visual subject matter than photographs for the same reason that drawn illustrations are often preferred in textbooks. Through the drawing medium, the artist can accentuate and manipulate subjects to ideally illustrate a specific characteristic or concept. Through the use of technology, however, if photos are the base reference for a project, photo-editing software can be used to process the images for the scientific illustrator's needs or as the start of a hybrid photo/drawn-painted image using a drawing or painting program in concert with the photo-editing software.

Other examples of projects that could make excellent use of this unit's project is the life cycle of butterflies, an activity that is also common to classrooms. The New York City Department of Education's "New Standards Performance Standards" document for science offers online a "Work Sample & Commentary: Butterflies" section (http://schools.nyc.gov/offices/teachlearn/documents/standards/science/es/47butterflies.html) that shows student drawings and observations that could easily have been presented through the techniques and approaches presented here. Such a project would have enhanced the paper-driven activity shown in that standards document by engaging the student in a high-motivation, authentic activity to be presented to a variety of appreciative audiences.

The same document contains other activities that might well be adapted as described above, among them the "River Cutters" activity, in which a student illustrated the effects of water in shaping the land with a series of drawings and descriptions. All of these involve the recording and presenting of information about change, yielding subject matter that is perfect for expression through drawn animation, the technique used in the digital zoetrope project.

UNIT **17**

Transformation
by **Clay Animation**

To create one's own world in any of the arts takes courage.

— GEORGIA O'KEEFFE

Please see the sections "Using this Book" and "Assessing Digital Art Projects" for more information about these standards, the interaction between them, and connecting these standards to the lessons in this book.

STANDARDS

NETS•S

Although all or most of the NETS•S are touched on in this unit, the connection is strongest and easiest to see and understand in the standards listed below:

1. a, b, c, d	4. a, b, d
2. a, b, d	5. a, b, c
3. c	6. a, b, c, d

Note: In this and other units, students engage in activities of broad scope that often require focus on group efforts in the production of works or in approaches to their sharing. Success requires students to *exhibit a positive attitude toward using technology that supports collaboration, learning, and productivity* (NETS•S 5.b).

National Standards for Arts Education (Visual Arts)

CS–1, AS–b

CS–2, AS–a, b, c

CS–3, AS–a, b

CS–4, AS–a

CS–5, AS–b, c

UNIT OBJECTIVES

Students will be challenged to:

- Understand the history of stop-action clay animation and its role as a visual art.

- Learn and apply the principles of animation.

- Understand how digital technology can be adapted to produce animations.

- Create an original work of art that applies the concepts and skills learned in this unit.

CENTRAL IDEAS

Although some of the early classic film animation was created through a sequential series of drawings, other pieces were made using stop-action animation. This technique, which developed into an important art form in its own right, relies on a two-part process. In the first stage a series of photographs of a model (usually of clay or a similar pliable material) that illustrate a change or movement of that figure are taken. The change is accomplished very gradually, with little difference between any two photographs. However, a significant cumulative change happens over the course of a large body of the photos.

In step two the photos are presented to the viewer, one after the other, in the same sequence they were shot and at a rapid pace. The effect is the illusion that the clay model is moving. In many ways this process is the same as the one used in drawn animation, but the principal difference is that these images are photographs and not drawings.

Many students find stop-action animation more accessible than drawn animation for the simple reason that clay modeling requires a less demanding level of skill. This is one technique that I found almost any student could use to produce a brilliant work of art if he or she was willing to plan, work methodically, and use some imagination.

This technique was tapped and used successfully by the film industry in its early days. Given the overall simplicity of the process, one would assume that stop-action animation could have been adapted for school projects; but few schools could provide students with the cameras, film, and other materials needed to produce clay animation projects in the traditional way. With simple digital technology, however, student artists can produce similar works of art. Clay model stop-action animation produced this way offers a unique set of art-making capabilities and challenges tht can form the basis of highly worthwhile activities for students.

TECHNOLOGY RATIONALE

Technology is used in this project to produce the individual elements and is used to tie them all together into a finished whole.

In years past, professionals who worked with clay animation used conventional film photography; however, this would be highly impractical for schools. Only a rare classroom could afford to acquire the number of film-based movie cameras needed, not to mention the high cost of film and processing.

Digital photography makes this easier and practical for today's classroom. The photography in this project works best through still photographs, which allows students to use common, inexpensive digital cameras. Software unifies the long series of still photos into a single continuous flowing movie. This software is commonly available as well.

The still images capture the very gradual evolution of a miniature clay sculpture. This project serves a good example of how common classroom technology can provide an experience that in the past could be experienced by only a very few well-financed professionals.

Principal Technology Skills Addressed

- Digital photography

- Stop-action animation

Technology Resources Needed

- Digital cameras

- Animation program

WEB RESOURCES

AnimateClay (collection of clay animation samples and information):
www.animateclay.com

Clay & Stop-Motion Animation How-To Page:
www.animateclay.com/modules.php?op=modload&name=Sections&file=index&req=viewarticle&artid=24&page=1

Claymation Station (comprehensive, student created, resource of background and how-to information):
http://library.thinkquest.org/22316/

Gumby World
www.gumbyworld.com

Claymation with PowerPoint:
www-bioc.rice.edu/precollege/msdaniel/claymation.html

Education Wichita (Clay Animation Made Easy—comprehensive collection of resources):
http://education.wichita.edu/claymation/resources.html

Head Gear Animation (examples of stop action animation):
www.headgearanimation.com/work/category/stop_motion

Tech4Learning (clay animation samples and information):
www.tech4learning.com/claykit/samples.html

Unit Conceptual and Pedagogical Overview

Stop-motion animation, the special effects approach that made successful such classic movies as *King Kong* (1933), *The Beast from 20,000 Fathoms* (1953), and *The 7th Voyage of Sinbad* (1958), is a much beloved art form. In later years, with the advent of television, clay animation made such cult classics as *Gumby and Pokey* and *Davy and Goliath* come alive. Today's students may be most familiar with *Wallace and Gromit*.

In the project presented in this unit, the same body of techniques and the applications that made these masterful works possible is available to students, although in a more practical digital version. In addition to digital still cameras and animation software, plastiline clay, a portable, storable, durable, and inexpensive material, completes the set of required materials.

Three elements of the act of making art are at work in this project: representation, the expressive quality of modeled sculpture; the narrative quality of art applied to storytelling; and animation. Clay animation projects bring each of these elements together to work simultaneously, and yet the individual elements offer three different challenges for student artists. However, as the elements work together in this project, the combination offers the added challenge of learning to manage a complex project.

ACTIVITIES

In this project students will make their own short clay animation films. This may be done as small collaborative group projects or as individual projects.

DAY 1

1. **Research and preparation**

   a. Direct the students to do Web-based research on the process of clay animation. (Alternately, this step may be assigned as homework prior to Day 1.)

   b. Present examples of clay animation to the class (examples can be found on the Internet—see the sites listed in Web Resources). Lead a group discussion afterward to foster focus, reflection, and understanding.

   Sample focus questions include the following:

   • How does clay animation work?

   • Have you found any clay animation films that are particularly interesting or inspiring? Why?

   • What does clay animation have in common with drawn animation?

   • What advantages does clay animation have for the filmmaker?

DAY 2

2. **Selecting theme and character**

   c. Students begin the project by selecting a theme and a character to star in the movie.

Note: Teachers can direct clay animation projects at many subjects across the curriculum, and examples of student work that illustrate this variety can be easily found on the Web (see the suggested links in the Web Resources section for this unit).

By setting the parameters of the project in terms of broad subject categories, teachers can allow the students to select a theme based on their interests and imagination, a dimension that fosters motivation and a high level of engagement.

As an example, a project might involve the study of pre-Columbian clay figurines. The figurines stem from a rich and long history in which animals or animal features are a principal motif. Their creators believed animals had special or totemic power. The production of these figurines as well as myriad other types of carved or modeled figures (Japanese Netsuke, for example) offers a particularly good entry point for this project because these traditional art objects involve a character (animal or hybrid human-animal) who portrays a story or specific quality. Also the figures were rendered by artists in a similar medium and on a similar scale to the plastiline figure that the student artist will create in this example.

Web-based research into the chosen area of study is the starting point for the students. In the case cited here, they would each choose a specific clay figure work of art, further research its significance, and print out a photograph of it.

Alternately, if the students are simply directed to follow their imagination, the steps of identifying a central character and Web searching for reference material on its appearance will prove invaluable, as well.

After the central character of their clay animation is selected, students should come up with a general idea of what action their film will feature (e.g., jaguar figure opens its mouth to roar, rattlesnake pipe coils, monkey vase grows, etc.). The group may want to create storyboards to define this animated sequence.

DAYS 3–4 +

3. Creating clay animation

d. The first step is to model a character that is based on the artifact selected in the previous step. This interpretation can be an attempt to faithfully reproduce the original or loosely interpret it, depending on ability levels, instructional focus, and the teacher's judgment.

Note: Because clay animation-based projects are generally long-term projects, thought and preparation must be given to preparing the classroom for the project. A major logistical consideration is storing projects in progress. A good approach would be to have each student provide, at the project's start, a shoebox or similar sized container (plastic tubs with lids are even better) in which to store the work. Once placed in the box, each student's work will be protected from damage (plastiline is by nature pliable if left exposed).

e. The next several sessions involve the students in a labor intensive process in which they continually alter the original figurine slightly (size, color, shape, direction, etc.), photograph it digitally, alter it slightly and photograph it again.

This process will call for the production of approximately 50 photographs to produce even a very short clay animation film in which a recognizable character performs an appreciable action or undergoes a noticeable transformation of some sort.

Project Sample

Process Used to Develop this Sample

The clay animation process is not difficult to understand. It does, however, require tightly controlled classroom logistics in order to implement projects for large numbers of students.

Essentially, the student animators develop a small-scale clay sculpture that undergoes a long series of incremental changes. They photograph each of these changes after it is made, and then another sequential change is implemented. The process therefore is one of sculpt, photograph, sculpt, photograph, and so on. Even an extremely short film will require several dozen photographs.

Figure 17.1.
Project Sample—
Transformation by
Clay Animation. These
frames are taken from
the animated piece
"Paul Bunyan."

One of the important challenges is controlling the position of the camera. A tripod set up in a fixed position (or one that moves only very slightly, so as to avoid a jerky motion when the photos are put together at the end of the process) would be ideal. Alternately, taping a camera to a fixed object such as a stack of books, or affixing it by another method can achieve the same result.

Another element to be mindful of is light. Consistent light will give a consistent visual effect. Fortunately, changing light will not present a challenge in most classrooms because bright overhead light is nearly ubiquitous.

It is unusual for classrooms to have the luxury of having enough of all the materials, equipment, and space for a clay animation project so that more than 30 students can work on individual projects simultaneously. Often, sharing materials is the key to implementation. A manageable approach demands a collaborative project in which five or six groups of four to five students each are provided with materials. An in-between approach allows each student to make an individual sculpture that is part of the many in the series, and then it is photographed at the group's single camera station. I have observed both scenarios work well, although I personally prefer the fully collaborative single project.

In the single collaborative project approach each student will be responsible for many steps, particularly if multiple characters (necessitating the creation of several sculptures) are part of the plan. Besides sculpting, managing the miniature set and props (something that inevitably becomes part of these projects), photography, maintaining story continuity, as well as keeping notes about the group's process and progress all become part of the joint workload. Each group should determine who's doing what before the day's work begins, which can be a good way to incorporate planning and managing into the lesson. It is helpful to have a story outline or storyboards to define the sequence and serve as a reference.

Time also is an important factor in any clay animation project. Unless a class has the luxury of leaving the work set up permanently in a self-contained classroom, distributing partially completed work, setting up equipment, and then putting it all away can consume a good deal of time. This project benefits from a double or extended class period. It is also the type of project that inevitably goes much better the second time a teacher attempts it, as the experience is invaluable.

When the students have taken all the photographs, they can import them into software that will present each one in rapid succession. Software titles commonly used for this include PowerPoint, Windows Movie Maker, iMovie, and Frames (a low-cost program from Tech4learning that has been specifically refined for student-made clay animation projects and is provided as part of their classroom clay animation kit). Essentially, the animation process is one of selecting and importing each frame into the software in the order they are to be presented to the viewer and then adjusting the timing of how fast the images will be presented.

Putting together the animation calls for the work scene to shift from the classroom as sculpture/photography studio to the classroom as computer lab/animation studio. The students will need a computer dedicated to each project (e.g., if a group of four is working on a single project, then a computer for those four students will be required).

The additional elements of titling and narration can be added to this project. The various software choices all include slightly different sound recording and generating capabilities, as well as the option to add text to the animation. Narration will require a microphone for each project-dedicated computer unless a more elaborate sharing scheme is worked out for the groups, although adding text instead will require only a keyboard. The Internet abounds with how-tos and tutorials for the sound and animation techniques of these programs.

In addition to brief, periodic demonstrations and explanations of work and classroom procedures, a short daily reflection discussion about how things are going, what discoveries have been made, how to solve simple problems, and so on, will go a long way toward making this a very rewarding activity.

Sharing the Work

Student projects can be shown in a formal theater setting with an LCD projector (e.g., a class- or schoolwide animation festival) or on a dedicated desktop computer set up as a kiosk (the film is run on a continuous loop or set up for the viewer to start manually). Additionally, the work can be published by burning it to disks and distributing it.

Student projects can also be uploaded to Web sites that host non-professional video. A Web search will reveal numerous examples, many of them free. The link to the video can then be shared through blogs, e-mail, free digital communities, and so on.

Assessment

The goals of this project are to produce a piece that has a natural-looking and flowing movement with an interesting character and storyline context for that movement. Although the procedural and technical aspects of the project are important points to assess, it is probably wisest to subordinate them to these broader goals of filmmaking.

Using Rubrics to Assess a Group Collaborative Project

Assuming the class will work on clay animation projects in groups, with each group comprised of about four students, the following approach to rubric-driven assessment is a possible method for grading.

Evaluating the product of the group's effort is one vital aspect of assessment. In this sense the work can be reviewed as if it were produced by a single student, with each student receiving the same grade for this portion of the assessment.

Suggested discussion questions: How might you alter the process you followed to: Produce this clay animation? Change the model? Change the way you took the still photos? Change the number of photos or the way they are linked? Make other changes?

Suggested General Assessment/Accountability Rubric for Unit 17

Project Components	Excellent	Proficient	Partially Proficient	Not Sufficiently Proficient or Incomplete
Completion of Project • Did the group generate the necessary clay models, props, and sets? Did they shoot the recommended number of photos? • Did the group edit the individual photos effectively into a finished animated sequence?	All portions of the project are completed successfully at a high level.	Most portions of the project are completed successfully at a high or satisfactory level.	Some important (and other) portions of the project are completed successfully at a satisfactory level.	Few of the project portions are completed successfully at a satisfactory level.
Research and Preparation • Did the group follow outlining and storyboard exercises to define its animated sequence?	Conducted the needed research/ preparation in a way that allows for a full level of participation in the project.	Conducted the needed research/ preparation in a way that allows for a high level of participation in the project.	Conducted the needed research/ preparation in a way that allows for a satisfactory level of participation in the project.	Conducted the needed research/ preparation in a way that allows for a minimal level of participation in the project.

(Continued)

Suggested General Assessment/Accountability Rubric for Unit 17 *(Continued)*

Project Components	Excellent	Proficient	Partially Proficient	Not Sufficiently Proficient or Incomplete
Theme and Concept Learning • Does the finished animation satisfy the project criteria in terms of format? Content? • Does the finished piece indicate a good understanding of the clay animation process? • Did the group plan a project that reflects an understanding of this process and that takes advantage of its possibilities?	Fully understood the concepts and goals of the project. Understood the contextual background content. Understood how to apply the above in the creation of an original work.	Understood a good deal of the concepts and goals of the project. Understood the contextual background content to a high degree. Understood how to apply the above in the creation of an original work to a high degree.	Understood some of the concepts and goals of the project. Understood the contextual background content to a degree. Understood how to apply the above in the creation of an original work to a degree.	Did not adequately understand the concepts and goals of the project. Did not adequately understand the contextual background content. Did not adequately understand how to apply the above in the creation of an original work.
Technical Proficiency • Did the group show proficiency in modeling, posing, and photographing the subject(s) of their project?	Demonstrated a high degree of understanding and mastery of the concepts and skills involved in the techniques required of the project.	Demonstrated a good degree of understanding and mastery of the concepts and skills involved in the techniques required of the project.	Demonstrated a satisfactory degree of understanding and mastery of the concepts and skills involved in the techniques required of the project.	Did not demonstrate an adequate degree of understanding and mastery of the concepts and skills involved in the techniques required of the project.
Technology Use • Did the group handle the digital photography effectively? • Did they save and manage files appropriately? • Did they import and edit files in the animation application appropriately?	Handled the technology portions of the project in a highly effective, insightful, and responsible fashion.	Handled the technology portions of the project very proficiently and in an effective, insightful, and responsible fashion.	Handled the technology portions of the project in a satisfactorily effective, insightful, and responsible fashion.	Did not handle the technology portions of the project in a satisfactorily effective, insightful, and responsible fashion.
Creativity-Expression • Did the group develop a unique work that reflects its joint concerns and taste?	Conceived, developed, and executed a work of art that is highly original and that takes full advantage of the medium's possibilities.	To a good degree, conceived, developed, and executed a work of art that is original and that takes full advantage of the medium's possibilities.	To a satisfactory degree, conceived, developed, and executed a work of art that is somewhat original and that takes advantage of some of the medium's possibilities.	Did not well conceive and execute a work that is original or takes good advantage of the medium's possibilities.

Note: Refer to chapter 7, "Assessing Digital Art Projects" for an overview of assessing technology-supported student visual art projects.

Cross-Curricular Connection

Clay Animation in Science

In addition to showing the phenomenon of transformation, clay animation is a good platform for the implementation of projects that enable students to illustrate movement, an important facet of life science.

A project commonly seen in elementary science classes involves the creation of illustrations or models of insects and their specialized body parts. The insects have specific modes of movement, which creates a natural theme for young scientists who are observing and counting body parts: eight legs for a spider; two antennae for an ant; a head, thorax, and abdomen for crawling insects, and so on.

This modeling project commonly revolves around drawings or the use of simple materials such as pipe cleaners and colored tissue paper. Clay animation, however, adds wonderful dimensions to the project, as the unique movements and behaviors of insects can be explained through stop-action animation of student-created models. An interesting twist to this project would have the insect characters explaining the functions and movements of their own bodies to the audience.

Sharing Student Art with an Audience
Archiving, Exhibiting, and Publishing

The painting has a life of its own.

— JACKSON POLLOCK

Please see the sections "Using this Book" and "Assessing Digital Art Projects" for more information about these standards, the interaction between them, and connecting these standards to the lessons in this book.

STANDARDS

NETS•S

Athough all or most of the NETS•S are touched on in this unit, the connection is strongest and easiest to see and understand in the standards listed below:

1. a, b   4. b, c, d

2. a, b, d   5. a, b, c, d

3. b, c, d   6. a, b, c, d

Note: When students share their artwork, the context for individual work is often best established through group exhibitions. By applying their creativity and hard work to whole-group sharing, students *exhibit leadership for digital citizenship* (NETS•S 5.d).

National Standards for Arts Education (Visual Arts)

CS–1, AS–a, b

CS–2, AS–a, b, c

CS–3, AS–a, b

CS-4, AS–a, b, c

CS–5, AS–a, b, c

CS–6, AS–a, b

UNIT OBJECTIVES

Students will be challenged to:

- Understand how the act of making art intended to be shared with an audience differs from making art intended solely for personal viewing.

- Understand the processes of planning and implementing exhibition, and publishing projects in order to share art with audiences.

- Learn technology skills used to prepare exhibits and publish art products.

CENTRAL IDEAS

The act of sharing art with an audience, along with reflecting on feedback from an audience and giving feedback as an audience member, provides a broader and more complete learning experience for the student artist. This chapter gives an overview of the broad range of extension activities that add meaning to art projects through public display. Although it is wise to keep the exhibition in mind from the planning stages of an art project, these projects actually begin once the art is completed.

Technology Resources Needed

Archiving: scanner, digital camera, digital video camera, video-editing software, QuickTimeVR software, photo/video/VR organizing, storing, posting software or online resources

Real-World Art Exhibits: digital camera, word processing software, printer, digital video camera and video-editing software, QuickTimeVR software

Virtual Art Exhibits: digital camera, scanner, slide show software (or multimedia software), LCD projector, desktop computers (to use as kiosks)

Hard Copy Publishing: scanner, digital camera, word processing/desktop publishing software, printer

Digital Publishing: digital camera, scanner, Acrobat (or other PDF producing) software

WEB RESOURCES

ePublishing

Creating eBooks with PowerPoint (or any other presentation software):
http://drscavanaugh.org/ebooks/creating_ebooks_with_powerpoint.htm

RealeBooks:
www.realebooks.com/#SlideFrame_1

Class Exhibits

Artsonia:
www.artsonia.com

Digital Edge Learning Interchange (VI):
http://ali.apple.com/ali_sites/deli/exhibits/1000680/Professional_Standards.html

Eduscapes:
http://eduscapes.com/Web/museum/studentexplore.html

Smithsonian Education (Creating a Classroom Museum):
www.smithsonianeducation.org/educators/lesson_plans/collect/crecla/crecla00.htm

Art & Design → Every Picture Has a Story

Hero Study/Projects

Hero Power:
http://library.thinkquest.org/CR0212302/famousheroes.html

My Hero: http://myhero.com/myhero/

Trading Heroes:
www.highbeam.com/doc/1G1:19084118/Trading+Heroes+-+developing+role+models.html?refid=SEO

Available in print:
Gura, M. (1993). Trading hero cards. *Educational Leadership 51*(3) pp. 79–80.
Gura, M. (1997). Trading heroes—Developing role models. *School Arts 96*(6) pp. 22–23.

Book Making

Children Creating Artists' Books: Integrating Visual Arts and Language Arts:
www.readingonline.org/newliteracies/guzzetti2/

Let's Book It with Tech'Knowledge'y:
www.vickiblackwell.com/makingbooks/index.htm

We Are All Related: A Bookmaking Activity:
http://64.233.187.104/search?q=cache:-eP0M4cOXhEJ:www.historysociety.ca/content/en/pdfs/Beaver.pdf+bookmaking+for+students&hl=en&gl=us&ct=clnk&cd=19

Technology How-To Resources

Adobe Web Tech Curriculum—Lesson 9.2 Scanner Basics:
www.adobe.com/education/webtech/CS2/unit_graphics2/sb_home.htm

CNET (Digital Video Basics—video information about digital video):
http://ecoustics-cnet.com.com/4660-10165_7-6510112.html?part=ecoustics-cnet&part=ecoustics-cnet&subj=video

Digital Camera Basics:
www.digitalcamerabasics.com

Photo.net (digital cameras—a beginner's guide):
www.photo.net/equipment/digital/basics/

Scanner Guide—First Time Users:
www.nuance.com/scannerguide/firsttimeusers/

Tech4Learning—Simply VR (samples and information on student virtual reality projects):
www.tech4learning.com/simplyvr/vr_samples.html

Unit Conceptual and Pedagogical Overview

Students can learn valuable lessons by creating original art works themselves. And, of course, in producing their own work, many opportunities exist for them to study and appreciate the work of great artists who've come before them. Over time, students should begin to see how art has been an essential facet of all human history. Still, as rich as this extended body of learning is, it is only part of the story.

To complete the cycle, student artists must present their art to an audience. The act of planning and preparing for messages to be heard and the receipt of and reflection upon the reactions of viewers will provide meaningful insight for student artists.

As is true in other facets of a well-balanced education, performances are essential. They can be seen as "proving behaviors," methods by which what has been learned is demonstrated and then analyzed. In visual arts education the function of performance is accomplished through exhibition and sometimes publication of student work. The feedback from audiences and peers from the exhibits, as well as student analysis and reflection upon that feedback, offer unique opportunities for further and deeper understanding.

Engaging in accountable talk—explaining and defending the ideas and decisions behind one's art—greatly enhances learning. Furthermore, it serves as preparation for the use of this challenging, yet well-rewarded behavior in the world beyond school. Learning to analyze and evaluate the work of peers and colleagues, to formulate focused criticism about it, and to articulate these are invaluable learning experiences, as well.

I view exhibiting the work of students to be an important part of the program I provide them. This concept goes much further than merely placing their work on the wall and showing off interesting and attractive objects created inside the classroom. It includes making students a part of the process of conceiving the exhibit and setting its goals, as well as planning, executing, and sharing it. At times it seems the learning that has taken place through these activities is as worthwhile as the creation of the art itself. The truth is more complex. The activities that happen around exhibiting, critiquing, archiving, and publishing student art combined with those involved in the creation of the work form a complete whole. It is this completeness that makes all of this extra work worthwhile, for after the cycle of exhibition activities is finished we can rest assured that our students truly *know* that wonderful aspect of life we call *art*.

This chapter offers a general discussion of methods for archiving and sharing student art, an essential dimension of student art programs. It may also be used as a resource to support the various projects in this book, as well as a great many others not presented in these pages. Additionally, this section is an instructional unit in its own right, culminating in the creation of a learning product that is an example of the approaches discussed here.

Archiving

Student art that is produced within the limitations of the materials and resources of typical schools is often unwieldy, impermanent, and fragile. Flat work, such as drawings and paintings, especially pieces created with student- or school-grade materials, deteriorates rapidly. School-grade paper yellows, becomes brittle, and breaks down within a relatively short period of time. School-grade paints and pigments quickly fade and flake from surfaces. Collages suffer from glues that cease to hold, as do cardboard sculptures and many other types of works. Furthermore, schools simply don't have an inexhaustible amount of space in which to store student work. A busy school, with hundreds or thousands of students, quickly runs out of space, and students who take their work home often encounter the same problem. Archiving student art through the use of digital photos, scanners, videos, and other means is a modern and highly practical solution to these challenges.

Two-dimensional work is easy to scan on inexpensive flatbed scanners. The maximum dimensions of what can be placed on the scanner, however, must not be larger than the scanner bed. Teachers may want to keep this fact in mind when they select a format for student work, rather than discovering this problem later on when they would like to scan oversized pictures.

Large-format scanners are available, but, of course, at a significantly higher price. These may be well worth the investment if scanning and digital storage of art becomes part of a school's program.

Items too large for scanners can be photographed using a digital still camera. Digital video may be the solution for archiving sculpture that moves, such as mobiles or masks worn by students in a presentation. Virtual reality software will prove useful for conventional, static, three-dimensional work such as origami or box sculptures. As we will see in the following section, the digital images produced by these processes have other uses beyond simple archiving and often can be used in other contexts for different purposes.

Once scanned or photographed, individual images of student work accumulate and must be organized. A wide variety of photo (and digital video) organizing and storing software and online resources are available. Some resources permit public posting of still and video images, offering a form of quick publishing. Many of these sites are no- or low-cost resources easily located on the Internet (e.g., Picasa, Flickr, Yahoo Groups, Photobucket, Ourmedia, Magic Gallery, etc.). A quick survey will reveal that within this category of resources different items offer different approaches, functions, and capacities. Some offer sortable catalogs while others provide thumbnail galleries; and some accommodate photos only while others accept various types of media.

Exhibiting

The following is a review of many of the possibilities available to today's typical school, one that has a modest amount of technology available for teachers and students. Through this idealized scenario, a full continuum of approaches is presented, although teachers are encouraged to pick and choose what strikes them as most practical and effective for their immediate needs. Projects undertaken down the road will likely present opportunities to circle back and try elements not implemented the first time around.

Sample Activity

Select a class art project to archive and share as both a hard copy and digital exhibition, as well as offering it as a digital publication. Alternately, any portion(s) of this project may be selected or adapted as a culminating phase of the project selected.

Many of the projects discussed in this book are adaptable for the entire continuum of activities described below, and virtually all of them for portions of it. However, for the sake of illustration, a brief description of the example project is necessary.

Our Heroes Trading Cards (lesson plan in brief)

1. Discuss with the class the concept of "Who is a hero and why?"

2. Have the students search the Web for images and information about a person they consider a hero.

3. Have them process the image they select to reflect their own tastes and sensibilities and to create a portrait that is uniquely their own.

4. Direct the students to write a short biography of their hero.

5. In a word processing program (such as Word), have the students use the auto shape function to draw a rectangle the same size as a trading card. Have them align this rectangle to a specified location on the page using the draw grid function. Import the processed image into the rectangle.

6. On a new page, draw another rectangle the same size and in the identical location as the illustration on the first page, and then import the text of the biography into the rectangle.

With the completion of the six steps above, the hero cards are ready for the final phase of production: the implementation of which is contingent on the manner in which the work will be shared.

Produce a Real World Exhibit

A Two-Dimensional Class Art Project

Gallery Exhibits

The hero cards, like all of the projects described in this book, call for the production of real-world works of art. These, in turn, offer the opportunity for the wonderful culminating activity of a real-world exhibition.

1. After preparing a unified body of work as the result of a single art project or an extended series of projects, the class is ready to mount an exhibition. Making this a formal portion of the project that is known to students from the beginning, instead of casually tacking it on at the end, will add urgency to all other phases of the work and will produce a better experience and finished work. Outlined below are suggestions for organizing and implementing a class exhibition activity.

   a. Bring the class to the gallery space (school library, lobby, spare classroom, etc.) to engage them in the process of pre-visualizing the exhibition. Discuss how many works can be shown in the gallery, how they can be hung or displayed, the types of framing or mounting and background material that can be used to show them off to good advantage, and so on. Alternately, photos taken of the space and presented as a digital slide show can be shown to the group.

   b. Make the inclusion of the work of each student in the class a standard for participation. Having more work on hand than can be practically exhibited is a good position for a class to be in before it begins work on the exhibition. Toward this end, a thorough review of the works considered for inclusion becomes an exercise in analysis and discussion.

   c. Class field trips to art museums are classic school activities to enrich the overall educational experience, as well as to achieve numerous specific goals in the instructional areas of art, social studies, and other subjects. A trip to a museum may also function as a motivational and informational experience upon which a class may plan its upcoming exhibit.

2. A brainstorming session will produce a list of discoveries about the variety of materials museums and galleries produce to support exhibitions. Among them are:

   d. A small sign accompanying each work lists the artist's name and class, the work's dimensions and date produced, and the media or technique used to produce it.

   e. An exhibition catalog—this would include the same information as the sign with the possible inclusion of more explanatory text, prices (if the works are for sale), and other information as needed. Each short passage may be accompanied by a small photographic reproduction of the work. Often a short biography of each artist, accompanied by a headshot photo, will appear in the catalog.

   f. A large poster with text explaining major segments of the exhibition (the genre, medium, challenge and goal or purpose of each major type of work, etc.). These oversized projects can be brought to any local copy shop on disk and printed to order at a reasonable cost.

g. A large sign at the entrance to the exhibit to announce it. This generally would include the title of the exhibit and/or the names of the group exhibiting. The date may be included as well.

h. A postcard, with a reproduction of a single or a small group of works included in the show that is representative of the quality or spirit of the work exhibited. On the reverse is the essential information about the date and location of the exhibit, and possibly a brief description of the art work and/or the artists. This card is often used as an invitation to attract visitors or supplied as a take away for those who attend.

Obviously, all of the elements described above need not be included in a single class exhibit effort. Student interest and practicality can dictate which elements are essential.

Note: All of the items above can be produced as word processed/desktop published documents. Scans of small-scale work or photos of larger or three-dimensional work can be sized and/or photo processed and imported into Word or other software used to edit, process, and lay out the finished piece.

These are important ancillary items that contribute to the overall experience and the transformation of a school event into an authentic and impressive one.

3. Additionally, these follow-up activities will enrich the overall experience:

i. Exhibit Opening and documentation. It is customary for major museum or gallery exhibitions to be accompanied by an "opening," a cocktail party–style celebration of the spirited life of an exhibit about to begin. This is an opportunity to use digital photography to document the event and to edit and process a document about it afterward.

Figure 18.1.
Invitation to a class art exhibit.

Figure 18.2. Project Sample—Hero Card. This example was used as the graphic to enhance the exhibit invitation on the previous page.

Note: Museum exhibits over the past several decades have featured gallery guide "audio tours" in which viewers rent or borrow devices to play back recorded docents' comments and explanations as they view the work. Podcasting now puts this type of enhancement within the reach of schools. Web research on how to produce educational podcasts will reveal a great amount of how-to information, as well as free resources (see author's free resource—PodcastforTeachers.org). Once recorded and uploaded, exhibit viewers can download the tour either from their home or class computer, from a single computer supplied at the exhibit, or if a monitor or aide is available, the school may provide loaner mp3 players to visitors at the exhibit. This may also be an opportunity to involve other school groups that have experience with podcasting, giving them a role in the exhibit, as well.

Produce a Virtual Exhibit of a Class Art Project

There are numerous varieties of virtual exhibits or digitally supported exhibits, which include digital exhibits in PowerPoint, online, on-site via LCD installations, or at kiosks.

One simple version of a virtual exhibit involves the creation of a single, unified digital slide show of a body of student work. Once selected, each work is either scanned or photographed digitally and the graphic files are imported into slide show software.

Over the past few decades it has become common practice for museums, both art museums and those devoted to science, history, and other aspects of culture, to make use of looped slide shows presented with an LCD projector. In addition to making the hanging or staging of an exhibit of many separate works of art infinitely easier, the slide show format has other advantages of an artistic and curatorial nature.

- Showing art through slides creates its own special atmosphere and feeling.
- The scale of the works can become an additional element of the viewing experience. Viewers can experience even small drawings as environmental—presented in such a large format as to give the viewer the experience of being in the work instead of looking at it.

- The viewer's attention can be better directed. The slide show is a linear experience and the designer of the exhibit can utilize this to determine for the viewer the order in which works are seen. Additionally, the amount of time each work is to be viewed can be established by the exhibit designers.

- Segments of works can be isolated and presented as slides, giving the exhibition designer a greater palate of visual possibilities with which to work.

- Transitional effects can be added, bringing an element into the exhibition that isn't possible in real-world exhibits.

Alternately, slide shows can be presented as kiosk experiences, in which viewers encounter the work individually or in small groups, viewing it on a computer screen. The result of this approach may be to make possible the presentation of many more works than in a traditional exhibit. If a number of kiosks are provided to viewers, different bodies of work can be presented on each. An end-of-year class exhibit, then, might utilize six kiosks, each loaded with a virtual exhibition of a different project or body of student work.

A variation on this would be to use presentation software that allows for hyperlinking (instead of a simple, linear slide show) and listing all the works on an exhibit home page (running locally on the computer; not uploaded to the Web). This would allow the viewer to select the order and viewing time of the works to be seen as his instincts direct.

One advantage of the kiosk approach is that a great deal of art can be made available in a small space. A table display at a parents' night function could sit in a school lobby, for instance, and offer guests a good experience in viewing student art. Once created, these virtual exhibits can be stored, moved, and easily presented again and again as school community needs dictate.

Produce a Hard Copy Publication of a Class Art Project

An alternative context in which student artists can present their work to a real audience is found in the world of publishing—both e-publishing and traditional hard copy publishing. Even hard copy publishing has, over the past two decades, become increasingly dependent on digital technology. Drawings, paintings, and collages, as well as photos of paper sculptures and constructions, have long been included in print media, as have photographs as illustrations and design enhancements for text. In the field of juvenile publishing, picture books have moved the status of graphics from enhancement to center stage player.

Ideally, the decisions about how a body of student art will ultimately be presented to its audience should be included in the planning of the project from its inception. Understanding how art will be presented and viewed are planning elements that are inextricably tied to the other aspects of projects.

In the case of the Heroes Trading Cards project, it is an easy matter to import the graphics and text into a program such as Word and center and adjust them to assume the identity of a page in a book. Many printers are capable of printing on both sides of the paper (duplexing), and this capabiltiy can be used to create a book-like hard copy.

A black-and-white project such as this one can be printed on 8.5 x 14 inch legal paper. A single sheet printed front and back will yield four pages when folded down the center. A class of 30, with each student contributing a single page, will require the printing of only eight sheets to accommodate the entire body of work. The extra page at the front can be used as a title page and the one at the end for the class biography or for other statements. A book of ten sheets will allow for acknowledgments, an index, citations, and other important information.

Many of today's laser and inkjet printers will allow printing on heavy stock, which can make a good cover for the publication. By using a long-reach stapler (an item already on hand in many schools, and easy to find at stationery stores) the ten sheets of legal printer paper and one sheet of heavy stock can be folded in half and fastened by student publishers. Alternately, today's neighborhood commercial copy shops offer many services besides the use of photocopy machines, and printing and binding services are frequently within the financial reach of school groups.

Student bookmaking projects and resources to support them are abundant on the Web. For most projects, ubiquitous word processing programs can handle all of the pagination, layout, and printing needs encountered.

The resulting class book on heroes will make an attractive and permanent artifact that focuses learning and demonstrates student competencies. It can be produced in conjunction with a real life gallery or virtual exhibit, as well. This format, and variations on it, can be made to fit a wide variety of student illustration projects that feature art, and they easily incorporate writing, as well.

Produce a Digital Publication of a Class Art Project

The publication aspect of sharing student art with an audience can take advantage of innovations in the area of e-publishing, as well. Staying with the heroes book project mentioned previously, it is not hard to imagine aspects of it that would benefit from e-publishing. It's easy to understand the difficulties and expenses encountered in producing the hard copy book, as well as the obvious limitations as to how many copies can be produced and how they can be effectively distributed over distances. E-publishing offers an alternative approach with specific advantages. By producing the book as a PDF document instead of printing it in hard copy, a finished product is produced (one that is fixed and can't be altered), and the work can be distributed without additional costs in whatever quantities are required. The book, as PDF, can be e-mailed or uploaded to a school Web site, making it available globally.

Beyond this simple approach, e-publishing is a growing field of its own and teachers with a particular interest in it can find much information about it on the Web.

Alternately, many sites on the Internet publish student writing, artwork, and books, and this avenue can be of use, as well.

Discussing Student Art Exhibits

To round out the picture, it should be stressed that a great deal of value may be had in structured, formal discussions with students about finished art. Students should be able to identify and articulate a number of core aspects of art works including:

- The type of art for which it is a emblematic (e.g., abstract, surrealistic, etc.)

- If the project is a picture, identify it as a portrait, landscape, still life, or other

- The medium and/or method used (photography, collage, drawing/painting)

- Whether it is two-dimensional or three-dimensional, and if three, is it a sculpture in the round, relief sculpture (mask), mobile, or other form

- The theme or motif

In addition to identifying it, a further dimension of value would be to evaluate it or make observations about its success or shortcomings in terms of:

- Comparing it to the work of artists associated with the movement or development to which it can be traced or related.

- Discussing the work's adherence to or variation from those qualities most associated with the type of work it embodies.

Furthermore, the work can be discussed in terms of design elements and the way they work together in a piece; for example, the way a dominant or secondary color harmonizes with the others in the piece, the angle or size of a sculptural element's relationship to the whole, or the choice of a quality for a line or pattern as part of a picture.

My personal experience with this dimension of teaching art is that this type of talk appears rather foreign to students the first few times they try it, but soon they begin to feel comfortable with it and look for items with which to increase their vocabulary as they discuss art works further. It is helpful for the teacher to model this behavior, especially if it is incorporated into the daily discussion that happens around the classroom. Above all, the ability to discuss art in a non-judgemental, supportive manner is a great breakthrough for students. As students become more adept at this teachers may choose to incorporate some of it in the overall assessment of a student's performance on a project.

Assessment

Assessing student performance for this project will vary from case to case depending on which of the suggested components the teacher opts to include. However the overall body of considerations will include the following:

- Did the student participate in the class discussions, field visits, brainstorming sessions, and other planning activities and sharing mechanisms selected by the class?

- Did the student choose an appropriate sample of work for inclusion in the class sharing of the project?

- Did the student follow directions to prepare the work selected for exhibition (real world or digital), complying with all parameters set and completing all aspects of the preparation?

- Did the student participate in the execution of the sharing mechanism (e.g., exhibition, publication, Web site, etc.)?

- Did the student contribute to class debriefings, reflections on feedback and other measures of success, inlcuding discussions of further learning based on shared ideas?

These points may be incorporated into a simple checklist or developed in a sliding scale rubric to facilitate and clarify student assessment.

Note: To select for specific projects, refer to chapter 7, "Assessing Digital Art Projects" for an overview of assessing technology-supported student visual art projects.

Cross Curricular Connection

The World

The class exhibit, real-world or virtual, can be viewed as a wonderful culminating event for a science, social studies, or other subject area unit of study, if the goal of the production of art Is to engage students in research, reflection, and reporting on a theme within that subject. This book gives many examples of how the student production of pictures and sculptures can be assigned in a way that they perform that function.

A visit to a museum or gallery can show how much ancillary material is produced to support an exhibit. In addition to invitations and signage next to the viewed objects and at the exhibit entrance, there are often catalogs, gallery guides, and reviews of the work present at many exhibitions. All of these represent literacy learning opportunities as well as those to make art.

UNIT **19**

Digital Storybooks

I found I could say things with color and shapes
that I couldn't say any other way—things I had no words for.

— GEORGIA O'KEEFFE

*Please see the
sections "Using
this Book" and
"Assessing Digital
Art Projects" for
more information
about these
standards, the
Interaction
between them,
and connecting
these standards to
the lessons in this
book.*

STANDARDS

NETS-S

Although all or most of the NETS•S are touched on in this unit, the connection is strongest and easiest to see and understand in the standards listed below:

1. a, b, d	4. b, d
2. a, b, c	5. c
3. b, c	6. a, b, c, d

Note: In this and other units, students publish their work on the Web in formats that are easily shared and exchanged with other groups around the world. Locating and inviting audiences from other cultures to view and interact with the work is a logical extension made easy by the use of Web-based technology. This type of sharing allows students to *develop cultural understanding of global awareness by engaging with learners of other cultures* (NETS•S 2.c).

National Standards for Arts Education (Visual Arts)

CS–1, AS–b,

CS–2, AS–a, b, c

CS–3, AS–a, b

CS–5, AS–a, c

CS–6, AS–a, b

UNIT OBJECTIVES

Students will be challenged to:

- Reflect on the importance of storytelling and the structures and processes of effective storytelling.

- Understand the relationship of illustration to presenting stories.

- Explore the role that technology can play in illustrating and directing the audience through the story experience.

- Create their own illustrated story through the focused use of technology.

CENTRAL IDEAS

Storytelling, one of humanity's most basic formats for social interaction, education, and entertainment, is closely associated with visual art. When stories are told in book form, the sharing of descriptions is greatly facilitated by the accompaniment of visual images that enhance and empower the words. This relationship is nowhere more apparent and well developed than in the illustrated storybook. These have become so popular and are so much a part of growing up that in order for students to fully understand their world they really ought to try their hand at creating a book of their own.

In many of the best illustrated storybooks we see a back-and-forth dialogue between writing and illustrating, each influencing the other. Today's students have a great appreciation for hard copy storybooks, but are also very involved with electronic media that enhance storytelling with animation, virtual reality imagery, special effects, hyperlinks, and other storytelling devices that have emerged. I developed the project presented in this unit to bridge the two literary worlds, hard copy and digital media, in which today's students live. I found that students responded favorably, accepting and appreciating the blurring of borders between the two, and enthusiastically rolled up their sleeves to get down to work on their own contribution.

Many colleagues agree that the technology-based storybook project is a perfect format through which students can understand the basics of stories, story illustration, and the complexities of the new media that storytelling embraces.

TECHNOLOGY RATIONALE

The use of technology in this project enhances it in several important ways; primarily establishing standard parameters for displaying the student work, so that the art of all class members clearly appears to be part of a uniform effort. This is achieved by importing all work into a frame that is standardized (or close to standardized) in size, line thickness, type, and spacing. While technology makes this easy to achieve, overcoming the challenges in doing this by traditional means would overshadow the project itself. Furthermore, by importing the student art into technologically drawn frames, a neatness and completeness is lent to them.

Using a program that facilitates the creation of slide shows will allow the finished drawings to become the individual pages of a digital book. A program such as PowerPoint allows the reader/viewer of the book to move at his or her own pace, advancing from one slide to another as desired. Furthermore, by hyperlinking the pages, the viewer can jump from one to another without having to follow a set order or shift between different organizing views of the program. Programs such as Microsoft Photo Story or other free photo management services offered by Kodak and Flickr, will give a steady-paced, linear presentation of the slides, as will Adobe's Photoshop Elements. Many of these programs allow for additional text to be added to the slide as captions or other ancillary text-bearing elements.

Principal Technology Skills Addressed

- Digital drawing/painting

- Importing and blending graphics and text in a graphics program

- Slide show and/or hyperlinked presentation

Technology Resources Needed

- Digital drawing/painting program

- Presentation program

WEB RESOURCES

Adobe Digital Kids Club (storyboard information and resources):
www.adobe.com/education/digkids/lessons/storyboards.html

DigiTales (Seven Steps to Create a Digital Story):
www.digitales.us/resources/seven_steps.php

How to Create a Digital Movie (Teaching Pre K–8):
www.findarticles.com/p/articles/mi_qa3666/is_200411/ai_n9465004

Schoolhousevideo: Blank Storyboard (informational resources on video and storyboards):
www.schoolhousevideo.org/Pages/Storyboards.html

Tech4Learning (MediaBlender sample projects):
www.tech4learning.com/mediablender/samples.html#langarts

Unit Conceptual and Pedagogical Overview

The narrative quality of art is one of the richest of its aspects in terms of creating exciting and worthwhile projects for students. This is a dimension of visual art that students come to school already quite familiar with and for which they have boundless appreciation. I've more often been challenged to get students to slow down and understand all the details of a project before jumping in to it than I have in motivating and getting them to begin work. Adding technology to the mix only heightens their excitement and special feelings toward it.

Telling stories through pictures and enhancing stories with illustrations is a natural outgrowth of two of mankind's most basic needs as a spiritual being: the relating of tales and the creation of images that represent important things in his or her world. The impulse to engage in these activities can be seen in the rituals and cultural life of early man through the digital media–driven world in which we live today.

The production of stories that are told in pictures is not so much something to be taught as it is a natural behavior to be liberated, brought out, and perfected. Furthermore, visual storytelling represents a series of activities that may greatly impact numerous dimensions of literacy learning, enhance social, global, and cultural studies, and serve as an important tool for students producing reports.

In effect, our media-drenched world has us continually immersed in digital storytelling. Broadcast TV, downloadable video files, widely distributed and shared DVDs, vlogging, video-enhanced online news resources, and so forth, have all of us absorbing stories told visually. In the interest of providing truly relevant educational experiences, it is valuable to guide students through the production of their own corollaries to the digital stories produced by others, the result being that their ability to analyze and evaluate the media items they consume is greatly facilitated. It's been my observation that this is the aspect of digital storytelling that is so motivating for students.

However, the students I've worked with over the years are not fully satisfied simply consuming the work of other storytellers. It's my observation that they want to participate directly—producing their own versions of what they see and honor in the world around them. Furthermore, and perhaps most importantly, the production of digitally enabled visual stories is fun!

The production of digital storybooks involves combining a number of visual technology techniques. Essentially, there are two categories of techniques: 1) production of individual static elements (a series of pictures), and 2) presentation of these elements via a digital engine that will hold them, keep them in order, and present them to the viewer in a way calculated by the artist to produce an effectively related story.

In the first category, technologies such as drawing and painting programs, scanners, digital cameras, image processing programs, as well as browsers and search engines to mine the Web for usable images and images to use as reference in the creation of original images, may be used.

In the second category, software for word processing, photo management, slide shows, Web authoring, multimedia, and digital video may be used. Before attempting this project, it may be wise to work on other projects that give background experience with some of these applications first.

Navigation

Before selecting a presentation format for the project there are some decisions about the navigational experience that the artist needs to make.

One of these decisions has to do with the flow of the story's content. Traditionally stories are told in a linear fashion, from start to finish. However, one of the great developments of technology is the development of the hyperlink. In a document in which links are embedded, the reader or viewer is invited to modify that linear experience, creating his or her own unique number of destinations (links may be followed or ignored according to individual tastes), and the order in which they are explored.

This type of navigation is commonly exploited in computer/video games and has established entire genres of storytelling that are unique to the digital age. If this type of navigation experience is the one that's desired, then a digital platform that enables this must be selected.

On the other hand, if the more traditional linear approach to storytelling is preferred, there is still an important navigation decision to be made. This has to do with the pace at which the story advances and whether or not the viewer can go back to review segments of the story easily or (for a cohesive understanding) must read and see it through from start to finish.

ACTIVITIES

This project involves a great deal more than the art of illustration and the technology by which the story is presented. The structure of stories: character, setting, plot, and so forth, is essential as well. Therefore, this project is ideally done as part of, or in collaboration with, the language arts program for which it can serve as an authentic activity and a means of portfolio or performance assessment. Conversely, it can be used as a way to introduce literary concepts in anticipation of their refinement in a more formal literacy setting.

DAY 1

1. **Research and preparation**

    a. Conduct a class discussion about storybooks. Have the students share their favorites and explain why they are so well liked.

    Some suggested focus questions:

    - What parts of the story do you learn from the illustrations and what parts do you learn from the words?

    - Which should come first when a story is created—the words or the pictures?

    - Can a story be presented in different versions? Have different endings?

DAYS 2–3

2. **Pre-writing: outlines and organizers**

    b. Students should engage in pre-writing planning before getting to work in earnest on their book. They can use various formats for this, such as a traditional written outline, a chart produced on a graphic organizer, or a storyboard format, which is probably the most effective for this purpose.

    Note: A number of free digital storyboard resources are available on the Web. These may prove especially useful if students can copy and paste (or otherwise transfer) the initial sketch done within them into the finished work space. Alternately, a digital storyboard can be created using a simple word processing program that has an auto shapes drawing tool. Using this, the page is divided into small rectangles with space below in which to write descriptions of the action.

    A literary story format will help focus and facilitate this activity. There are many possibilities, but a useful basic framework for fiction that I've used to good effect is as follows: An appealing character overcomes significant difficulties to achieve a worthwhile goal. Countless stories ranging from fairy tales to classic mythology conform to this structure, Jack and the Beanstalk being one example. Using this framework, students are directed to do a drawing to accomplish each of the following:

    - Present the protagonist—the central character or hero of the story. Use this drawing to help establish the character's personality and character traits, physical characteristics, group identity, etc.

- Introduce a problem or challenge that he or she must overcome (e.g., Dorothy finding her way home from Oz; Harry Potter locating the philosopher's stone, etc.).

- Introduce a sidekick or companion to accompany and assist the hero (e.g., Dorothy's Tin Man, Cowardly Lion, and Scarecrow; Batman's Robin; Shrek's Donkey; etc.).

- Present a villain or antagonist (e.g., Captain Hook in Peter Pan, Cinderella's stepmother, etc.).

- Illustrate a few attempts (some failed and one successful) to overcome the difficulty.

- A picture to announce the resolution of the problem and the conclusion of the story.

DAYS 4–6

3. Writing and illustrating the story

c. From the storyboard outline, students refine and flesh out their story, and illustrate each item on a separate full page. They can create illustrations in traditional art materials then scan them to produce a graphics file, or create them in a drawing/painting program directly.

The publishing industry standard calls for more than the eight to ten pages (title page included) called for in this project, but a shorter length project will fully illustrate the concepts involved for young artist/authors.

Note: One of the artistic challenges of this project is that of continuity. The project calls for numerous pictures of the same characters, all of whom must retain the same look in each page they appear. A drawing/painting program can be a help in this regard if the images are composed of basic shapes pulled from the auto shapes function. On the other hand, freehand drawing is difficult enough with a pencil, and infinitely harder with a mouse. Whether to draw directly with the computer or use it to scan, save, and process traditionally done drawings is an important implementation consideration.

DAYS 7–9

4. Creating the storybook

d. The students import the finished drawings into a program that allows each to be shown as a full screen/page. Students can write text-based captions in a word processing program and then copy and paste them into a text box inserted on those pages.

If a linear presentation of the story is desired, the finished piece can be held in a simple slide show application. If a nonlinear approach is wanted the project will have to be done in a program that allows for the creation of hyperlinks. One of the following two options can be selected.

Note: PowerPoint is a slide show program that also permits the insertion of hyperlinks.

Hyperlink Option 1. A "button," "icon," or "thumbnail" (a greatly reduced version) of each of the illustrations is placed on a master or home page of the book. A hyperlink is established between each of these and the corresponding full page illustration.

Note: These may be placed on a solid-color or textured background from the standard palate provided or an additional illustration may be used as a "wallpaper" background for that page.

Hyperlink Option 2. Using a graphic organizer all navigational paths that the author would like to offer the reader can be worked out and then established using hyperlinks between buttons and/or icons. This is an involved process of trial and error and will take a session or two longer than the nonlinear version of the project.

Project Sample

Figure 19.1. Project Sample—Digital Story Book.

Figure 19.2. Project Sample—Digital Storybook. This screen offers the viewer/ reader the option of a happy or a sad ending to the story.

Process Used to Develop this Sample

Following an outline in storyboard format, the artist executed a series of drawings to strategically illustrate the plot and action of a well-known fairy tale.

The artist did the first version of the drawings traditionally, in pencil and crayon; then scanned them using a digital scanner and saved them as JPEG format files.

The artist imported the JPEGs into a painting program (Paint, in this case) in which he reworked them to give them a harder edge and a more cleanly defined drawing quality than a crayon scan would yield without enhancements. He used the Brush tool to give a defining black outline where needed. He also enhanced colors by going over them with the Brush tool, as well. He cleaned up smudging in the areas around the figures by using the Eraser tool and the Brush tool with the white tone selected.

He next imported the finished illustration files into a program with word processing features (PowerPoint used here). Using the AutoShapes tool, he drew a rectangular frame on the page in which to place the illustrations and selected a heavy line from the Line Style menu. He imported the JPEG drawings into this frame and using the Captions feature he typed and positioned them (alternatively captions might have been created directly in the painting program). He created subsequent slides the same way making certain to use the rulers on the sides of the page to ensure that the frame dimensions, position, and line weight was identical in each slide.

To complete the digital storybook he created a slide show (in this case, in PowerPoint). He ordered the slides for story continuity and then hyperlinked a number of them to enable the reader to re-order them according to whim. In this case the artist created two ending slides, a happy ending and a sad ending. By using the links the reader can select the ending desired.

Sharing the Work

This project offers opportunities within two basic approaches for sharing:

1. Hard copy versions of the finished books can be shared with other classes of students. There they will be consumed as part of the ongoing reading program, alongside the commercially prepared materials used. Feedback from the consumer group may prove exceptionally enlightening for the creators.

Figure 19.3. The project uploaded to the Flickr photo-sharing site, a free Web-based resource.

Figure 19.4. Close up of the digital storybook launched in the slide show feature of Flickr.

2. The storybooks, through the use of an LCD projector, large screen monitor, or inter-active white board, can be presented to the class. It may prove useful to implement this approach "in house" before handing the work off to other classes, as the feedback gained from peer creators may help further refine the product before it is presented to an outside audience.

It is an easy matter to upload the drawings (when saved as JPEG or other graphics file format) to a free, user-friendly Web 2.0–based resource such as Flickr. Once this is accomplished, students can share the link to this site in a variety of ways including simply e-mailing the link to others, and/or embedding the link in the class blog, Web site, or e-newsletter.

Note: See unit 18, "Sharing Student Art Work" for an overview of opportunities in sharing technology-supported student art projects.

Assessment

Presenting the project to peer authors/illustrators in the same class can provide many forma-tive learning opportunities. One approach would have the teacher craft a short checklist for peers to use as they review one another's work (e.g., Is it clear who the hero is? Do they understand what the challenge is and how the hero overcomes it? Does the story finish in a way that resolves all important issues?). By having the creator receive direct audience feed-back, the intended communication of the book can be compared to the actual experience of the readers.

Suggested General Assessment/Accountability Rubric for Unit 19

Project Components	Excellent	Proficient	Partially Proficient	Not Sufficiently Proficient or Incomplete
Completion of Project • Student uses a storyboard • Student creates original drawings • Student scans drawings (if done directly by student) • Student digitally reworks drawings • Student creates framed, captioned, sized versions • Student creates slides • Student orders and hyperlinks slide show	All portions of the project are completed successfully at a high level.	Most portions of the project are completed successfully at a high or satisfactory level.	Some important (and other) portions of the project are completed successfully at a satisfactory level.	Few of the project portions are completed successfully at a satisfactory level.
Research and Preparation • Student selects an appropriate theme for a story and identifies major elements of character, plot, setting, etc.	Conducted the needed research/preparation in a way that allows for a full level of participation in the project.	Conducted the needed research/preparation in a way that allows for a high level of participation in the project.	Conducted the needed research/preparation in a way that allows for a satisfactory level of participation in the project.	Conducted the needed research/preparation in a way that allows for a minimal level of participation in the project.
Theme and Concept Learning • Student understands that a complete story (intro, development, resolution) is to be constructed, first by identifying key segments, then by creating captioned pictures that will be produced and presented by digital means	Fully understood the concepts and goals of the project. Understood the contextual background content. Understood how to apply the above in the creation of an original work.	Understood a good deal of the concepts and goals of the project. Understood the contextual background content to a high degree. Understood how to apply the above in the creation of an original work to a high degree.	Understood some of the concepts and goals of the project. Understood the contextual background content to a degree. Understood how to apply the above in the creation of an original work to a degree.	Did not adequately understand the concepts and goals of the project. Did not adequately understand the contextual background content. Did not adequately understand how to apply the above in the creation of an original work.
Technical Proficiency • Student used traditional drawing and digitally enhanced drawing techniques to illustrate the action and other qualities of the narrative.	Demonstrated a high degree of understanding and mastery of the concepts and skills involved in the techniques required of the project.	Demonstrated a good degree of understanding and mastery of the concepts and skills involved in the techniques required of the project.	Demonstrated a satisfactory degree of understanding and mastery of the concepts and skills involved in the techniques required of the project.	Did not demonstrate an adequate degree of understanding and mastery of the concepts and skills involved in the techniques required of the project.

(Continued)

Suggested General Assessment/Accountability Rubric for Unit 19 *(Continued)*

Project Components	Excellent	Proficient	Partially Proficient	Not Sufficiently Proficient or Incomplete
Technology Use • Student used the scanning, painting, drawing, and word processing functions of software to complete the project tasks. • Student saved and managed files and the digital work environment to complete tasks as directed	Handled the technology portions of the project in a highly effective, insightful, and responsible fashion.	Handled the technology portions of the project very proficiently and in an effective, insightful, and responsible fashion.	Handled the technology portions of the project in a satisfactorily effective, insightful, and responsible fashion.	Did not handle the technology portions of the project in a satisfactorily effective, insightful, and responsible fashion.
Creativity-Expression • Student used the project as an opportunity to make a personal statement • Student execution of project shows a degree of originality	Conceived, developed, and executed a work of art that is highly original and that takes full advantage of the medium's possibilities.	To a good degree, conceived, developed, and executed a work of art that is original and that takes full advantage of the medium's possibilities.	To a satisfactory degree, conceived, developed, and executed a work of art that is somewhat original and that takes advantage of some of the medium's possibilities.	Did not well conceive and execute a work that is original or takes good advantage of the medium's possibilities.

Note: See chapter 7, "Assessing Digital Art Projects" for an overview of assessing technology-supported student visual art projects.

Cross-Curricular Connection

Digital Storybooks in Language Arts

Many language arts standards documents call for students to write their own stories. Producing either a fictional or autobiographical narrative account are often the two categories of writing assigned for this. Subsidiary to these, the documents often list plot development, organizing structure, and sensory details to develop characters and settings, as well as the sense of closure in an ending as elements by which to measure student achievement in writing stories.

For many professional writers of books for young students, the act of illustration is deeply associated with other aspects of creation. In fact, works by author/ illustrators comprise a major and high profile portion of the genre. Art to accompany or drive the text narrative therefore is essential. Furthermore, producing and managing graphics for such publications currently involves a good deal of technology.

Consequently, this is a perfect project on which to base an interdisciplinary/ interdepartment collaboration among teachers. Ideally this would include the language arts teacher, the visual art teacher, and the technology teacher. However, any two of these three groups could effectively work on this with their students to produce a successful project.

UNIT **20**

A Virtual Sculpture Exhibit
Sharing 3-D Student Art Work

Sculpture occupies real space like we do... you walk around it
and relate to it almost as another person or another object.

— CHUCK CLOSE

Please see the sections "Using this Book" and "Assessing Digital Art Projects" for more information about these standards, the interaction between them, and connecting these standards to the lessons in this book.

STANDARDS

NETS·S

Although all or most of the NETS•S are touched on in this unit, the connection is strongest
and easiest to see and understand in the standards listed below:

1. a, b, c   4. a, b, d

2. a, b, d   5. a, b, d

3. c   6. a, b, c, d

Note: In this unit and others, students *apply existing knowledge to generate new ideas, products or processes* (NETS•S.1.a) by which already finished art works are made accessible to audiences. To accomplish this, students reexamine and reconceive the works, research, and processes that went into producing the art work.

National Standards for Arts Education (Visual Arts)

CS–1, AS–a, b

CS–2, AS–a, b, c

CS–3, AS–a, b

CS–4, AS–a, c

CS–5, AS–a, b, c

CS–6, AS–a, b

UNIT OBJECTIVES:

Students will be challenged to:

- Understand the concepts and techniques of virtual reality imaging.

- Participate in the creation of an original VR image to capture and exhibit three-dimensional work.

- Contribute to the creation of both a real-world and virtual reality class exhibition of sculpture.

CENTRAL IDEAS AND TECHNOLOGY RATIONALE

Sculpture in the round has an experiential as well as a visual aspect to it. This is established by the dimension of time, the time it takes to travel around a sculpture and understand it from a series of angles and points of view. Similarly, the experience of seeing panoramas or defined spaces in the round requires a continuum of visual impressions that unfold over a period of time.

Until recently, this was impossible to capture in a two-dimensional or published medium. The emergence of QuickTime Virtual Reality (QTVR) technology however, has changed that by establishing digital virtual reality images of real spaces and objects. These have become extremely popular.

Virtual reality, or VR, images can serve the purposes of students who need to capture a time-based multi-view experience, like that of appreciating a freestanding sculpture, so that it may be saved, published, or disseminated. VR is of particular value to student artists in archiving and presenting sculpture in the round or spatially dependent and site-specific works in galleries and other spaces.

Furthermore, because of the increasing popularity of VR-based products, understanding and producing VR is a skill set that is well worth the time and attention that students invest.

Principal Technology Skills Addressed
- Digital photography
- Virtual reality presentations

Technology Resources Needed
- Digital cameras
- QTVR software

WEB RESOURCES

Adobe (digital photography information and resources):
www.adobe.com/cfusion/search/index.cfm?loc=en_us&term=digital+photos

NOVA (information and resources—virtual reality):
www.pbs.org/wgbh/nova/novatech.html#qthowget

QuickTime Virtual Reality (information on virtual reality):
www.quicktimevirtualreality.com

University of Texas at Austin—Teachnet (Virtual Reality information and resources):
www.edb.utexas.edu/teachnet/qtvr/

Unit Conceptual and Pedagogical Overview

Artists express their ideas as either flat, two-dimensional works (drawings, paintings, prints, etc.), or as sculpture. The design decisions involved in choosing between the two are numerous, but the difference in the experiences the selected form gives the viewer is the defining issue. Artists who create sculpture gravitate toward it because it affords many views of a subject, something not possible from a painting or photograph, a format that is purely frontal.

True, one could produce different views of a subject as a series of two-dimensional works, and these would give the viewer much of the same information about the subject as a sculpture in the round would. Still, even though the visual data might be there, the feeling would unmistakably be that of a flat, two-dimensional work. There simply is no way to duplicate in two dimensions the experience of walking around a piece of sculpture or of turning a small three-dimensional piece around in one's hand. Or rather, there hasn't been a way to do this until recently, with the advent of virtual reality software.

Referred to as 360-degree panoramic photography, QuickTime Virtual Reality (or simply QTVR), can be used inexpensively, is easy to use, and is a perfect platform on which many wonderful art experiences can be made to happen for students.

QTVR is a way of stitching together a series of images to produce a single image that can be viewed through a (browser-like) digital viewer. Essentially, the student artist produces a series of digital photos, something that has become increasingly easy and common for all of us in and out of the classroom. Next, the student imports these photos into a piece of software in which they can be aligned, edited, stitched together into a seamless whole from the separate files, and saved as a single document.

There are two varieties of virtual reality products that students can use to capture, archive, and digitally display three-dimensional work. One gives a 360-degree "in the round" experience, basically a virtual trip around a 3-D-object, allowing the viewer to direct his own visual tour of all sides and facets. The other is a 2-D panoramic view. In this variety, the artist places the camera in the middle of a scene and takes photos of segments in the full-circle field of view.

The product of the panorama process is not a movie, but a virtual experience directed by the viewer. When opened in the viewer software, the computer's mouse actions can pull the image to reveal a portion of a 360-degree view. Thus, the viewer holds down the mouse button and drags the image from angle to angle, moving at will through a panorama-like field of view. The result is that the viewer experiences being at the center of a panorama that wraps around him. The effect is startling and is well described as virtual reality.

The project that follows will incorporate both approaches and illustrate their value.

ACTIVITIES

This project will involve each student preparing a piece of sculpture in the round (already completed as part of a previous assignment) for inclusion in a virtual class sculpture exhibit.

DAY 1

Activity I: Creating Digital Virtual Sculpture Pieces

1. **Preparation**

   a. Begin the project by having a class discussion.

   Some suggested points to cover include the following:

   - Which project(s) should the class include in its sculpture exhibit?

   - Which piece(s) should each member of the class contribute as part of the group exhibit?

   - What are the advantages and disadvantages of real-world gallery and virtual exhibits of sculpture?

DAY 2

2. Creating a virtual sculpture

Having selected a piece of sculpture to represent each member of the class, each student will create a virtual reality version of that piece.

   b. Direct the students to set up their desk space as a temporary photo studio. Students are assigned to bring in to class a cardboard box (or other appropriate item) that will function as a base or stand for their sculpture. These may be painted, covered with a textured material, or draped with fabric (as the aesthetic needs of showing off their sculpture to good advantage dictate).

   c. When ready to photograph the pieces, they can be placed on an inexpensive kitchen cabinet turntable or lazy Susan that has tick marks placed strategically around its perimeter, segmenting it into eighths or sixteenths. The idea is for the camera to remain stationery as the turntable holding the sculpture is revolved an increment for each photo taken.

Note: It may be best for the teacher to set some standards for the bases of the sculptures or provide a uniform set of materials so that the variations between how the students satisfy this requirement don't produce too disparate a set of visual elements.

Students should experiment with a variety of bases on which to place their sculpture (they may wish to swap bases with another student), a variety of backdrops, and a variety of lighting situations in order to arrive at a satisfactory photographic result. A series of photos should be taken, showing the sculpture from every angle. It may prove fruitful to assign some Web research on how to photograph sculpture as background information for this step.

Note: It may prove effective to organize students in small work groups (three to five students) for this step of the project. This will enable them to share cameras and materials and to assist one another with the work.

DAY 3

3. Creating a virtual sculpture

d. Students load the photos they took in the previous step into the QTVR software, and produce the virtual reality piece of their sculpture.

Implementation Note: It will be necessary to acquire QTVR (QuickTime Virtual Reality) products like Simply VR (tech4learning is the distributor) in order to do this phase of the project. A Web search will reveal different sources, some of which are free downloads. For a complete step-by-step walkthrough of the process, there are numerous examples of this on the Web.

DAY 4

Activity II: Creating a Group Virtual Sculpture Gallery Exhibit

4. Creating a virtual gallery

e. This is to be done as a class group activity: The students set up the classroom as a temporary sculpture gallery, clearing unnecessary furniture from the classroom. What remains should be student desks or work tables (perhaps covered or draped) with the sculpture bases and sculptures on top. Adjust the lighting for maximum effect.

Again, the students will need a base on which to set their personal sculptures. This may be the same base they used for Activity I, in which they created an individual virtual reality piece of their individual work.

A student team should be selected to set the camera up on a tripod at the center of the exhibition to rotate in increments as the panoramic series of photos is taken. Photos showing students as viewers in the exhibit are fine depending on the final product desired. Obviously, a good deal of experimentation may be required until a satisfactory product is produced.

DAYS 5–6

5. Producing the exhibit

The student team(s) that took the whole exhibit photos returns to the computers and QTVR software, this time producing a panoramic VR piece of the exhibit instead of the individual sculpture.

Project Sample

Figure 20.1. Project Sample—Virtual Sculpture. One of 16 photos of the African theme-Box Sculpture taken to produce the archived Virtual Reality version.

Figure 20.2. Several of the sequential photos taken of the African-theme Box Sculpture imported into Simply VR software to produce the spinning, 360-degree virtual reality version.

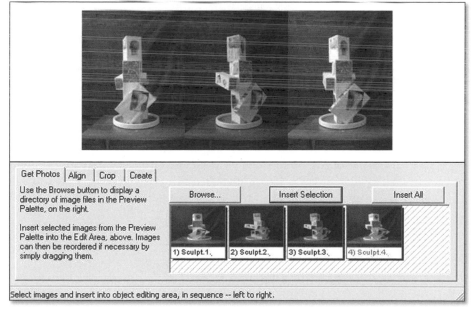

Examples of Virtual Reality for Sculpture Gallery Tours

Better than providing static two-dimensional images here of digital virtual reality movies, this section lists Web sites that host good examples. These may give teachers and students good ideas about the possibilities of using QuickTime Virtual Reality to archive and share student sculpture.

These sites fall into two categories: 1) exhibits of individual objects, captured in 360-degree VR, and 2) those with panoramic views of exhibitions with multiple objects (replicating the gallery experience).

Individual Object Sites

These links are to museum Web sites, some os which are of sculpture and some are of other types of museum objects.

Arizona State Museum 3-D Pottery Storeroom:
www.statemuseum.arizona.edu/exhibits/pproj/pots.asp

Northport-East High School:
http://admin.northport.k12.ny.us/qtvr.html

Maya-Archaeology.org / Copan Museum—Honduras:
www.maya-archaeology.org/museums/copan/copangate.html

Myriad Productions:
www.myriadproductions.com/vrPRO.html

Nakasato Virtual Museum:
www.dino-nakasato.org/en/vm/indexVM-e.shtml

Virtual Collection of the Royal Alberta Museum:
www.royalalbertamuseum.ca/vexhibit/virtcoll/index.asp

Washington University Museum of Medicine:
http://beckerexhibits.wustl.edu/3D/movies/index.html#VC703110

Exhibition Sites

National Gallery of Art—Alexander Calder: 1898–1976:
www.nga.gov/exhibitions/caldbro.shtm
www.nga.gov/exhibitions/caldwel.shtm

National Gallery of Art—Van Gogh's Van Goghs Virtual Tour. (This exhibition was on view at the Gallery Oct. 4, 1998–Jan. 3, 1999. See also, exhibition overview and its related links.):
www.nga.gov/exhibitions/vgwel.shtm

National Park Service—Eleanor Roosevelt Visionary:
www.cr.nps.gov/museum/exhibits/elro/

National Park Service—Virtual Tour/Frederick Douglas:
www.cr.nps.gov/museum/exhibits/douglass/panoramics/vr_main.html

Oriental Institute Virtual Museum (University of Chicago):
http://oi.uchicago.edu/museum/virtual/as/cen2.html

Panorama of Rodin Sculpture Garden nr2:
www.virtualparks.org/scenes/Z2WXltBVd42VPU0sjL5H_Mg.html

Sharing the Work

As culminating products, the class produces a virtual reality piece of each sculpture in the exhibit, as well as a single piece that gives the experience of the exhibit as a whole. One particularly effective approach would be to create a thumbnail gallery of the group of VR pieces. When an individual sculpture is selected, a mouse click can launch the respective VR experience of it.

These can be presented as a kiosk experience when loaded on a single desktop computer or they can be uploaded to the class or school Web site or blog. Alternatively, they can be distributed as copies of a disk that the class produces.

Note: See unit 18, "Sharing Student Art Work" for an overview of other possibilities in sharing student projects.

Assessment

In assessing the virtual reality representation of the student sculptures the perspective should focus on how functional it is in terms of conveying the experience of the original. In addition to completeness in presenting all important sides and angles of the piece, does it convey a sense of the scale, weight, texture, warmth or coldness, and so forth, of the original?

Items to include in a checklist:

- Was an appropriate representative piece of sculpture chosen from the student's overall body of work for the exhibit?

- Was the piece presented effectively in the photo shoot? Was an effective and appropriate base and backdrop created for it?

- Were the photos taken effectively (e.g., properly illuminated, the appropriate distance of piece from camera, appropriate and effective increments of rotation, etc.?)

- Were the photos effectively incorporated into the VR experience of the sculpture?

Suggested discussion question: Ask the student to explain why the viewer will get an accurate experience of the original sculpture by viewing only the virtual reality version. Presenting both versions side by side may make this activity more enlightening.

Note: See chapter 7, "Assessing Digital Art Projects" for an overview of assessing technology-supported student visual art projects.

National Educational Technology Standards

National Educational Technology Standards for Students (NETS•S)

The National Educational Technology Standards for Students are divided into six broad categories. Standards within each category are to be introduced, reinforced, and mastered by students. Teachers can use these standards as guidelines for planning technology-based activities in which students achieve success in learning, communication, and life skills.

1. Creativity and Innovation

Students demonstrate creative thinking, construct knowledge, and develop innovative products and processes using technology. Students:

    a. apply existing knowledge to generate new ideas, products, or processes

    b. create original works as a means of personal or group expression

    c. use models and simulations to explore complex systems and issues

    d. identify trends and forecast possibilities

2. Communication and Collaboration

Students use digital media and environments to communicate and work collaboratively, including at a distance, to support individual learning and contribute to the learning of others. Students:

    a. interact, collaborate, and publish with peers, experts, or others employing a variety of digital environments and media

    b. communicate information and ideas effectively to multiple audiences using a variety of media and formats

    c. develop cultural understanding and global awareness by engaging with learners of other cultures

    d. contribute to project teams to produce original works or solve problems

3. Research and Information Fluency

Students apply digital tools to gather, evaluate, and use information. Students:

    a. plan strategies to guide inquiry

    b. locate, organize, analyze, evaluate, synthesize, and ethically use information from a variety of sources and media

    c. evaluate and select information sources and digital tools based on the appropriateness to specific tasks

    d. process data and report results

4. Critical Thinking, Problem Solving, and Decision Making

Students use critical-thinking skills to plan and conduct research, manage projects, solve problems, and make informed decisions using appropriate digital tools and resources. Students:

    a. identify and define authentic problems and significant questions for investigation

    b. plan and manage activities to develop a solution or complete a project

    c. collect and analyze data to identify solutions and make informed decisions

    d. use multiple processes and diverse perspectives to explore alternative solutions

5. Digital Citizenship

Students understand human, cultural, and societal issues related to technology and practice legal and ethical behavior. Students:

    a. advocate and practice the safe, legal, and responsible use of information and technology

    b. exhibit a positive attitude toward using technology that supports collaboration, learning, and productivity

    c. demonstrate personal responsibility for lifelong learning

    d. exhibit leadership for digital citizenship

6. Technology Operations and Concepts

Students demonstrate a sound understanding of technology concepts, systems, and operations. Students:

    a. understand and use technology systems

    b. select and use applications effectively and productively

    c. troubleshoot systems and applications

    d. transfer current knowledge to the learning of new technologies

APPENDIX **B**

National Standards
for **Arts Education** (Visual Arts)

Content Standard 1: Understanding and applying media, techniques, and processes

Achievement Standard

a. Students select media, techniques, and processes; analyze what makes them effective or not effective in communicating ideas; and reflect upon the effectiveness of their choices

b. Students intentionally take advantage of the qualities and characteristics of art media, techniques, and processes to enhance communication of their experiences and ideas

Content Standard 2: Using knowledge of structures and functions

Achievement Standard

a. Students generalize about the effects of visual structures and functions and reflect upon these effects in their own work

b. Students employ organizational structures and analyze what makes them effective or not effective in the communication of ideas

c. Students select and use the qualities of structures and functions of art to improve communication of their ideas

Content Standard 3: Choosing and evaluating a range of subject matter, symbols, and ideas

Achievement Standard

a. Students integrate visual, spatial, and temporal concepts with content to communicate intended meaning in their artworks

b. Students use subjects, themes, and symbols that demonstrate knowledge of contexts, values, and aesthetics that communicate intended meaning in artworks

Content Standard 4: Understanding the visual arts in relation to history and cultures

Achievement Standard

a. Students know and compare the characteristics of artworks in various eras and cultures

b. Students describe and place a variety of art objects in historical and cultural contexts

c. Students analyze, describe, and demonstrate how factors of time and place (such as climate, resources, ideas, and technology) influence visual characteristics that give meaning and value to a work of art

Content Standard 5: Reflecting upon and assessing the characteristics and merits of their work and the work of others

Achievement Standard

a. Students compare multiple purposes for creating works of art

b. Students analyze contemporary and historic meanings in specific artworks through cultural and aesthetic inquiry

c. Students describe and compare a variety of individual responses to their own artworks and to artworks from various eras and cultures

Content Standard 6: Making connections between visual arts and other disciplines

Achievement Standard

a. Students compare the characteristics of works in two or more art forms that share similar subject matter, historical periods, or cultural context

b. Students describe ways in which the principles and subject matter of other disciplines taught in the shcool are interrelated with the visual arts

© *1994 National Art Education Association, www.naea-reston.org*

Index